THE GOD

OF SEX

How Spirituality Defines Your Sexuality

PETER JONES

MAIN ENTRY EDITIONS

Escondido, CA

To my wife, Rebecca

To my seven children and their spouses,
David and Eowyn Stoddard
Gabrielle Jones
Julien and Christina Jones
Andrew and Myriam Hertzog
Tessa Reed
Zoe Jones
Toby Jones

and

to my grandchildren
Jesse, Liam, Alethea, Emma and Ethan Stoddard
Kellen, Maya and Finnan Jones
Aidan, Lewis and Michael Hertzog
Miranda Reed

Behold, children are a heritage from the LORD, the fruit of the womb a reward. Like arrows in the hand of a warrior are the children of one's youth. Blessed is the man who fills his quiver with them! He shall not be put to shame when he speaks with his enemies in the gate.

—PSALM 127:3–5 ESV

Contents

Introduction

GOD AND SEX: AN ODD COUPLE

₪

God and sex make an odd couple. In fact, these two realities seem to stand at opposite ends of the values spectrum. God represents disembodied, ethereal holiness; sex is the very essence of hard-driving material pleasure—and never the twain shall meet!

Sex and gender are delicate subjects for church people.[1] Some claim the issue is of marginal importance to the gospel. Even in orthodox circles, some duck out of the debate with the argument that it is "not a confessional issue." Of course it is not, since our sixteenth-century confessions were written before the 1960s "liberation of sexuality." Since then, however, sex has become the driving issue of the culture. If Christians do not find the courage to address the biblical teaching on sex, they will wake up one day to find themselves and the gospel completely marginalized. "Spiritual" gays rightly see the deep and organic connection. Says Christian de la Huerta, a gay activist, "Sexuality encompasses or imbues all other aspects of being human; it is an integral component of who we are."[2]

Meanwhile, our Christian young people plead with the church leaders for an honest discussion of the subject. A pastor to university students says, "Our twenty-somethings are immersed in a culture of sexual deviancy, and the church has remained silent."[3] Cara Hunt, a twenty-eight-year-old television news anchor in Fairbanks, Alaska, and a committed Christian, is "particularly bothered by euphemisms and other tactics to avoid frank discussion of gender roles and sexual activity."[4]

Mainline churches have no problem since they long ago gave up worrying about confessions. They therefore baptize sexual liberation as the new work of the Spirit and come out in favor of the lordship of Christ, the centrality of the cross—and gay marriage![5] But such cutting and pasting has been called religious "commodification." In our consumer world we eat chocolate but never think about where that chocolate was grown or the workers who harvested it or the process that finally brought it to our supermarket. Chocolate is simply a contextless commodity we consume when the desire arises. We do this with religion too.

Many Christians are like an Episcopalian I read about who loves the liturgy of his church but also spends hours in yoga exercises. At least some of those Christians are represented in a Canadian survey that reports almost half of yoga participants assert beliefs in both reincarnation and resurrection. One perceptive observer notes, "Even a slight understanding of either concept would recognize them as incompatible, but in removing each from their traditions, the consumer mindset...groundlessly insists on finding a way to embrace them both."[6] The world expects a better response from those claiming to be Christian.

God and sex are inextricably related. For the sake of our young people, our churches, our society, and our world, it's imperative that we understand the connection between theology and sexuality. It is time to deal with sexuality in the context of worldview. Lauren Winner, who wrote a courageously honest book on sex, titled *Real Sex*, understands this need. She writes:

> We need to ask whether the starting point for a scriptural witness on sex is the isolated quotation of "thou shalt not," or whether a scriptural ethic of sex begins instead with the totality of the Bible, the narrative of God's redeeming love and humanity's attempt to reflect that through our institutions and practices...If we see scripture not merely as a code

of behavior but as a map of God's reality...the church needs not merely to recite decontextualized Bible verses, but to ground our ethic in the faithful living of the fullness of the gospel.[7]

The God of Sex is an attempt to explain why our newly "spiritual" modern culture liberates sex and why the Bible restricts sex to heterosexual marriage. Its goal is not to restore the America of the fifties. Ultimately, the debate about sex is not a conflict between uptight traditionalists and cutting-edge futurists. Rather, two views of sexuality emerge from two timeless religious options tied to two fundamental worldviews.

In the words of psychiatrist Jeffrey Satinover, how we order sexuality is "one of the most revealing indexes of a civilization."[8] Actually, how we do it will determine whether our civilization survives.

THE BEGINNING OF THE STORY

₪

It was cold and windy that night in the Midwest university town, but I sensed as my lecture progressed that the temperature had continued to rise. My subject was, after all, controversial. As I descended from the platform, I noticed a giant of a man striding toward me out of the audience. As I stared up at the six-feet-ten-inch colossus from my five-feet-seven-inch vantage point and noted the look on his face, I wondered if I had just finished my last lecture on that particular subject. He said nothing, but thrust a crumpled paper into my hand and walked away. Those few scribbled words are now pinned to my office wall, and they still speak to me:

> I am angry, so angry! I realize that the things driving my temptations are...fueling this whole paganist [sic] movement...but at the same time I still have these desires—Damn it!

He walked out of my life, and I never saw him again.

As a Christian, do you wonder how to talk to someone who is gay? Do you have gay acquaintances who insist that you endorse their lifestyle if you want their friendship? Declaring homosexuals "lawbreakers" will not help, since the moral underpinnings of our society have been redefined. A placard carried in the San Diego Gay Parade says it all: "He's *your* God. They're *your* rules. *You* go to Hell."[1] We can no longer appeal to a commonly held ultimate authority or notion of God. Quoting Bible verses at gays and other sexual sinners may indeed be counterproductive. This is ironic, since Christians always try to preach the gospel, and that gospel affirms that "all [which definitely includes me!] have sinned and fall short of the glory of God."[2]

Jeffrey Satinover—who has counseled many gays and has written with wisdom and authority on the homosexual movement—warns that while the present normalization of homosexuality increases the likelihood that a young person will adopt a homosexual lifestyle, he also believes that "ridicule, rejection, and harsh punitive condemnation of [the homosexual] as a person will be just as likely to drive him to the same position."[3] We face a delicate situation in contemporary Christian witness.

As the culture begins to normalize homosexuality and "progressive" churchmen hurl dismissive accusations of "irrationality," "religious bigotry," and "hate speech" at those defending a biblical view of sex, the specter of serious conflict between faithful biblical witness and a powerful pagan religious ideology looms large on the horizon. Christians who have a love for the lost and fortitude for the truth must come to understand the profound "theo-logic" of the Bible's worldview with regard to sexuality.

This is what was suggested that cold night in my encounter with my tall, gay interlocutor who, in saying nothing, said it all.

PART ONE

SEXUALITY ACCORDING TO THE PAGAN VIEW OF GOD

INTRODUCTION

₪

Part 1, "Sexuality according to the Pagan View of God," is an invitation to ask the deep questions concerning the reasons behind the notions of sexuality taught to our children in many schools and seen on today's television screens. Those who think this view of liberated sex is a spanking-new idea need to know that, in reality, it is a return to a much more old-fashioned worldview. In fact, the worldview proposed today is the same as that proposed by equally old-fashioned pagan religions. Oddly, in the third millennium we are given a choice of two equally "old" worldviews.

There is a deep correlation between a monistic understanding of God and the practical issues of spirituality—particularly, sexuality. The pagan understanding of God as a spiritual force within nature produces a deconstruction of heterosexual norms. Poly*theism* produces "poly*gender.*" Behind the many sexual choices are many gods. If we are to make wise decisions in a time of cultural insanity, we at least need to understand the deep issues that explain where our culture is going.

Chapter 1

OUT WITH THE OLD: MAKE LOVE, NOT WAR

₪

Come mothers and fathers
Throughout the land,
And don't criticize
What you can't understand.
Your sons and your daughters
Are beyond your command.
Your old road is
Rapidly agin'.

—BOB DYLAN

THE SIXTIES SEXUAL REVOLUTION IN "CHRISTIAN AMERICA"

Somehow, Dylan (the bard of what I have come to consider the true American revolution) caught the "apocalyptic" character of the times in his 1963 song "The Times they Are a-Changin'." Another hit song of that time described it as "The Age of Destruction," or as "The Eve of Destruction,"[1] and another song from the hit musical of the 1960s, *Hair*, ominously welcomed the dawning of the "Age of Aquarius"—though it seemed nobody really understood what that meant. For the 1960s revolutionaries, the old had to go and the new be installed. This included deconstructing the normative sexuality of the *ancient regime*.

We should note two steps in the deconstructive process: (1) the normalization of heterosexual excess and (2) the normalization of homosexuality. "Traditional" sexual morality is in tatters, in large part, through the impact of one man, Alfred C. Kinsey.[2]

ALFRED C. KINSEY AND THE DESTRUCTION OF "NORMAL" SEX

Long before the cultural revolution broke out at street level in the 1960s, Kinsey spoke to overflow crowds in universities across the nation and the world, persuading them that traditional sexual norms were false and that the American male was promiscuous, self-pleasuring, and significantly homosexual. Today, few remember Kinsey (1894–1956). Even a major Hollywood movie about his life, starring Liam Neeson, failed to revive his memory, since it turned out to be a financial bust. However, Kinsey's studies, beginning with his blockbuster, *Sexual Behavior in the Human Male* (1948), enthroned him as the father of the sexual revolution.

How objective was Kinsey's science? Some lionize him as a great fact-based researcher who liberated sex from the shackles of puritanical thought. Others "revile him as a fraud whose 'junk science' legitimized his own personal preference for degeneracy."[3] Even scholars sympathetic to Kinsey disagree. Leftist scientists such as Abraham Maslow, Lionel Trilling, and even Margaret Mead condemned Kinsey for betraying science by creating false data about American sexual life. Both of his biographers regard him as a brave pioneer and reformer,[4] but one reveals that Kinsey "had affairs with men, encouraged open marriages among his staff, stimulated himself with urethral insertion and ropes, and filmed sex in his attic."[5] He goes on to justify Kinsey's work by saying, "It shouldn't surprise us that pleas for sexual tolerance would come from a person who couldn't be himself in public."[6] One reviewer of Kinsey's work believes Kinsey's great interest in deviant sex stemmed from the fact of "his own sexual ambiguities,"[7] indicated by the odd witness of one homosexual interviewee who claimed to have spent seven hundred hours alone with Kinsey.[8]

As he sought to demonstrate via research that "pansexuality"[9] was the norm, personal considerations clearly motivated Kinsey. He was also motivated by ideology. Reacting against a strict Methodist father who made him go to church three times on Sunday, Kinsey, as an adult, believed himself to be a scientist, free of ideology. For him, "religion and morality were the hated enemies that stand in the way of sexual freedom...no sex was abnormal...man was merely an animal with a high degree of intelligence."[10] This, too, of course, is an ideology. E. Michael Jones identifies that ideology more clearly as a deep-seated commitment to "biological and social evolution." Kinsey argued that deviance and/or difference was the material "out of which nature achieves progress...in the differences between men lie the hopes of a changing society."[11] It is now obvious that this ideological pre-commitment determined what Kinsey would find in his research.[12]

Only one generation after Kinsey and the 1960s cultural revolution, the bedrock sexual values in American culture were collapsing. The normalcy of male-female sexuality and of heterosexual marriage had been abandoned. This cultural, spiritual collapse constitutes the *real* American revolution.

Kinsey's biographer, James H. Jones, has this to say about his legacy:

> Kinsey died believing that his crusade to promote more enlightened sexual attitudes had not succeeded. Yet in 1957, a year after his death, the Supreme Court's Roth decision narrowed the legal definition of obscenity, expanding the umbrella of constitutional protection to cover a broader range of works portraying sex in art, literature, and film. In 1960, the birth control pill was introduced, offering a highly effective method of contraception. In 1961, Illinois became the first state to repeal its sodomy statutes. The next year, the Supreme Court ruled that a magazine featuring photographs of male nudes was not obscene and as therefore not subject to censorship.

Then, in 1973, in a dramatic reversal, the American Psychiatric Association removed homosexuality from its list of psychopathologies. *Kinsey, the anguished man of science, had prevailed.*[13]

The Deconstructive Power of Heterosexual Excess

The history of the sexual revolution has been well documented.[14] The phenomenon is so huge it is difficult to measure. Many ordinary men and women, according to the promises of the revolution, changed their private lives, believing those changes would help create a better, more open society. Prior to Kinsey, people called sexual love "the marital act." After Kinsey, sexual expression knew no bounds. Here are a few examples of where we have arrived after this deconstructive period.

Destruction via Pornography

When our culture left behind the norm of one man-one woman sexuality, one of the unexpected effects was the eventual meeting of pornography and cyberspace. This techno-sexual rendezvous unleashed an unprecedented wave of sexual liberation through Internet pornography. We have not begun to measure the consequences this voyeuristic obsession—which sees the opposite sex merely as an object for self-pleasure—will have on the moral soul of our culture.

Internet Pornography

Bus stations are depressing places, especially late at night, and they always seem to be located in the seediest parts of town. While in seminary, I waited for a bus late one Sunday evening after having spent a great day at church with my friends, including my future wife. As I leaned wearily against the wall, I saw him. He wore the classic raincoat, collar turned up and hat pulled down—the ultimate sleuth. But his disguise was not good enough. I recognized one of my respected professors making straight for the red-light district. Though raised as an evangelical, his theological world collapsed with the onslaught of liberalism, and he eventually became a vociferous spokesman against the faith of his youth. Did his visits to prostitutes come before or after his spiritual decline?

I show my age when I say that in those days he had to go to the red-light district to fulfill his lust. Had he lived now, he might have stayed in his comfortable study and received illicit sex piped over the Internet. His students would never have known. CBS confirms what I say. "In the space of a generation, a product that once was available in the back alleys of big cities has gone corporate, delivered now directly into homes and hotel rooms by some of the biggest companies in the United States."[15] As the "dot-coms" of the nineties collapsed, online pornography flourished—one of the few industries successfully charging money for online content. A recent survey found that *one-third* of German Internet users regularly visit pornographic sites. The figures are similar in the rest of the West and in the United States. Here are some frightening facts about the invasion of pornography.

₪ Media Metrix, which tracks Internet usage, affirms that porn sites are the favorite destinations of internet users.[16]

₪ In 2002 it was estimated that the adult online industry in the United States generated approximately $1 billion in revenues annually, and some in the industry expected this figure to grow from $5 to $7 billion over the following five years, barring unforeseen change.[17] In 2005 it is estimated to be a $13 billion industry.[18]

₪ European pornographic firms are exploring the possibility of a stock market listing.

₪ In the United States, Playboy Enterprises paid $70 million for three pornographic TV networks. On its decision to abandon its soft-porn-only policy, its shares shot up by 12 percent.

₪ The latest development, erotic games and porn video clips for cell-phone users, will, when everything is in place, double the industry profits, granting to pornography the attribute of unlimited ubiquity. The depressing news, according to legal experts, is that it is now virtually impossible to turn back the tide of Internet porn.[19]

Pornography is often justified as a way of breaking out of the narrow confines of "uptight" morality to discover one's true, sexually liberated, natural self. That is why, in deconstructing sex, pornography *must* be taken to the high schools—to liberate our children!

Pornography in High School

Diversity is a mandatory element of student orientation on most American college campuses and is now pushed in high schools. Patriotic bells ring at the sound of phrases such as "one man–one vote," "freedom and personal choice," or "tolerance"; but *diversity* can be a pretext for introducing *perversity*. Radical educators are trying to undermine any notion of normative Judeo-Christian moral structures in the minds of the rising generation. Deborah M. Roffman, a sex educator, discussed students' clothing in this "quote of the day" from the *New York Times*:

> Kids are supposed to test the limits; you worry about it if they don't do that. But the message now is that there are no limits.[20]

"Teens are having more sex—and getting more diseases" by "turning to sexual behaviors that were once considered taboo," declares *U.S. News & World Report*.[21] Even *USA Today* complains: "The fact that we have high school kids videotaping sex acts and in effect producing pornography is a sad comment on what is happening to our culture...It's probably not an isolated situation."[22] Though some call for the full extent of the law to be applied to these young pornography-producing students, instead of going to jail, they can simply go to college.

Pornography in College—College as Sex Carnival[23]

Anyone with children in college should be concerned about the state of sexuality on the campus. I doubt we could have ever seen, in the history of America or in the entire history of the "Christian" West, an article like the one titled "Dorm Brothel: The New Debauchery, and the Colleges that Let it Happen."[24] In our institutions of "higher learning" that educate the elite of the next generation, all hell has broken loose. The author, a respected professor at Loyola College in Baltimore, gives a particularly moving *cri-de coeur* as he provides a firsthand report of the animalistic behavior of contemporary undergrads. What bothers him even more than the sophomoric behavior of the students, is the attitude of the administration of his Roman Catholic school, which does all it can to facilitate the sexual carnival. Dating is out, hooking up is in. Almost like animals, young people make genital contact without ever making friends. Gone are any institutional structures that would keep sexuality from being anything other than an appetite to be satisfied. To quote the author, "In most American college coed dorms, the flesh of our daughters is being served up daily like snack jerky."

In such a context, pornography (and not only heterosexual) is honored as a subject worthy of academic study, especially now that academic feminists have given it the green light.[25] The available pornography includes images of heterosexual and homosexual intercourse, masturbation, bestiality, sadomasochism, bondage, rape, incest, and much, much more, all justified in the name of the high goal of sexual liberation.

Wesleyan University in Middletown, Ohio, begins with the basics, offering a seminar called "Pornography: Writing of Prostitutes." At Wesleyan and elsewhere, a rehabilitated sex industry is now part of the curriculum. Porn stars work the college lecture circuit. For instance, Annie Sprinkle, a "performance artist" as she is euphemistically known, packed a Wesleyan auditorium to extol the value of prostitution and told students, "The answer to bad porn is not no porn, but to try to make better porn."[26] Students are giving it their best college try, making pornographic films of themselves and their friends and showing the results in class—just like those high school boys but this time for academic credit. Parents must wonder why they pay more than $30,000 a year to send their children to a university that teaches them to indulge in and create porn. Some shrug and say, still somewhat surprised, "That's what kids do these days, they make porn at school"[27]—as part of the academic curriculum. Hartford's Trinity College offered a new philosophy class in the fall of 2000 on the legal and political issues surrounding pornography and prostitution.[28] The sanction of the ivory tower has created transgression without shame—higher education for the lower nature.

With the academic normalization of lust, it is little wonder that Western European governments are granting health and retirement benefits to state-accredited prostitutes—in the name of democracy.[29] It helps explain the United Nations document, the Convention on the Elimination of All Forms of Discrimination, adopted in 1969. This document—called and international bill of rights for women and already ratified by one hundred eighty countries—recommends the decriminalization of prostitution and the elimination of the traditional stereotypes of women in the role of mother.[30] In all of human history, no rising generation has been so inundated with pornography or so coaxed into thinking it normal. A book by a twenty-one-year-old says it all in its two-word title: *Porn Generation*.[31] I say the following after much thought: Only a clear understanding of the way the Creator meant things to be can stop the rot. Otherwise we are doomed as a civilization.

Abortion—the Deconstruction of Motherhood

In once Calvinistic Scotland there is now one abortion for every four live births and in some regions one abortion for every three.[32] In the United States, approximately 1,370,000 abortions occur annually, according to the Alan Guttmacher Institute.[33] Abortion has brought great numbers of young women under the spell of transgression and into the entangling web of self-justifying moral impotence. Dr. Beverly McMillan, an obstetrician-abortionist in Jackson, Mississippi, finally had to admit:

> I was depressed to the point of suicide, and I think the abortions had something to do with this...With the technique I used, we had to reassemble the parts. It just got too real...[what got me out] was looking at the bodies and realizing [that] five minutes earlier, this was all together in one beautiful piece.[34]

Dr. McMillan finally quit after years of abortion practice. She could no longer justify her work. A Christian ethicist observed that when conscience, provoked by guilt, is suppressed, it loses none of its force. The force is only redirected, driving a person into more and more wrongdoing.[35] The phenomenon is illustrated in the lyrics of the song performed by folk artist Mary Prankster, at a National Organization for Women (NOW) event: "Gonna hook me up to that great big suction pump, and bust that little piece of dust that's growing deep inside of me."[36] The dehumanization and destruction of delicate babies and of fragile moral sensitivity are essential in the deconstruction of traditional values and the promotion of the goals of the sexual revolution.

The Deconstruction of the Traditional Family

Though sexual relationships outside of marriage have always been a temptation, something definitive happened in America in the 1960s. Sexuality was "liberated" from its conjugal confines, and as a result, marriage has never been the same. Even children needed liberating. In an article published in November 1973 in the *Harvard Educational Review*, Hillary Rodham—who became first lady and then senator from New York Hillary Clinton—advocated liberating our "child citizens" from the "empire of the father."[37] With notions like that, it is not surprising that a well-known sociologist could observe "the ideal of the nuclear family died during the 1960s and 1970s."[38] One should note some of the factors that have produced it:

₪ Unlimited and easy contraception pushed sex outside of marriage.

₪ Feminists persuaded countless young women that careers, not family, really matter.

₪ Bastardy and divorce were destigmatized.

₪ The commercialization of sex and the sexualization of commerce separated sex from marriage and successfully sold immorality.

₪ "Morally neutral" sex education in the schools encouraged experimentation.

₪ The MTV youth culture promoted hedonism.

₪ The elimination of transcendence made morals and the family structure a purely relative and personal affair.

₪ Divorce, which now occurs in 50 percent of marriages, became easily accepted.[39]

We have a generation of liberated "sluts," "sacred prostitutes," and "shameless gigolos," freed from the chains of marriage and the restraints of conscience, responsible to no one, "living in sin," on whom the future of our nation must be built. This is democracy gone nuts! Said a college student, "The sexual revolution is over and everyone lost"[40]—everyone, that is, except the pagan agenda of liberation from the creation's norms.

The Deconstruction of Normal Sex by the Promotion of Homosexuality

In raising the issue of marriage, we've already embroiled ourselves in the discussion of homosexuality. In recent years the promotion of homosexuality and bisexuality—which are now protected and even promoted by the state—has destroyed normal heterosexuality. Though presented in the righteous robes of civic justice, homosexuality represents a complete distortion of creation's sexual structures. We cannot understand the radical implications of homosexuality's acceptance until we realize that homosexuality turns the blueprint for life inside out and upside down.

For having made that last statement, I am classified as a bigot and a homophobe. Much confusion exists. The average person is naturally confused upon reading a booklet called *Just the Facts*, which was sent, in cooperation with the Interfaith Alliance, to 14,500 school board presidents by fourteen mainstream mental health establishments. The booklet declared homosexuality to be "normal behavior."

The confusion is deliberately sown. Take Barnes and Noble, for example. This highly visible bookstore chain cooperated with the Anti-Defamation League to promote homosexuality through a booklet sent out with all its orders. *Close the Book on Hate: 101 Ways to Combat Prejudice* starts with a pledge to which we would all adhere without hesitation: "I will speak out against anyone who mocks, seeks to intimidate or actually hurts someone of a different race, religion, ethnic group or sexual orientation." But as you read on, the 101 "Ways to Combat Prejudice" turn out to be at least ninety-three ways to normalize sodomy.

Homosexuality on the High School Campus

The Barnes and Noble booklet recommends specific actions that will help achieve the goal "at home, in your school, in the workplace, in your house of worship, in the community." To close the book on hate in your school, the booklet recommends that you "encourage representation of all students on every school board, committee, group publication, and team...create a school calendar with all the holidays and important civil rights dates represented." (Obviously, a place for gay pride week will be found.) High school kids are encouraged to "poll your teachers about their ethnic-cultural backgrounds...and their experiences with prejudice. Ask each to write a short paragraph on the subject that can be compiled along with their photos in a teacher 'mug book.'" The problem is there is a real opportunity to "out" and publicly denounce teachers who do not affirm a politically correct doctrine.

In this document, valid protection of the homosexual is used to promote the homosexual lifestyle, even among young, impressionable children. Under the guise of "moral neutrality," our schools have become places where traditional values may *not* be taught, and immorality *must* be. The strategy of protecting in order to promote is exemplified in two cases, one from each coast.

Former Massachusetts governor—and then US Ambassador to Canada—Paul Cellucci, set in motion at taxpayer's expense a pro-homosexual annual Gay, Lesbian and Straight Education Network (GLSEN) Conference, which one observer described as a thinly disguised gay sex festival and recruitment fair. Of the 650 attendees, 400 were public school students, bused in for the occasion on taxpayer's money. One astute observer noted:

> The homosexual groups backing the programs justify them on grounds of "making schools safer for gay children."...The *Boston Globe* gave the official spin to the conference in its Sunday edition under the headline, "Alert against threats to gay teens." The first paragraph repeated the canard about suicide and safety in schools. The conference, said the *Globe*, was merely an attempt to overcome homophobia.[41]

If this were true, then why was so much attention given to explaining to students the various techniques of homosexual lovemaking? Here is the reason.

Four years later, on April 30, 2005, GLSEN sponsored an event at Brookline (Massachusetts) High School where a booklet called *Little Black Book: Queer in the 21st Century* was distributed to middle and high school students.[42] The book—which was made available to children as young as thirteen—contains phrases such as "You have the right to enjoy sex without shame or stigma." This booklet glorifies the riskiest of behaviors and then suggests that the students get tested for STDs every three to six months. It contains photos of full frontal nudity of men applying condoms, sexual profanity is used throughout, and abstinence is dismissed with the comment, "But how much fun is that?" One sidebar in the book lists gay bars in the Boston area "for the discerning queer boy," with the following annotations: *Campus/Manray Bar*: "Dancing, young guys and those who like young guys"; *Paradise Bar*: "Strippers dancing on the pool tables...porn on the television, the old, the young, something for everyone."[43]

Homosexuality on the College Campus

On the college campus, voyeuristic homosexuality is raised to an art form. Consider, for example, this course description for a fall 2002 class at UC Berkeley:

> QUEER CINEMA, Film 140: This course examines what performance is...as a live event that takes place on a stage or equivalent space...By examining queer cultures,...we will also look at the relationships between queer audiences and the cinema.[44]

At Hartford's Trinity College, mentioned above, the Gay and Lesbian Studies Department is brimming with enthusiasm. The Web site describes the difference between the college's present offerings and what was available in 1985. In 1985 there was nothing offered, but

> today, the course catalogue lists nearly 50 courses—offered by no fewer than 14 different departments and programs—that are related to gay and lesbian studies. In addition, the past two years have seen the development of a handful of new courses—all heavily enrolled—that specifically focus on the manifestation of sexuality in the fields of art, culture, science, and society.[45]

The progress of the pro-homosexual juggernaut shows no end. Generally, I have limited my comments to the United States, but the homosexual machine is rapidly moving forward in other nations as well. In 2001 in the United Kingdom, the age of consent for homosexuals was reduced to sixteen, and the following clause added to the amendment: "A homosexual act by any person shall not be an offense if he is under the age of sixteen years and the other party has attained that age." Suggested future reforms call for legalizing gay sex in saunas, public toilets, and "cruising" areas.[46] Social commentators need no special genius to recognize that gay marriage is the defining moral issue of the twenty-first century. In spite of serious efforts, which I support, to defend traditional one man–one woman marriage,[47] state-sponsored, legalized homosexual marriage will surely put the final touches on the social destruction of biblical, creational marriage.

The Feminization of Men

In the short-lived CBS sitcom, *Some of My Best Friends*, a straight, bridge-and-tunnel guy mistakes "GWM" for "Guy With Money" in a roommate ad and unwittingly moves in with a gay man. But by the second episode, he's learned to play gay, laugh out loud at the femme friend's campy jokes, and even prance around in silky, tight workout pants. This new sitcom demonstrates that the gay makeover of the straight American male has reached primetime.[48]

This process has been evident for years in big cities where gay men are rewriting the rules of what it takes to be the ideal man. Glossy magazines have noticed that straight men are looking more gay, but the influence is more than a matter of working out, waxing, and wearing Prada. It involves a profound change in consciousness, reflected in everything from greeting gay buddies with a kiss to treating women the way other women and most gay men do. In the trendier zones of New York, Los Angeles, Miami, and Montreal, the gay sensibility is influencing receptive straights.

There is a sobering lesson here. The homosexual lobby first gains access to the media and thus, to people's living rooms and bedrooms. Through the media, it recreates reality and begins to redefine what is "normal."[49]

POSTMODERN SEX: ENDLESS PERMUTATIONS

When normal male-female sex stops being the social yardstick, and when sex is separated from its essence—its created function for marriage and childbirth—the only standard left is the free-floating desires of each individual. And postmodern sex is exactly that—the expression of various forms of gratification and fantasy but with a horrendous loss of identity. Mark Taylor, the postmodern philosopher, states, "The lawless land of erring, which is forever beyond good and evil, is the world of Dionysus, the Antichrist, who calls every wander[er] to carnival, comedy and carnality."[50]

Such desires become the democratic right of the individual. No civic theory can put the brakes on our runaway sexual engine. We must accommodate more and more sexual eccentricities.[51]

The 1960s called for gender equality for women. Such equality must now be extended to all five sexes! The elite have enumerated them—male, female, gay, lesbian, and bisexual. (Some find as many as fourteen.) Says Charles Colson, "The gay-lesbian transvestite crowd wants to smash gender categories and obliterate the social norms within those categories. They say gender is artificial, a mere invention of society. So, they want your school to teach that kids are free to adopt any sexual identity."[52] Apparently they are succeeding.

An issue of the *UTNE Reader*, a chic magazine of the intellectual Left, promotes the active involvement of the Gay-Straight Alliance in schools. Specifically the Alliance wants to encourage children as young as thirteen to "come out as gays or lesbians." The argument goes that for young people, "Sexual identity can be fluid...It's not so absolute...This means rejecting the labels of male *and* female. If you erase those lines, then the whole thing changes."[53] High school students now describe themselves as "postgay," that is, they feel free to be anything they choose for the moment, sliding out of homosexuality into bisexuality and back as the whim occurs. Here are a few contributions to the colorful diversity now on offer.

₪ *Deirdre N. McCloskey.* A few years back, Deirdre was Donald N. McCloskey. Now she claims her moment in the sun: "I want the courtesy and the safety of a *why*less treatment [that has been extended to gays] [to be] extended to gender crossers."[54]

₪ *A fifteen-year-old boy from Massachusetts.* The nameless campaigner fought for his democratic right to attend class while wearing a dress, high heels, a wig and a padded bra. His therapist suggested that forcing the teenager to wear boys' clothing could endanger his mental health! At a court hearing, the sensitive lesbian judge, Linda Giles, overruled the school authorities. She argued that for the school to bar the boy from class amounted to "the stifling of a person's selfhood, merely because it causes some members of the community discomfort."[55]

₪ *A Church of England vicar.* The first vicar to undergo a sex-change operation, she returned to a warm welcome from parishioners. Ms. Stone, who was married twice and has a daughter, this time rose in the pulpit as a female priest, dressed in purple clerical robes and sporting a flashy pair of gold earrings and ruby-red lips.[56]

₪ *Lesbian prom king.* A senior girl who claims to be the only open lesbian at the school nominated herself for king "to defy the gender bias" of the traditional contest. The principal declined to oppose the nomination, saying, "We don't want her to be discriminated against."

Savoring this new diversity, Jungian, gnostic psychologist June Singer waxes apocalyptic: "A new sexual theory is in order, because of the dissolution of the old order [which] attempted to keep sexuality under moral and rational paradigms."[57] Indeed, this deconstructed sexual landscape needs the help of religion, a "new" kind of religion, such as the one that can be espoused by the American Humanist Association. This classic bastion of old-fashioned atheism now states, without the least hint of embarrassment:

> The battle for humankind's future must be waged and won in the classroom by teachers who correctly perceive their role as the *proselytizers*

of a new faith: a religion of humanity that recognizes and respects the spark of...*divinity in every human being.* The classroom must and will become an arena of conflict between the old and the new—the rotting corpse of Christianity...and the new faith of humanism.[58]

Contemporary "humanism" now throbs with spirituality. Mikhail Gorbachev, the last leader of the Soviet empire and a pure product of the atheistic Marxist system, now preaches a certain form of religious conversion:

We need a new synthesis that incorporates...democratic, Christian and Buddhist values,...which affirms such moral principles as...the sense of oneness with nature and each other...a kind of Ten Commandments that provides a guide for human behavior...in the next century and beyond.[59]

The materialist has become a mystic, at the cost of throwing out the original Ten Commandments for a substitute version that celebrates boys in dresses, thirteen-year-old gays and lesbians, sex-changed and twice-divorced Christian ministers, and lesbian homecoming kings.

This new religion intends not only to save the planet but also to deliver a new, liberating sexuality for everyone. But first the earth must be rid of that "ol'-time religion."

Chapter 2

Out with the Old: The Death of God

₪

W hen I had lots of hair and knew everything, I thought the 1960s "Death of God" theology was a minor irritant, or a joke. As one of my divinity school friends quipped, "I didn't even know he was sick!" But the "Death of God" was no laughing matter. In 2002, Steve Bruce, Head of the Department of Sociology at the University of Aberdeen, published a book, God is Dead: Secularization in the West, documenting how the 1960s belief that the God of the Bible is on the way out has become a reality.[1]

Feminist Naomi Goldenberg, who has become a witch, gladly confessed to her part in God's elimination. Feminists, she said, are engaged "in the slow execution of Christ and Jahweh...We women are going to bring an end to God."[2]

A book on pedagogy, popular among teachers of religion, has the provocative title *Teaching to Transgress: Education as the Practice of Freedom*.[3] This rebellious approach to teaching typifies the current attitude toward the norms of sexual ethics. Radical feminists seek freedom from the system of "patriarchy" in deliberate, unapologetic, deconstructive transgression. It is an effective, rapid way to destroy the old world and its God. Thus they demand that their sisters be "sinarticulate," have the "courage to sin," and "liberate the inner slut." "Erotic Feminist" Deena Metzger tells women, "We must allow ourselves whatever time it takes to reestablish the consciousness of the Sacred Prostitute."[4] Under the guise of Christian freedom, sin and spirituality are ritually wed. One speaker at a conference of two thousand mainline "Christian" women held up an apple, bit into it, and then, encouraged by cheers from the audience asked, "What taboo have you broken today?"[5] At another "Christian" convention, conferees were told to "discover and cultivate sacred Eros in all its ecstatic connections."[6] In a society in which prostitutes claim it is high time for them "to function as respected members of modern society,"[7] God really is dead.

In 1998 sociologist Alan Wolfe told a group of journalists during a visit to Washington, "We've [recently] gone from a predominantly Christian country to one of religious toleration."[8] "We used to be a Christian nation. Recently we have become a nation tolerant of all religions"[9]—all except one.

For proof of the deconstruction of God in contemporary society I call to witness a most unusual candidate, Tammy Bruce, the "conservative" lesbian talk-show host. A card-carrying member of the sexual revolution, Bruce documents the destructive agenda with great insight. From inside the movement she testifies that "the first step of the Intellectual Elite is to unmake and then remake history itself."[10] From that same insider position she reveals that the specific enemy has been and continues to be Christianity.[11] She proves her point by showing that Christianity is "the last approved prejudice" that can be viciously attacked without fear of social disapproval. Serrano's *Piss Christ,* a photo of Christ crucified submerged in the artist's urine, and Ofili's *Window to the Divine,* containing an image of the Virgin Mary covered in elephant dung and pornographic images, are lauded as "high art." Christian nativity scenes are banned from school "winter holiday" displays while symbols of other religions are allowed to remain.[12] NOW accuses Promise Keepers of a "right-wing 'misogynist' agenda," while defending pornography, which is so obviously anti-woman, as a "free speech issue."[13] All this strikes the non-Christian Bruce as clear evidence of a determined effort to erase the Christian God from the cultural scene.

The sexual college coursework already mentioned is joined to an equally distressing obliteration of all references to the Christian

God. A curriculum revolution is rewriting American history. At all the top colleges in the United States today, students can graduate without taking a single course in American history—replete as it is with endless references to God.[14] As an example, some years ago Stanford University ditched its Western civilization course curriculum at the demand of students who no longer wanted to learn of the oppressive history of Western and Christian civilization.[15] What does this produce? Historical amnesia. Freed from serious ideological and moral impairments from the past, college students are taught to reconstruct our cultural failure. Latin has a term for this—*tabula rasa*, a "clean sweep." Modern English has an equivalent term, *brainwashing*. You deconstruct a culture by destroying its memory of the past.

We need to understand recent cultural history as a program of both theological and sexual deconstruction. Did it succeed? Think about this one example. At the same time that many hotels have removed the Gideon Bibles from bed-table drawers, they have also installed pay-per-view pornography at the click of a remote. "Out with the old, in with the new" has never been more clearly depicted.

In With the New: Meet the "New" God of Religious Paganism

"Death of God" theologian David Miller, professor of religion at Syracuse University, understood that the funeral of the God of the Bible was *not the death of the divine*. It marked the rebirth of the gods and goddesses of ancient Greece and Rome.[16] Triumphantly announcing in 1974 the return of polytheism, Miller stated with unusual foresight and unabashed glee what would happen at this liberating moment:

> When released from the tyrannical imperialism of monotheism by the death of God, man has the opportunity of discovering new dimensions hidden in the depths of reality's history.[17]

The new god would not be one but many and would come in many forms.

Ancient Paganism at the Palmer House, Chicago

The British witch—a frail, middle-aged woman with skin as pale as her white robes—had flown in for the occasion. This priestess emerged from the rainy mists of Manchester, England, to recount the story of Isis, whom she served. As the story goes, Isis, the Egyptian goddess of magic, descended into the mystical underworld of deceased spirits to wrest her lover, Osiris, from the domain of death.

I listened with rapt attention to this official seminar presented by the Fellowship of the Healing if Isis at the Parliament of the World's Religions, held in an enormous hotel in downtown Chicago in 1993. Could this be happening in "Christian" America? Suddenly this fragile little woman became possessed of an unusual spiritual power and began wailing. Others in the audience took up the strain. A young black man sitting next to me, followed by a plump and otherwise jolly matron in the row behind me, stood and spoke with similar ecstatic energy. Soon the drab green seminar room in the Palmer House Hotel began to resemble the initiation ceremonies of an ancient pagan temple. When the moment came to "move into the second chamber," as in the ancient temples, I made my move—to the exit! I needed time to reflect on my first direct meeting of paganism in America.There I also heard Jean Houston speak for the first time.

Paganism: From Bumper Stickers to the White House

On bumpers in California, "Ankh If You Love Isis" is replacing "Honk If You Love Jesus."[18] Why is Isis appearing on bumper stickers? In Jean Houston's book, *The Passion of Isis and Osiris: A Gateway to Transcendent Love*, the author explains the attraction to what she calls, "sacred psychology":[19]

> In this journey of transformation...we form a powerful sense of identity with the mythic character...Symbolic happenings begin to appear in our

lives that bear undisguised relevance not only for our own existence but also for the remaking of society.[20]

Jean Houston first came to the public attention as a friend of Hillary Clinton when news reports told us that she and Hillary had met at the White House as "a couple of intelligent women...to discuss critical issues and employ a *rather ordinary inward turning exercise* [emphasis mine] to help focus their ideas,"[21] specifically by visualizing what Eleanor Roosevelt would have said and done. Houston denied that she was a "psychic."[22] However, in her lesser-known writings, Houston clearly claims shamanistic powers.[23] A modern lesbian witch defines a shaman as "a charged, potent, awe-inspiring, and even fear-inspiring person who takes true risks by crossing over into other worlds."[24] Draw your own conclusions. With self-proclaimed powers like these, Houston was doubtless helping the first lady get in touch with the departed spirit of Eleanor Roosevelt. Paganism in our time has reached the highest echelons of political power—without forgetting the masses.

Paganism at the Movies

My bizarre experience in the Palmer House Hotel in 1993 took place some years ago. Since then, these strange expressions of paganism have moved out of the obscure seminar rooms and the hushed corridors of political power into the American heartland. The society has cut itself loose from Christian standards and has followed a "trip" that led it first through drugs and highs in Haight-Ashbury, San Francisco, to Katmandu and Hindu-Buddhist meditation. One generation later, it is a common thing for "boomers" to seek light within rather than seeking it in "the Light of the World." To help the quest for light within, Hollywood has bequeathed all its technical savvy and endless wealth.

Hardly an American alive is unaware of the wisdom of Obi-Wan Kenobi, the Jedi warrior of George Lucas's *Star Wars* movies who explains the mystery of life to young Luke Skywalker: "The Force... is an energy field created by all living things. It surrounds us and penetrates us. It binds the galaxy together...it is all-powerful [and] controls everything."[25] That statement alone would be sufficient to suggest that the *Star Wars* trilogy essentially introduces the basics of Buddhism to America. The essence of Buddhism and of pagan religion in general is the conscious and consistent denial of God the Creator.

> You're not going to find truth outside yourself...You become a Buddha by actualizing your own original innate nature. This nature is primordially pure. This is your true nature, your natural mind...it is always perfect, from the beginningless beginning. We only have to awaken to it.[26]

The new mythology for the mass culture, robed in Hollywood dazzle, turns out to be pagan-Buddhist. Lucas did not act alone.

The Missionary Zeal of Religious Paganism

Buddhists say that there can be no enlightenment until all are enlightened.[27] At the first Western Buddhist Teacher's Conference in the 1970s, a group of Buddhist meditation teachers met in Dharamsala, India, to discuss the transmission of dharma (Buddhist teaching) in the modern world. By the 1990s, they pronounced this evaluation of their progress: "Strong bridges have been built from East to West, and the dharma has arrived in the New World."[28]

Buddhism has become so popular among Jews that there is a new category of spirituality books called "Ju-Bu" books. One is delicately titled *The Jew in the Lotus*.[29] bell hooks, a very influential black philosopher, writer, and educator—from an evangelical Christian home—now finds spiritual life in Buddhism. Little wonder the modern Buddhists rejoice in their achievements:

> Who but the enlightened Buddha could have imagined that yoga, tai chi, and meditation would be taught at the local "Y" [Young Men's Christian Association], the local synagogue, church, senior facility, and adult education class? Who could have imagined the spiritual bookstores and book clubs, graduate programs in Buddhist studies, and more than two thousand Buddhist centers in the US alone?[30]

Christians seeing a similar interest in Chrisitanity in Buddhist Japan, for example, would surely speak of a wildfire Christian revival.

THE NEW ECUMENISM

Although the vast majority of Americans have not converted to Buddhism or to other overt forms of pagan spirituality, many have converted to "syncretism," that is, to the belief that all religions say pretty much the same thing. Such tolerance is the seedbed of syncretism, which has become as American as apple pie. The pollster, George Barna, stated in 1996 that "America is transitioning from a Christian nation to a syncretistic, spiritually diverse society."[31]

In Salem, Massachusetts, the Salem Religious Leaders Association received a warlock as a member. The warlock is the high priest of a two-hundred-member Wicca coven, the Temple of the Black Rose. When asked why the warlock was allowed to join, Randal Wilkinson, a minister at Saint Peter's Episcopal Church, said that nobody could think of any compelling reason to forbid him from joining.

Barna documents the realization of a prediction made about America in 1888 by respected church historian Philip Schaff:

> America, favored by the most extensive emigration from all other countries, will become more and more the receptacle of all the elements of the world's good and evil, which will there wildly ferment together, and from the most fertile soil bring forth fruit for weal or woe for generations to come.[32]

Though the battle rages for spiritual and cultural health or decline, much of it is hidden from view. In particular, America has become fertile soil for all the pagan gods, while the God of the Bible—the true Lord of heaven and earth—is pushed to the margins.

Already in 1985 at a religious feminist conference titled "Women and Spirituality," keynote speaker and popular "Christian" theologian Rosemary Radford Ruether acknowledged that over the years

39

she had recommended the worship of pagan goddesses as more beneficial to women than Christianity.[33] Ruether is uncomfortable with Judaism and Christianity because they are "linear" religions that see history moving from past to future. She is happier with the cyclical approach of "the nature and fertility religions, pagan religions." The pagan monism of Ruether is slightly less radical only because, like ancient Gnosticism, it is dressed partly in Christian clothing.[34]

In these radical feminist circles, paganism has become the essence of Christianity. "The whole word [paganism] is taking on new meaning," says a leading feminist Roman Catholic nun. Basing her remarks (correctly) on the sense of the word *pagan* as "of the earth," she says, "It is not the belief we condemned in the past...I believe that was where Jesus was coming from...We are part of the earth, and we must work out our evolution into the beings we must become, in harmony with the earth".[35]

Unfortunately, this blending of God and the earth becomes worship of the earth and denial of the Creator, which is the essence of the paganism that Jesus himself denounced.[36]

A NEW GOD FOR A NEW WORLD

The new world is just around the corner. Many seers and spiritualists now adopt a rosy view of the future. For a generation, New Age prophets have talked about the earth tilting on its axis at the dawn of the Age of Aquarius (around AD 2000 to 2020), kick-starting the birth of a new spiritual humanity on a transformed planet.

Contemporary worshippers of Isis believe that the third millennium should be called the "Sophianic Millennium," because the goddess (also known as Sophia) is returning to lead us into marriage with the divine.[37] In a similar vein, Jean Houston, whom we met earlier, has a deep sense of the importance of what is going on: "Other times in history thought they were it. They were wrong.

This is it."[38] Such assurance betrays a wild-eyed utopianism of the most intolerant kind.[39]

You may think that such myths are only for distraction as sources of movie and book plots. Can anyone take such fabrications seriously?

Cutting-Edge Theologians and Futurologists

Many do, including serious religious thinkers who describe the pending change in human life and behavior with sophistication and who propose the dream as part of a major reorganization of society.

Huston Smith, one of the leading professors of religion in America, believes that the present work of the Spirit is producing an "invisible geometry to shape the religions of the world into a single truth."[40] Other "cutting-edge" theologians speak of "reinventing ourselves at a profound level [in order to] release the Earth community from its present impasse."[41] A growing conviction among futurologists is that, "We are witnessing the sudden irruption of a new civilization on the planet..."[42] One speaks of "a new ideology struggling to be born—a new global consciousness."[43]

A Foremost Thinker

How have such ideas become so plausible? In part, it's because our global humanity has the means to connect through Internet and the media. Lloyd Geering, Professor Emeritus of Religious Studies at Victoria University, is considered one of New Zealand's foremost thinkers and described by retired Episcopal Bishop John Spong as a "Presbyterian heretic."[44] Geering takes this new moment of human history very seriously, setting tomorrow's global culture in the context of Western intellectual history. Promoted by the Jesus Seminar, Geering's books[45] are blueprints for the future earth community—all written from the viewpoint of an apostate Christian. Geering predicts that tomorrow's global culture will be post-Christian and religiously pagan.

The God of Sex

Post-Christian

Tomorrow's culture will be post-Christian because evolution supposedly "proves" that human beings, as they evolved, created language, then symbols, and then religious explanations. The most recent human religious inventions are the monotheistic divine Creator of all things and the dualism between the spiritual realm and the realm of created life. Christian theology has called this the Creator-creature distinction. However, Geering says, "The other-world of the dualistic picture...has been slowly dissolving from Western consciousness" not least "through the most serious condemnation of traditional monotheism...by feminist thought." Feminist thinkers have shown that:

> The transfer of the seat of sacred power from the earth to the heavens, and the demise of the earth mother occasioned by the victory of the heavenly father, upset the balance of values in the gender relationship... [which] in the premonotheistic cultures...were conceived to be in a state of complementary harmony.[46]

Geering is categorical in his rejection of the God of the Bible: "The time for glorifying the Almighty [male] God who supposedly rules is now over." Notice how new sexual categories redefine "God." The end of Christianity is so evident "that some future generation may well be moved to discard the Christian calendar entirely, and rename the year AD 2000 as 1 GE, the first year of the global era."[47] Soon the Lord's Supper will only signify human fellowship, and Christmas will be a holiday for the celebration of family.

Religiously Pagan

According to Geering, tomorrow's culture will be religiously pagan. "Unlike the dualistic character of the Christian world, the new global world is *monistic* [italics mine]. That means that the universe is conceived as essentially [being] one."[48] Such thinking is classic spiritual paganism, and Geering, in spite of his all-pervading explanatory principle of evolutionary progress, has to admit with surprise that "the new story has...link[s] with the pre[monotheistic]...nature religions in which the ancients thought of themselves as the children of the earth mother." In an odd turn of events contemporary "spiritual" evolution goes backward! More than fifty years ago C. S. Lewis remarked on religious paganism's perennial character, calling it pantheism. He recognized its appearance in Nazi ideology as he wrote, "By a strange irony, each new relapse into this immemorial 'religion' is hailed as the last work in novelty and emancipation...so far from being the final refinement, pantheism is, in fact, the permanent natural bent of the human mind."[49]

Geering must not have read these remarks of Lewis. He believes that the "new" paganism will serve as the new religion for the future global society. In the future religion, "Mother Earth would be the consciously chosen symbol referring to everything about the earth's eco-system."[50] He notes that, "The loving care of Mother Earth is in many quarters replacing the former sense of obedience to the Heavenly Father.[51] In the religion of the coming global society, the forces of nature, the process of evolution and the existence of life itself will be the objects of...veneration."[52]

This is pure paganism, as defined by the New Testament—"worship of the creation rather than the Creator."[53] It should not be surprising that this new religion fits naturally "the Buddhist, Hindu and Chinese notions of nontheistic spirituality."[54] It would seem that a unification of all pagan religions is in the cards.[55] Sounding like a paragon of tolerance, Geering states, "There will not be 'only one way'...Groups must learn to be inclusive."[56] In other words, there will only be the "one, inclusive, pagan way," and this "must" be the case. Geering is not advocating tolerance, as he claims, but a veiled and hence dangerous form of intolerance—but for the survival of the planet, this is the way it *must* be!

Getting rid of God, this one-dimensional norm includes, as events proved, getting rid of one-dimensional sex. Welcoming the many gods of syncretistic polytheism and higher powers of the personal spiritual quest has also, and at the same time, signaled the arrival of a new era of multidimensional sex. How is that? Implicit within Miller's 1974 declaration about polytheism is feminist Shulamith Firestone's 1972 call for "a reversion to an unobstructed pansexuality."[57] Polytheism gives us polysexuality;[58] religious syncretism gives us the multicolored rainbow of sexual options. It took only a generation for the reality to arrive.

Between God and sex, however you define them, there is a deep connection.

Chapter 3

IN WITH THE NEW:
THE COMING SEXUAL UTOPIA

₪

SEX IN THE UTOPIAN KINGDOM

W e hear from many quarters an optimistic, spiritual view
of the future. In previous chapters we considered the "necessary
stage" that tears down both traditional sexual theory and practice
and the God of theistic spirituality. We then considered the upbeat
stage of global reconstruction based on a new view of God. In this
pagan, planetary utopian kingdom what will happen to sex?

The short answer is virtually anything. In South Africa one out
of every three children is having sex at the age of ten.[1] A Cambridge
professor writes a book on the goodness of lust.[2] Over the Internet,
teenage girls buy portable stripper poles as a symbol of "woman-
power," a way of saying, "I'm in charge of my body and my destiny." To say this with a straight face, you need religion, and pagan
religion gives an aura of spirituality to "anything goes" sex. Bishop
Spong admits that the two are intimately linked. He explains
his apostate Christianity: "The death of the God of theism has
removed from our world the traditional basis of ethics."[3] Radical
feminists argue that we must change our consciousness about sexuality, and they see such change as *spiritual* transformation. In its
popular version, sexual liberation is associated with "civil rights,"
but its real inspiration proceeds from the age-old dogmas of pagan
religion. Charles Pickstone, a radical Anglican priest, sets the tone

in his book *The Divinity of Sex*: "Sex is the spirituality that reveals the sacramental richness of matter."[4] In this new-look Christianity, as in old paganism, beds become altars and altars become beds. The spirit guide of Neale Donald Walsch, author of the best-selling *Conversations with God*, dangles the same forbidden fruit, as it urges, "Mix what you call the sacred with the sacrilegious, for until you see your altars as the ultimate place for love, and your bedrooms as the ultimate place for worship, you see nothing at all."[5] People are mesmerized by a vision too good to be true, of spiritualized, liberated, anything-is-possible, anything-is-moral sex.

AQUARIAN SEX

What will happen to sex in this pagan, planetary utopian kingdom? Leading psychologist and popular write June Singer believes she has the answer. The title of her 1977 book says it all: *Androgyny: Towards a New Theory of Sexuality*.[6] Why do we need a new theory about sex? Because we are entering a new period of human history. Singer actually says that the Age of Aquarius *is* "the Age of Androgyny."[7] Since Eros—the double-sexed god of love—knows no boundaries, as Singer states,[8] the future spiritual human being will be delivered equally from the constraining boundaries of male or female heterosexuality. Thus true spiritual liberation includes the liberation to be *both* male and female at the same time, in the same person—*andros*, male; *gyny*, female. In the coming Age of Aquarius all things are unified, so that in the sexual domain,

"[t]he archetype of androgyny appears in us as an innate sense of... and witness to...the primordial cosmic unity, that is, it is the sacrament of monism, functioning to erase distinction...this was nearly totally expunged from the Judeo-Christian tradition...and a patriarchal God-image."[9]

With Singer there is a deliberate attempt to redefine sexuality in terms of the new aquarian *spirituality*. We must look toward a whole way of being...no longer as exclusively "masculine" or "feminine" but rather as whole beings in whom the opposite qualities are ever-present.[10] Is it any wonder that thirty years later we have "postgay" sexually indefinable high school kids?

A New Moral Vision

A new morality will undergird the coming utopia. Sexual perversion is justified as the progress of democracy, of First Amendment freedoms and civil rights. What American dares to speak against such values? But democracy is unable to explain the complex issues of human behavior. "One man-one vote" does not define a foundation for morals.[11] It is often noted that Hitler came to power through a democratic vote. Though both left and right want to be seen as democratic, each side knows that democracy is not enough. If the pagan sexual makeover is to happen, it needs a new moral and spiritual vision. Singer noted in 1977, "There are no conventions and laws as yet that take into account the emerging consciousness [of sexual practice] of the Aquarian Age."[12] This emerging consciousness will only come about when the "arbitrary" Christian notions of good and evil are destroyed and a new "morality" is adopted.[13] Where can the program turn for such a moral vision? To change morality, you have to change people's thinking in general, and especially their thinking about God. We have traveled a long way down this road.

The Original American Pagan

Paganism is not so foreign to American soil. Ralph Waldo Emerson, the homegrown American pagan of the early nineteenth century, already described the essence of pagan morality, emphasizing its malleability: "No law can be sacred to me but that of my nature. Good and bad are but names very readily transferable to this or that."[14] The brilliant Emerson understood that the relativization of good and evil is essential to pagan well-being. Conscience must be silenced and guilt denied.[15]

THE GOD OF SEX

A NEW AGE EMERSON

Walsch's spirit guide sounds Emersonian too: "There's no such thing as the Ten Commandments...God's Law is No Law."[16] "Understand that 'right' and 'wrong' are figments of your imagination."[17] "No kind of evolution ever took place through denial. If you are to evolve, it will not be because you've been able to successfully deny yourself things you know 'feel good,' but because you've granted yourself these pleasures."[18]

Today we have the occultist, liberating "Jesus" who channeled messages to Helen Shucman, author of the best-selling New Age text, *A Course in Miracles.* This "Jesus" says to the reader about his unfortunate death: "Do not make the pathetic error of clinging to the old rugged cross...Your only calling here is to devote yourself with active willingness to the denial of guilt in all its forms."[19] Not surprisingly, Marianne Williamson—a woman who has greatly popularized *A Course in Miracles*—is known as the "guru to the stars," those social luminaries, so many of whom want spirituality and significance without moral purity.

The pagan solution proposes that we embrace our evil, accept it, justify it, and come to love it. In *Conversations with God* (which are actually conversations Walsch has with himself) the author embraces evil for himself and for everyone else. He assures us that "Hitler went to heaven...His deeds were mistakes, not crimes. The mistakes did no harm to those whose deaths he caused because they were released from their earthly bondage."[20] The radicals already push the envelope to show where such a program can go—as far as exonerating Hitler.

"Discover[ing]...sacred Eros in all its ecstatic connections," as radical feminists propose,[21] also includes for these kinds of "Jesus followers" the joys of pornography. At the beginning of their movement, feminists were against the sexual exploitation of the woman's body. Now, some promote pornography if it helps in the destruction of the normativity of the Bible's view of sexuality. In her lecture at the University of Minnesota Law School, Nadine Strossen, president of the American Civil Liberties Union told her audience, "Not only does [censorship] violate free speech, but it undermines the fight for women's rights."[22] In the same vein Christie Hefner, who is, according to her father, Hugh, "a strong feminist," took over the running of the Playboy empire in 1982 and has endorsed Playboy's decision to promote hard-core pornography.[23] Thus, pornography is made part of the new sexual morality.

The New Morality of Planned Parenthood

Notice the oxymoron in the following paragraph:

> New Hampshire homosexual Bishop V. Gene Robinson said during Planned Parenthood's fifth annual prayer breakfast [Planned Parenthood holds prayer breakfasts?] that Planned Parenthood should target "people of faith" to promote abortion rights and comprehensive sex education [people destroy babies by faith?].[24]

Planned Parenthood has got religion: "Our defense against religious people has to be a religious defense...We must use people of faith to counter the faith-based arguments against us," said Robinson. "We have allowed the Bible to be taken hostage, and it is being wielded by folks who would use it to hit us over the head. We have to take back those Scriptures," he said. "You know, those stories are our stories. I tell this to lesbian folk all the time: The story of freedom in Exodus is our story...That's my story, and they can't have it."[25]

This necessarily must be a morality of relativism, where good and evil finally merge. Thus Robinson affirms,

> The world is not black and white. We need to teach people about nuance, about holding things in tension, that this can be true and that can be true and somewhere between is the right answer. It's a very adult way of living, you know. What an unimaginative God it would be if God only put one meaning in any verse of Scripture.[26]

This homosexual bishop needs a malleable kind of moral system in order to live with himself and smooth over the "tension" caused when he left his wife and two young daughters in 1986 and moved in with a male lover. He also needs a new form of revelation and claims to find it in his own soul. "I know, in the end, that I'm going to heaven—and so are you."[27] Of course the classic Christian source of revelation, namely the Bible, says the very opposite: Do you not know that the unrighteous [including]...*men who practice homosexuality*...will not inherit the kingdom of God?[28]

You may wonder if this relativism, masquerading as morality, is making progress in our modern society.

Even Tammy Bruce, the lesbian talk-show host cited previously, is not fooled by this "new morality." Though she was once president of the Los Angeles chapter of NOW and served on their national board of directors, she has since distanced herself from the movement. She states in no uncertain terms that "a moral vacuum is engulfing the Left...moving through the body of society like a cancer, putting us all at risk."[29] She calls the god of this movement "malignant narcissism."[30] The bisexual high priestess of this god is surely Madonna, who in her hit song "Hollywood" declares, "I am bored with right and wrong."[31]

THE DISAPPROVAL OF DISAPPROVAL

Sociologist Alan Wolfe notes that Americans are reluctant to pass judgment on how other people act and think and have added an eleventh commandment: "Thou shall not judge."[32]

Such an unwillingness to judge became apparent during the Clinton scandal of the 1990s. Columnist Ellen Goodman fearlessly and self-righteously applied this new morality to the Left: "We liberals do not approve of the immoral life of President Clinton but we refuse to disapprove."[33] Here is a form of the eleventh commandment: "Thou shalt disapprove of disapproval."[34] This disapproval relativizes the original commandments (such as "Thou shalt not commit adultery") and absolutizes the eleventh, producing the situation many deplore, as Wolfe's findings demonstrate.

The rising generation apparently does not see this, having been brainwashed by radical teachers. A national survey of college seniors, conducted by Zogby International in 2001, showed that three-quarters of them had been taught by their professors that what is right and wrong depends on differences in individual values and cultural diversity.[35] In the insightful words of Tammy Bruce, "Like God, right and wrong are dead."[36]

According to Judge Edith H. Jones of the U.S. Court of Appeals for the Fifth Circuit, the practice of law is just as demoralized. At present "the question of what is morally right is routinely sacrificed to what is politically expedient." According to this respected judge, "[T]he American legal system has been corrupted almost beyond recognition...The integrity of law, its religious roots, its transcendent quality are disappearing...The historical soil of the Western legal tradition is being washed away, and the tradition itself is threatened with collapse."[37]

In this "new" moral context of "individual freedom," the liberation of sex is having a field day.

Liberated Sex—Sex with Everybody and Anybody

Neal Donald Walsch, a "moral" spokesman for the spiritual Left and also for the god of the spiritual Left, also brings deep revelations about the nature of sex in the coming utopia. Walsch, speaking for himself, rather than quoting his "god" (though this is doubtless the same thing) says, "I envision a world where we can make love to anyone, any way we wish to, at any time, anywhere."[38] Walsch's "god" approves of masturbation, even as a kind of religious ritual: "Give yourself abundant pleasure, and you will have abundant pleasure to give others. The masters of Tantric sex knew this. That's why they encourage masturbation, which some of you actually call a sin."[39]

Sex with anybody by anybody is also the utopian citizen's birthright. Walsch's god approves of sexual activity by children and teenagers, saying, "In enlightened societies offspring are never discouraged, reprimanded, or corrected when they begin to find early delight in the nature of their very being...sexual functions are also seen and treated as totally natural, totally wonderful, and totally okay."[40] Walsch's god does not say whether the enlightened little ones are doing it solo, with their friends, with their siblings, or with adults. To ensure that the kids get the message, Walsch's god says schools should replace the current "facts-based curriculum" with a "values-based curriculum," including "value-laden" courses on "Celebrating Self, Valuing Others, and Joyous Sexual Expression."[41]

Liberated Marriage—Married to Everybody

Barbara Marx Hubbard, once a Democratic presidential candidate and now a spiritual teacher at the State of the World Forum (organized annually by Mikhail Gorbachev), sees marriage this way. Her "familiar spirit" says that in the new age, fidelity of the partners is for the sake of their chosen act, whether it is to be a godly child or godly work in the universe. When the act is completed, the partnership is renewed if there is more to be done. It is lovingly ended if there is nothing more to be created by that particular couple. Each discovers the next partner or partners with no hint of sorrow, for nothing is separated among those totally connected with God.[42]

Early feminist Jessie Bernard, in her influential 1972 book *The Future of Marriage*, adopted the same value system: "To be happy in...traditional marriage...a woman must be slightly ill mentally."[43] True to form, Lloyd Geering argues that in the post-Christian global age about to arrive "because of the growth in human autonomy...there will be no permanent adhesion to any form of association [club, church, marriage partner]."[44] Walsch's god denounces fidelity and marriage vows as "the Highest Betrayal" and a "blasphemy."[45] This divine message Walsch heard fits perfectly his situation of having been married five times. In the coming sexual utopia, an essential element of stability in past societies will become gloriously unstable.

Liberated Families—Raised by Everybody and Anybody

In the utopian sexual kingdom, traditional families will disappear, and tribal elders will raise the children. Barbara Marx Hubbard says, "The breakup of the 20th century procreative family structure is a vital perturbation needed for the breakthrough of the 21st century co-creative family structure."[46] Already in 1932, Aldous Huxley in his famous novel, *Brave New World*, describing the utopia to come, wrote, "Everyone belongs to everyone."[47] In 1997 A. Cornelius Baker, the executive director of the National Association of People with AIDS, openly admitted that the goal of the homosexual movement was not so much inclusion in society but the profound redefinition of society. He declared that homosexuals are now "engaged in redefining the society in which we live—how marriage is viewed, how family is viewed."[48] This redefinition of marriage and family—which limits the stringent demands of faithfulness associated with traditional, heterosexual marriage[49] while opening marriage to include all kinds of groups and people[50]—renders marriage so diffuse that the specter of the "nanny state" as the ultimate family looms ominously large.

Walsch's god proposes that parents should turn the care of their children over to the "entire community":

> Place the raising of children in the hands of your respected Old Ones. Parents see their children whenever they wish [we call it "quality time"], live with them if they choose, but are not solely responsible for their care and upbringing. The physical, social, and spiritual needs of the children are met by the entire community, with education and values offered by the elders.[51]

In the rosy world of tomorrow's sexual utopia, "it takes a village."[52]

Indeed, family members who refuse to move into the liberty of this glorious freedom should be left behind. Barbara Marx Hubbard says, "If members of our family choose to remain where they are, we have no more obligation to suppress our own potential on their behalf. In fact, the suppression of potential is more 'immoral' than growing beyond our biological relationships."[53] So just leave! The nanny state will take care of the ex-spouse and kids, and everyone will live happily ever after.

Liberated Gender—Sex with Every Body and Any Body

In chapter 1 we discussed the call for gender freedom. The contemporary norm is a fluid sexual identity. Bisexuality is hip. "Gender blur" for teenagers is cool. Radicals encourage the rejection of labels such as "male" and "female," demanding freedom to organize their lives without such a straightjacket. June Singer's invitation to androgyny is embraced by the music group Garbage, which catches the contemporary mood in its powerful song "Androgyny."[54] "Nobody wants to be alone, Everybody wants to love someone...Why can't we all just get along? Boys in the girl's room, Girls in the men's room, You free your mind in your androgyny." The song ends with the repetition of the words, "boys, girls" so that the two become indistinct. The message is that the mind is freed by bisexuality.

What is driving this agenda?

THE END OF GENDER—FROM POLYTHEISM TO POLYSEXUALITY

What happens when you change a society's religion? What happens when those deep religious notions are overthrown and replaced by conflicting religious ideas?

In the last generation, bishops such as Episcopalian John Shelby Spong and Anglican David Jenkins have called for a new (pagan) view of God, denying the resurrection and rejecting all other major doctrines of Christian orthodoxy without censure. It should thus come as no surprise that in August 2003, the Episcopal Church USA voted by a two-to-one majority to ordain Gene Robinson (a divorced minister living with a homosexual lover) as a bishop. Again, ideas have consequences—especially our ideas about God. "Without God," said Dostoevsky in the *Brothers Karamazov*, "all things are permissible."[55]

Jeffrey Satinover uses the term "polysexuality," noting that "many gays themselves...have cogently argued that the gay lifestyle is not so much 'homosexual' as 'pansexual.'" Satinover further notes that "'human sexuality' in the 'state of nature' is enormously diverse and polymorphous...What we call the 'gay lifestyle' is, in large measure, a way of life constructed around *un*constrained sexuality."[56] An unconstrained pagan view of the divine (polymorphous polytheism) will produce unconstrained polymorphous pansexuality, as Virginia Mollenkott clearly demonstrates. This represents the ultimate "freeing of the mind."

Omnigender: A Trans-religious Approach

Virginia Ramey Mollenkott is an ex-Bible Presbyterian professor of literature who is now an openly practicing lesbian. She offers a radical paradigm for the future liberation of sexuality, an "omnigender" society of "allosexuality [other sexuality]...an arrangement of many erotic patterns in no particular hierarchy"[57] where virtually all sexual choices are normalized. Such choices would include:

- ₪ intersexuals or hermaphrodites (people with both sets of sexual organs, male and female)[58]
- ₪ transsexuals (sex operation changes)
- ₪ drag queens and kings (cross-dressing performers)
- ₪ transgenderists or bigenderists (cross-dressing or cross-living part or full time)

₪ androgynes (both male and female gender roles at same time)[59]

₪ heterosexuals

₪ homosexuals

₪ bisexuals

₪ Those who enjoy various fetishes (oral or anal, group sex, sadomasochistic sex, which is mentioned without judgment)[60]

₪ autoerotics

₪ asexuals

₪ pansexuals

₪ pedophiles[61]

It is becoming increasingly clear that the national debate over same-sex marriage is broader than homosexuals getting "married." Homosexuals are beginning to admit they want what Mollenkott proposes, namely, the destruction of the concept of monogamy and traditional marriage altogether. What they really are after is a society that recognizes every sexual arrangement as normal—even group sexual liaisons and polygamy.[62]

For Mollenkott, this diversity is a utopian "world worth fighting for...[where] people [a]re appreciated in their complexities instead of being attacked for not sorting out neatly into one or two possible genders."[63] Here are the "new dimensions" that become possible when we eliminate the God of the Bible. The goal is "to move society toward attitudes and *policies* favoring liberty and justice for all."[64] For Mollenkott, the legal division of people into male and female is as wrong as the legal division of people into black and white.[65] In such a (utopian, just) society, "everybody would have their own unique sexuality, falling in love with another person's...entire being, not just that person's genitals...People would be unisexual, choosing to identify themselves anywhere on the whole spectrum of sexuality."[66] Children would be raised according to the sex choice of parents.

3: In with the New: The Coming Sexual Utopia

FROM BATHROOM HUMOR TO BATHROOM POLITICS

I once spoke in Australia about the importance of sexual distinctions. Five professional engineers videotaped the lecture. As I warmed to my subject, helped significantly by the wires under my coat and the spotlights focused on my person, I exhorted the men in my audience to respect male-female distinctions and "stick to their urinals." As the place erupted in laughter, I got myself into even more trouble by apologizing for my "off-the-wall remark." All caught on videotape from a professor of theology!

Bathroom issues often bring a chuckle, but they have become serious policy. In the 1960s when I visited my future wife at her sophisticated all-women's college on the East Coast, there was one tiny bathroom for men on a stairwell called "The Euphemism." When my daughters attended that same college a generation later, males used the women's bathrooms! Mollenkott's proposal for unambiguously unisex bathrooms is a reality on the university campus[67] and in some parts of the new American army.[68] The movement is spreading. Some seventy municipalities nationwide are producing ordinances that would allow "bathroom choice" based on a person's psychological self-appraisal. In other words, if a man feels like a woman, he has the right to use the women's bathroom.[69] For the sake of social engineering, sophomoric bathroom humor is giving way to serious bathroom politics.

Does this new bathroom behavior improve things? The youthful Wendy Shalit, author of *A Return to Modesty: Discovering the Lost Virtue*, denounces the oversexualized generation of which she is part. Her firsthand testimony is poignant: "When...bathrooms are co-ed, and we are all thrown together...there's no escape from the culture of immodesty. When everything is integrated...there's no mystery, and there's no separation, and there's no reverence between the sexes."[70]

In spite of this plaintive cry, the lesbian Mollenkott calls for the elimination of oppressive gender-specific pronouns like "he" and "she,"[71] and the end of Sir and Madam and Mr. and Mrs. in polite speech.[72] In such a society we would no longer see the "M" and "F" boxes on government application forms, drivers' licenses, passport applications, or marriage forms.[73] According to Mollenkott, all prisons and competitive sports will be unisexual. Such physical and legal changes will produce a just society without norms. "When all the variations of human gender and sexuality become acceptable...then everyone will be 'normal' and 'normalcy' sill lose its coercive power."[74]

Are Mollenkott's musings the imagination of marginals with no hope of success? She does not think so. As proof she mentions the Platform for Action of the United Nations Conference on Women in Beijing, 1995. This action plan was drawn up by the American delegation headed by Hillary Clinton and proposed the *five* genders I mentioned earlier: male, female, homosexual, lesbian, and bisexual. The plan was defeated only because of an alliance between the Vatican and a number of Muslim states.[75] At Brookline High School on April 30, 2005, at a GLSEN (Gay, Lesbian, Straight Education Network) homosexual conference for middle- and high-school kids, an eyewitness gave this report:

> It was kind of sad and disheartening. For example, one girl, who looked like an 8th or 9th grader, was dressed like a hooker, in boots, stockings, suggestive blouse, and lipstick. She started talking about "multiple types of genders" and how it bothered her when she filled out online forms that there was just male and female to choose from. "No, it's NOT just male or female," she said to the group. The workshop coordinators agreed, and responded that, "They're just keeping a stereotype alive," indicating that limiting society to two genders is almost like a crime.[76]

In similar fashion, in some of our top women's colleges, students have voted to do away even with the *feminine* pronoun, for it excludes women students who do not feel particularly feminine.[77]

Mollenkott believes her vision of society will eventually win, and, in light of what is happening in our state schools, she is probably right. The old stereotype is barely being kept alive. In 2001 she predicted:

In all probability, official church policies will be the rear guard on gender, being dragged along towards gender justice kicking and screaming when the secular society will no longer tolerate anything else.[78]

What does Mollenkott know that the average person fails to see?

The apostle Paul indicates in Romans that the pagan rejection of God produces perverted sexuality as an ultimate and inevitable consequence. The Greco-Roman society of his day was living proof. Mollenkott's trajectory suggests that the process also works the other way. The polysexualist Mollenkott has become a polytheist, finding the "truth" she is promoting in all the religions.[79] Her sexual perversion has led her far from the God of the Bible.

The call for "omingender" policies, when stripped of its disguise as civil rights and human dignity, appears for what it is:[80] a pagan religious agenda to change the spiritual character of Western, once "Christian," society.

BACK TO THE FUTURE: THE UNTHINKABLE EXTREMES

If any example shows that we are faced with two mutually contradictory worldviews, it is surely pedophilia. Adults engaging in sex with children have no place in a theistic universe. However, in a monistic universe, such behavior is as natural as breathing.

Mollenkott is guarded about the implications of an omnigendered society and does not endorse sex anywhere, anyhow. However, she allows for the possible value of pedophilia. "In our culture," she says, "pedophilia absolutely cannot be expressed relationally" because of the age of consent.[81] For her, intergenerational sex is "not likely to have tragic repercussions" and is only dangerous when adults instigate guilt feelings.[82] In other words, pederasty could well be part of our enlightened sexual future, just as it was an accepted part of the elite society of ancient Greece and Rome. Its legitimacy seems to depend only on public acceptance, and the radicals are working on that. The University of Minnesota Press recently published a book by Judith Levine, *Harmful to Minors: The Perils of Protecting Minors from Sex.*[83] The book argues that children are entitled to safe, satisfying sex lives. Five academic experts assured the University Press of the book's validity. In a culture with no limits, once there is no age limit for sexual activity, pedophilia is an obvious next step.

One more indication of the contemporary clash of worldviews is bestiality, which Mollenkott oddly omits. Bestiality is a thriving cottage industry on the Internet. At Halloween in our local Barnes and Noble, right up there at the entrance, you could not miss the book of Fiona Horne, *Witch: A Magickal Journey: A Guide to Modern Witchcraft.* In it, the physically beautiful Horne describes the spiritual possibilities granted by "Lulu," her snake "familiar."[84] She explains: "In ritual, an animal can be used to facilitate the forging of links to the supernatural forces...and commune with nature."[85] Her snake represents the serpentine, sexual energy of Kundalini, a Hindu technique for joining sexuality and pagan spirituality. Horne makes the connection explicitly. For the sake of Barnes and Noble readers everywhere she explains how she had herself photographed with the animal coiled around her naked body, herself in a mystical (kundalini) trance, with the snake's face breathing into hers. "One thing I like to do," she adds, "is to breathe her breath. She puts her head under my nose and we breathe together."[86] Though delicately avoiding the more lurid details, all the sexual innuendoes are present in this "idyllic" account of a witch and her familiar.

New Age teacher Terence McKenna believes that nature's various species communicate with one another via chemical signals. Animals provide a bridge because they too are divine.[87] In Native American spirituality, the eagle and the owl are "messengers that bring instructions from the spirit of the night [which is] everywhere [and] has no name."[88] Thus the shaman, who is in touch with the powers of the earth, has a more-than-ambiguous relationship with animals. Eliade explains:

The shaman can turn himself into various animals, and it is sometimes a question to what extent the animal cries uttered in the course of a séance belong to the familiar spirits or represent the stages of the shaman's own transformation into an animal, that is, the manifest revelation of his true mystical personality.[89]

Bestiality has always had its place in some forms of occult spirituality because of the need to experience the divinity of nature in all its forms. In other words, in this extremist form of sexual "liberation" there is also a deep connection between "god" and sex.

THE POWER OF POLYAMORY

Stanley Kurtz is a research fellow at the Hoover Institution. The Hoover Institution, a think tank on the campus of Stanford University, hardly expresses the views of right-wing gay-haters. Kurtz himself cannot be called homophobic, since he believes "our increased social tolerance for homosexuality is generally a good thing."[90] Kurtz nevertheless writes with deep insight into the decisions we are making as a culture that could spell irreversible disaster for civilization.

His thesis maintains that the core issue today is not homosexuality as such but gay marriage, which he believes, will destroy marriage as we know it. "Marriage is a social institution. Stable families depend on it. Society depends on stable families...marriage means monogamy. Gay marriage will break that connection. It will do this by itself, and by leading to polygamy and polyamory. What lies beyond gay marriage is no marriage at all."[91]

Kurtz documents the powerful lobbies that are ready to demand equal rights for polygamy (many marital partners) and polyamory (literally, "many loves," that is, more than two people in a long-term committed sexual relationship). Polyamory is more chic than the old-fashioned polygamy, for it involves all kinds of sexual combinations: one woman and two men; two women and one man; groups of more than three; heterosexual group marriages; groups in which some or all members are bisexual; lesbian groups, homosexual groups; and many more.

Kurtz's research shows that this is a cutting-edge issue among scholars of family law. As states approve "marriage" for a greater and greater variety of exceptional arrangements, they are moving to a state-sanctioned polyamory. Kurtz identifies a number of leading legal experts who favor just such legalization. He mentions, among others, longtime National Gay and Lesbian Task Force policy director Paula Ettelbrick, who believes that promoting polyamory is the ideal way to "radically reorder society's view of the family."[92] Ettelbrick teaches law at the University of Michigan, New York University, Barnard, and Columbia. Others in this movement include Nancy Polikoff (American University Law School), Martha Fineman (Cornell law professor), Martha Ertman (University of Utah law professor), Judith Stacey (Barbra Streisand Professor in Contemporary Gender Studies at USC), David Chambers (University of Michigan law professor), and Martha Minow (Harvard Law School). Kurtz says that "together these scholars represent what is arguably now the dominant perspective within the discipline of family law. They have plenty of followers and hold much of the power and initiative within their field. There may be other approaches to academic family law, but none exceed the radicals in influence." This is a sobering statement, which Kurtz backs up with factual evidence.

How far these ideas have penetrated into mainstream society is indicated by Al and Tipper Gore's 2002 book *Joined at the Heart*, in which they define a family as those who are "joined at the heart" (rather than by blood or by law).[93] According to Kurtz, the notion that a family is any group "joined at the heart" comes straight from Harvard's Martha Minow, mentioned previously, who worked with the Gores.

Mainline churches are also receptive to polyamory. The WOW (Witness Our Welcome) 2003 conference in Philadelphia, and ecumenical gathering for "sexually and gender-inclusive Christians," celebrated the spiritual aspects of polyamory. "Having multiple sexual partners," said one of the leaders, Debra Kolodny, "can be 'holy'...there can be fidelity in threesomes. It can be just as sanctified as anything else if all partners are agreed."[94] The conference was supported by groups within the Presbyterian Church (USA), including McCormick Theological Seminary as well as Dignity USA (Roman Catholic), People for the American Way, the Human Rights Campaign, Episcopal Divinity School, Chicago Theological Seminary (United Church of Christ), and Wesley Theological Seminary (United Methodist).[95]

Kurtz directly ties this socially explosive movement to homosexuality. He believes homosexual marriage will open the door for all other permutations. Some do not believe this. "The 'conservative' case for gay marriage holds that state-sanctioned marriage will reduce gay male promiscuity," but the opposite will doubtless happen if the well-documented promiscuous character of gay relationships is to be believed.

> What if, instead of marriage reducing gay promiscuity, sexually open gay couples help redefine marriage as a nonmonogamous institution? There is evidence that this is exactly what will happen...Married gay couples will begin to redefine the meaning of marriage for the culture as a whole, in part by removing monogamy [marriage to just one person] as an essential component of marriage.[96]

FLASHBACK

It is ironic that in the much-vaunted, highly evolved sophistication of contemporary culture, we are reaching back to the ancient world for its spirituality. As we embrace the spirituality associated with the mystery religions of the Greco-Roman Empire, we also assume its expressions of unrestrained sexuality.

The polytheism of ancient Greece was intimately tied to the spirituality of the Mysteries.[97] The amoral gods of Mount Olympus were personifications of the forces of divine nature, in particular the fiery force of sexuality. Initiation into the powers of nature was the essence of pagan spirituality, and sexual trance was one powerful means to that end. Some early church fathers saw the essential spiritual conflict as the confrontation between the God of the Bible and the goddess of unbridled, erotic sexuality, Aphrodite.[98] We face a similar conflict today.[99] This "aphrodisiac" view of sex was especially evident in the lewdness and violence of the "Hollywood of the ancient world," the Greek theater. Greek public plays were notorious for use of cross-dressing, gen-der-bending, and androgynous themes.[100] Needless to say, such provocative images found a reflection in the popular culture in the use of erotic charms, spells, and potions for the provocation of lust.

In real life, sex between wife and husband was just one of many choices available—at least to the male. (Before the advent of DNA testing, the wife was kept under lock and key to ensure the purity of the progeny.) Men could avail themselves of slaves of both sexes, concubines, and *hetairai* (high-class courtesans, available for a fee). They could also try to entice a young man just out of puberty. These relationships were celebrated on vases, in much of Athenian literature, and on the stage.

The term *lesbian* is derived from the story of the Greek female poet Sappho, who lived on the island of Lesbos in the sixth century BC. She wrote pornographic poems to accompany images on the Greek vases, lustfully portraying love between women. Though such lesbian influence was not as widespread as homosexuality, this literature suggests a certain interest in and probable practice of lesbianism in the ancient Greek world.

Since there were no religious strictures, disordered sex was not limited to the popular scene. Even the great Stoic philoso-pher Zeno declared that wise citizens "ought to engage in sexual realtions with adolescent sexual favorites and nonfavorites, both male and female...[because] the same treatment for all is decorous and fitting."[101] Both Plato in the *Laws* and the *Republic* and the early Stoics proposed both the end of marriage and free sexual expression for all, which would solve the problem of jealousy and sexual possessiveness due to adultery.[102] Family values, said the Stoics, prohibited the attainment of wisdom and virtue.[103] In that ancient, sexually liberated world, children were also a problem. Like some radical politicians today who call for massive daycare programs, Plato and Zeno argued that the upbringing of children should "be a community project, in which all adults must show a parental kind of love for all the children alike in the city."[104] With this notion of irresponsible sexuality, it was true also in the ancient world that "it took a village." Plato also defended pedophilia and homosexuality.[105] Beyond that, as we shall note below, ribald and salacious parades of homosexual priests calling passersby to the liberating experience of gender-bending excess, were common occurrences on the social calendars of the empire's major cities.

After accepting heterosexual monogamy for almost two millennia as the unquestioned cultural norm, we are now moving "forward" to the sexual chaos of the ancient world. Because it is accompanied by a revival of ancient pagan spirituality, Mollenkott's "omnigendered society" is closer to reality than we ever imagined.

This pansexual polytheistic era draws ever closer, due to the progress of the powerful political and religious homosexual movement.[106] In this coming sexual utopia, Christians may soon be hiding in the closets so recently vacated by gays.

Chapter 4

HOMOSEXUALITY: THE SEXUAL SACRAMENT OF RELIGIOUS PAGANISM

₪

A PERSISTENT PROBLEM

My computer chirped one day, announcing a new e-mail. It came from a visitor to my Web site:

> Subject: Gay marriage. Sexual orientation is genetic and everyone has the right to pursue happiness in this country! To push your beliefs on someone else sill only spread fear and intolerance. If you are truly a "Christian" you would believe that we are all God's children. Obviously, you are not practicing what you preach.
>
> SIGNED, GL

This person, perhaps a homosexual, thinks me unchristian because of my beliefs about homosexuality. I have tried to examine my motives to eliminate bigotry. But Christianity is a consistent worldview, and homosexuality is an integral part of the system of pagan thinking, so I have no choice but to state my case as clearly and as lovingly as possible.

Homosexuality is not a marginal fad of Western culture. Like the Sodomites who pounded on Lot's door a millennia ago, the modern gay movement gathers at the doors of our churches and academies, demanding entrance and full recognition. In spite of the mere one or two percent of people involved, *homosexuality is not a blip on the graph of sexual fashions*; here today, gone tomorrow.[1]

The power of this agenda cannot be ignored. It is strident, insistent, and backed by influential political and financial groups. Because homosexuality is explained as an unalterable, genetic condition (like being Hispanic, Caucasian, or African American), it claims special civil rights as a "minority" group. But those who do not agree with this theory refuse to be pressured into silence. In a private conversation one well-known psychiatrist told me that ninety-five percent of his large clientele is made up of homosexuals seeking reparative counseling.[2] Such therapy is based upon the notion that homosexuality is a treatable, psychological disorder. Jeffrey Satinover, author of *Homosexuality and the Politics of Truth*, has practiced psychiatry since 1986. A graduate of MIT (humanities and science), Harvard (clinical psychology), and Yale (physics), Satinover received an MD from the University of Texas Medical School. He declares unambiguously that homosexuality is not a stable behavioral trait: "The notion that 'homosexuals' are in effect a 'different species' (different genes) is ludicrous beyond belief. There is not the slightest evidence for that, as anyone who actually reads the studies (not reports on the studies) knows."[3] Even well-known gay researchers have repudiated their early findings. Dean Hamer was forced to admit that "the genetic markers [for homosexuality] were found to be nonsignificant."[4] Simon LeVay, in a study of the hypothalamic differences between the brains of homosexual and heterosexual men, offered the following analysis of his own research: "I did not prove that homosexuality is genetic, or find a genetic cause for being gay. I didn't show that gay men are born that way—the most common mistake people make in interpreting my work. Nor did I locate a gay center in the brain."[5]

In spite of the lack of scientific proof, the American Psychiatric Association removed homosexuality from the list of psychological illnesses,[6] and even from the list of subjects to research and debate.[7] The United States Supreme Court has decriminalized it,[8] preparing the way for legal recognition of homosexual marriage.[9] Our culture is making homosexuality perfectly normal (as it was in pagan Greece) or even the superior sexual choice.[10]

It's been said that "All's fair in love and war," but fair play is rare in this war. Homosexual forces are on the attack, seeking to deconstruct the dominant heterosexual culture. The bully tactics of the prohomosexual forces are ironic, since they gained a place in society by denouncing such tactics. Since on one approves bullying, we might expect discussion and the free flow of ideas no such a behavior as novel and abnormal as homosexuality. But opposition to the homosexual agenda is dismissed as "fascist" by the associate dean of the Annenberg School of Communications of the University of Southern California.[11] Ex-homosexuals may not address meetings of the National Education Association and the Parent Teachers Association, while Parents and Friends of Lesbians and Gays (PFLAG) are granted the platform.[12] Planned Parenthood has access to the schools, but alternate voices are rarely heard. This is a spiritual war, not a polite exchange of ideas.

WATCH OUT FOR THE UNSEEN TRAIN

In France where I lived with my family for many years, we often used the excellent train system. At the station, where you can cross the tracks, we used to see a sign: *"Attention: un train peut en cacher un autre"* (Caution: one train can hide another). The obvious train so big you cannot see anything else is the one we see without realizing that an unseen one may be the real danger. The homosexual agenda warns us of the bully train, but fails to warn us of the train that will deconstruct normal heterosexuality and promote the normalcy of gay marriage.

Who can resist the appeal to build programs that eliminate harassment and bullying? Opponents of homosexuality do not encourage the bullying of homosexual students. However, once the antiharassment card is slapped on the table, no one, whether teacher, student, parent, or staff may even express an opinion on the issue (unless the opinion is progay). Homosexuality becomes a moral, natural, "inborn" quality beyond criticism. Moral objections are dismissed as "homophobic." Free speech on the subject is forever banished. The program of antiharassment becomes the ideological imposition of homosexual orthodoxy. End of discussion!

During the 2006 uproar over cartoons criticizing Islam, journalist Robert Spencer made this statement about the Western notion of free speech: "Freedom of speech encompasses precisely the freedom to annoy, to ridicule, to offend. If it doesn't, it is hollow. The instant that any person or ideology is considered off-limits for critical examination and even ridicule, freedom of speech has been replaced by an ideological straitjacket."[13] Apparently this notion, so dear to the liberal West in the critique of fundamentalist Islam, does not apply to the debate about homosexuality.

It is the same with gay marriage. Many "middle of the road" people are swayed by the discourse of fairness. Canada has legalized gay marriage. The Canadian Prime Minister, Paul Martin, a Roman Catholic, against the teaching of his church, states that "all Canadians should be granted the same right to marriage."[14] Who could oppose the argument that democracy demands equal civil rights for every citizen? Certainly not Karl Giberson, the evangelical editor of the influential *Science and Theology News*, who fails to see why allowing gays the right to marry represents a problem for heterosexual marriage.[15]

This issue hides not one train, but two. Even more hidden and more dangerous than the legalization of homosexual marriage is the more powerful agenda behind it. The new, liberated sexuality, including homosexuality, hides a thundering, high-speed twin: a potent, life-changing spirituality.

According to Christian de la Huerta, a gay theorist, "Queer people often function as catalysts, acting as agents of change, helping to bring about reform, inciting social movements, and supporting the advancement of society."[16] For him, making homosexuality and gay marriage legal will deconstruct the norms of heterosexuality and traditional marriage altogether and make all sexual expressions valid (including polyamory and polygamy).[17] Traditional marriage is "a merely heterosexual, patriarchal construct, developed out of the need to establish paternity and property."[18] Marriage is emptied of its original meaning and redefined as the state consecration of all and any sexual alliances.[19] Such legal recognition removes the language of "husband and wife" from the law and eclipses the rights of children to be raised by a mother and a father.

Those who oppose this agenda for motives of conscience of religion are considered antigay bigots and homophobes. In Canada and Sweden, pastors have been threatened with jail for speaking about homosexuality in the pulpit, and some Pennsylvania pastors, after the state added "sexual orientation" to its hate crime laws, were considering liability insurance to protect themselves from prosecution. The train of civic fairness hides the second train that destroys heterosexual marriage, which hides the third train that brings religious transformation. If we cross this track, this third, spiritual train may well be a killer for the future of civilization.

A WORLD-SHAPING IDEOLOGY

Homosexuality is no longer a simple request for the right to sexual privacy or for a little unchaperoned "fun." It has become a program for social engineering, and all-consuming ideology. Hear Paula Ettelbrick again: "Being queer is more than setting up house, sleeping with a person of the same gender, and seeking state approval for doing so...Being queer means pushing the parameters of sex, sexuality, and family, and in the process transforming the very fabric of society."[20] T. E. Schmidt begins his book *Straight and Narrow?* by describing homosexuality as "an issue so important that it increasingly appears to be the battleground for all the forces seeking to give shape to the world of the next century."[21] Publicly accepted, state-recognized, socially normalized homosexuality sees itself as a necessary contribution to the *spirituality* of the culture. Chris Hinkle of Harvard University argues that "Homosexuality must make its moral case, not merely its civil-social rights. It must show the deep spirituality of homosexual love."[22]

THE SPIRITUAL POWER OF HOMOSEXUALITY

How is the movement doing in making its "moral case" and showing its "deep spirituality"?

Liberal Christianity

Liberal Christians have fallen in line. Many mainline churches already endorse homosexuality.[23] According to a new Anglican catechism commissioned by the ex-Archbishop of York, "Homosexuality may well not be a condition to be regretted but to have divinely ordered and positive qualities."[24] The day after the archbishop made this statement, the largest Presbyterian body in the world voted to overturn a theological conviction honored since the appearance of Presbyterianism in the sixteenth century. The General Assembly voted to lift the church's ban on the ordination of gays and lesbians as ministers and other clergy of the church.[25] In 1987 this same Presbyterian denomination called for "the elimination of [civil] laws governing private sexual behavior between consenting adults."[26] The Supreme Court picked up on this theme in 2003 in its decision in Lawrence versus Texas, making it illegal for states to have laws that seek to legislate sexual behavior.[27] Meanwhile, as we noted above, the Episcopalians ordained as bishop a divorced man openly living in a homosexual relationship. Those in favor appeal to the Christian principles of love, acceptance, honesty, and tolerance for all.[28] They vilify those who use Scripture to oppose their agenda, treating them as spiritual Neanderthals "spewing out blind prejudice and ugly hate in the name of Jesus."[29] They even set Christian opposition to homosexuality in parallel with Ku Klux Klan lynchings and Nazi anti-Semitism.[30]

However, moderate liberals quickly disappear into the vortex of the pagan sexual and spiritual utopia, unaware that they are being torn away from their gospel roots by the logic of the radical, pagan religious agenda. They do not understand that there is no halfway house, no compromise. Warmed-over liberalism, which has lost its sense of the transcendent God of Scripture, has no ground on which to stand to oppose the church's fall into paganism. Pansexuality brings in its wake pantheistic religious paganism for only pantheism offers religious justification for pansexism.

Spiritual orientation affects the sexual. The rendezvous of "god" and "sex" shows us what is on the horizon. If homosexuality gains global acceptance[31] as part of the agenda to bring "peace and understanding to the earth," the future moral and spiritual arbiter of the planet will be pagan religion, and homosexuality will be its sexual sacrament.

WHAT PEOPLE SAY ABOUT THE SPIRITUAL POWER OF HOMOSEXUALITY

Whatever conclusions we draw about biology and psychology,[32] the practice of homosexuality contains a profound spiritual component. This thesis is not the invention of "hateful" right-wing bigots. While not every homosexual understands the connection between sexual practice and religious assumptions, the elite do, and say so without ambiguity.

Gay Leaders

A gay spokesman at a Pagan Spirit gathering in 1985 made this claim: "We feel there is a power in our sexuality...[a] queer energy that most cultures consider magical. It is practically a requirement for certain kinds of medicine and magic."[33] Once the male-female distinction falls, other creational categories also become irrelevant.

As another gay pagan puts it, "It is simply easier to blend with a nature spirit, or the spirit of a plant or an animal if you are not concerned with a gender-specific role."[34] Here is a statement from a spiritual gay: "I think the future of the world, the hope of the world depends on us, that men who love men are the only people who can save this planet. That is...our purpose."[35]

Gay pride parades contribute to the spiritual fiber of the culture, says Christian de la Huerta of the National Gay and Lesbian Task Force.[36] The wild mix—of "go-go boys," topless lesbians, and endless other sexual variations, "all throbbing to tribal drumbeats" in an outrageous and provocative display of self-indulgence—actually constitutes "the pressing back of cultural boundaries by a people uniquely qualified for spiritual exploration...modern day shamans... who have walked between the worlds."[37] This sexual excess is not a sin but "a gift, a blessing...a privilege...and a sacred service."[38] The author exhorts gays to exercise their spiritual gift, taking up their "responsibility to continue bringing light, healing, and spirit to the world, even if the world does not yet realize or fully appreciate our value and contributions."[39]

Did you ever imagine that our thinking about social "progress" would take us *backward*? What de la Huerta celebrates as a new possibility for our culture has already been seen in the decadent culture of ancient Rome. Fast forward to the past. In the fifth century AD, St. Augustine mentions parades of obscene actors who role-played disgusting acts, joined by the public display of homosexual priests, *galloi*, "in the presence of an immense throng of spectators and listeners of both sexes."[40] These *galloi* were "well known for their cross-dressing, outrageous make-up, flamboyant hairstyles, ritual ecstatic dancing, characteristic mannerisms, and the gift of prophecy."[41] Nothing has changed. In the twenty-first century we will face a form of that ancient sexual decadence, clothed in the power of occultist pagan spirituality.

One day soon we may see the deconstruction of the heterosexual culture (Gen. 1:27), empowered by pagan spirituality. Biblical

Christians may find themselves surrounded by a compromised and "tolerant" society and by an apostate mainline church, intoxicated by notions and potions of civil rights and fair play. They will find themselves alone, locked in a struggle for social survival with politically powerful homosexual shamans. The Lutheran scholar Frederic Baue asks the question, "What comes after the Postmodern?" He answers: "A phase of Western/world civilization that is innately religious but hostile to Christianity...or worse, a dominant but false church that brings all of its forces to bear against the truth of God's Word."[42]

New Ager Shirley MacLaine

Shirley MacLaine, one of the early and articulate proponents of the new spirituality, wonders aloud in *Going Within* whether "the point of life itself," from a new age, pagan perspective, is to "balance both the masculine and the feminine in ourselves." She answers: "Then we will have spiritualized the material and materialized the spiritual to express ourselves for what we truly are—androgynous, a perfect balance."[43] The notion of "balance" is an essential component of pagan spirituality, as we will show below.

Modern Witches

The same balance is advocated in different terms in a massive volume on the goddess by Wiccan scholars Monica Sjoo and Barbara Moor:

> Creative women and men in all ages have found rigid heterosexuality in conflict with being fully alive and aware on all levels—sexual, psychic and *spiritual* [emphasis mine]...We are split against ourselves, and against the "self" in the other, by this moralistic opposition of natural polarities in the very depth of our souls.[44]

If within ourselves we are a mix of male and female, then men do not need women to complete their sexual needs, and women do not need men. Endless creative experiments with all kinds of sexuality become part of the agenda of being "fully alive."

Emily Culpepper, presently Associate Professor of Women's Studies and Religious Studies and Director of Women's Studies Program at the University of Redlands in Southern California, is an ex-Southern Baptist. She is also a lesbian pagan witch, replete with a "familiar" (a cat possessed by a spirit). She sees gays and lesbians, in her words, as "shamans for a future age."[45] In other words, she sees in homosexuality a spiritual component that functions to bring an experience of pagan religion. Culpepper left the church and repudiated Christianity.

Apostate Christians

Others stay in the church but say essentially the same thing. In more familiar but comparable terms, Virginia Mollenkott, calling herself "an evangelical lesbian feminist," speaks for gays and lesbians when she says, "We are God's Ambassadors."[46] Indeed, Mollenkott claims she "was told" by her "guardian angel, a Spirit Guide, the Holy Spirit of Jesus" that "a great shift is occurring in the world, and you are a part of that shift."[47] This "shift" includes her "shift" from biblical heterosexuality to pagan homosexuality and from biblical to monist spirituality, which now includes such techniques as meditation on the New Age as described in *A Course in Miracles* and the use of tarot cards and I Ch'ing.[48] For Mollenkott, homosexuals hold the key for a coming spiritual revival—of paganism.

A sign of the times is the portrait of Jesus painted for the *National Catholic Reporter*. Artist Janet McKenzie used a black woman as a model saying, "My goal was to be as inclusive as possible."[49] This inclusiveness was not only sexual. Jesus is presented against a pale pink background, strongly suggesting a homosexual motif. Details in the picture include a yin-yang circle representing perfect balance and a feather symbolizing American Indian spirituality. Describing herself as a "devout atheist" with an interest in many faiths, McKenzie has devoted much of her work to images of strong, spiritual women. The new, iconic Jesus for many Roman

Catholics turns out to be an ambiguous male whose deep essence derives from a strong woman of pagan spirituality.

Rosemary Radford Ruether, the leading "Christian" feminist theologian mentioned earlier, explains the nature of the pagan-homosexual revival. Androgyny is the model for a coming human species liberated from "dualistic" gender into "psychic wholeness."[50] Such a vision has already made it to Broadway in the "Vagina Monologues." This wildly successful feminist-lesbian show has already been exported to twenty-five foreign countries, including Turkey and China, and at one performance at Madison Square Garden, had eighteen thousand women whipped into a frenzy, shouting over and over the four-letter word for their private parts! In his review, Henry Makow makes the telling observation:

> The "Vagina Monologues" presents a sad picture of life at the dead-end of feminism. It is an anguished cry for male love by a generation of women deceived by feminism, who now have no choice but to become lesbians...We must face the fact that feminism is a homosexual movement in deadly competition with heterosexuality.[51]

Said another advocate, "the church has always been blessed by gays and lesbians,...witches...[and] shamans."[52]

The close connection between pagan esoteric spirituality and androgynous sexuality is limited neither by era nor by place, as many gays and lesbians are proud to affirm. Homosexuality has never been a mere biological issue. It has always been deeply associated with a particular kind of religious commitment.

THE HOMOSEXUAL PRIEST-SHAMAN IN HISTORY

In many eras and in many cultures, pagan cults have held up as their sexual representative the emasculated, androgynous-homosexual priest.[53] Michael York, and expert on pagan religions states, "In many traditional settings, the shaman is someone with sexually deviant preferences, and sometimes transvestite dress becomes characteristic of the shaman's differences."[54] Mircea Eliade, an expert in comparative religions, argues that androgyny as a religious archetype appears almost everywhere and in every age in the world's religions.[55] The androgynous shaman is thought to occupy the space between the living and the dead, between chaos and order, where the opposites are reconciled.[56] Much evidence exists to support this judgment.[57]

Texts from Mesopotamia in the nineteenth century BC tell of androgynous priests associated with the worship of the goddess Istar from the Sumerian age (1800 BC).[58] Their condition was due to their "devotion to Istar who herself had 'transformed their masculinity into femininity.'"[59] They functioned as occult shamans who released the sick from the power of the demons just as they had saved Istar from the devil's lair. "As human beings," says a contemporary scholar, "they seem to have engendered demonic abhorrence in others;...the fearful respect they provoked is to be sought in their otherness, their position between myth and reality, and their divine demonic ability to transgress boundaries."[60]

The pagan religions of ancient Canaan maintain a similar view of spirituality and sexuality. The goddess Anat preserves many of the characteristics of Istar.[61] Like the Syrian goddess Cybele, Anat is headstrong and submits to no one.[62] She is both young and nubile but also a bearded soldier, so that many commentators conclude that she is either androgynous or bisexual.[63] She symbolizes the mystical union celebrated by her worshippers as a ritual enactment of the "sacred spiritual marriage."[64] At the beginning of the fifth century AD, the cult of the goddess Cybele continued to have success as Augustine vividly describes in his *City of God*,[65] noted previously.

WORLDWIDE PHENOMENON

The organic connection between pagan spirituality and homosexuality persists in the remnants of those ancient religions. The

Siberian shamans, known as *chukchi*, and the shamans of Central Asia engage in ecstatic rituals and dress as androgynes.[66] Among the Ngadju Dyak, a pagan people group living deep in the dense bush of southern Borneo, the *basir*, "asexual priest-shamans...the true hermaphrodites, dressing and behaving like women, have a priestly function."[67] This behavior also characterizes Amazonian shamans, Celtic priests (ancient and modern), and Indian *hijras*. The *hijras*, who go back into the mists of Hinduism, are a religious community of men who "dress and act like women and whose culture centers on the worship of Bahuchara Mata, one of the many versions of the Mother Goddess worshipped throughout India."[68]

In another form of Hindu spirituality, Tantric Yoga, androgyny is also the goal, when the two contrary principles of Shiva and Shakti are joined. Eliade explains: "When Shakti, who sleeps in the shape of a serpent (*kundalini*), at the base of his body, is awoken by certain yogic techniques, she moves...by way of the *chakras* up to the top of the skull, where Shiva dwells, and unites with him."[69] The yogin, through powerful techniques of sexual-spiritual meditation, is thus transformed "into a kind of 'androgyne.'"[70] In Buddhism the true human, the archetype called a *bodhisattva*, is androgynous.[71] These yogic practices and mystical teachings concerning androgyny may be as old as the Mesopotamian and Syrian examples discussed previously.

In Mesoamerica and South America, homosexual and trans-gendered shamans served in the temples of the Aztecs, Chimu, Lacke, Lubacas, Manta, Mayas, Mbaya, Moche, and Tupinambas.[72] In Alaska, native tribes regarded homosexual shamans as special:

> Yup'ik culture is especially notable.... Homosexual shamans and medicine women were felt to occupy a special place between the masculine and feminine as well as between the spirit world and the mundane, and thus could serve as intermediaries between men and women, and between the spirit world and the mundane world.[73]

In American Indian religion, homosexual transvestite males (*berdaches*)[74] function as shamans.[75] Amongst the Navajo, the *nadle,* a feminized male, serves as a peacemaker. According to Navajo myth, the original hermaphrodite went to the underworld to be associated with the dead and the devils of the lower world.[76] Among the Zuñi tribe, the Anawilona ("he-she") is a powerful mythological figure.[77] Similar figures are to be found in African and Australian Aboriginal cultic practice.[78] "Some African societies," observes an ethnographer, "have developed intermediary genders of men-women and women-men who, like their Native American counterparts, are seen as sacred and as spiritually powerful individuals."[79] Other examples of spiritual-physical androgyny include the homosexual priests of the Yoruba religion in Cuba and "young gay witches in Manhattan."[80]

A history of gay male spirituality states with obvious pride that "gender-variant men have fulfilled a sacred role throughout the millennia."[81]

What is the relationship between homosexuality and pagan spirituality?

HOMOSEXUALITY: RELIGIOUS SIGNIFICANCE

A monistic, pagan view of existence will work itself out in all the domains of human life and especially in the domain of sexuality.[82] This relationship has been noted by thinkers both straight and gay, Christian and pagan.

Francis Schaeffer, Christian Apologist

Writing during the "student revolution" of the 1960s, Francis Schaeffer noted, "Some forms of homosexuality today...are a philosophic expression...a denial of the antithesis. It has led in this case to an obliteration of the distinction between man and woman. So the male and the female as complimentary partners are finished."[83] At the heart of pagan monism is a mystical, unitive experience, a state in which distinctions disappear and opposites are joined. Androgyny, on the sexual level, reflects and confirms such an experience.

C. G. Jung, Influential Psychoanalyst

Carl Gustav Jung (1875–1961), one of the most influential thinkers of modern times, taught that to become a mature human being one had to reject the biblical notion of God.[84] Jung embraced paganism and believed that the homosexual androgyne is a model of spiritual maturity who willingly assumes his physical tendencies and thus joins what the biblical God has separated.[85] Indeed for Jung, spiritual androgyny symbolizes "the integration of the opposites or the state of the individuation of the autonomous individual."[86] Therefore, homosexuals are (though some unconsciously or only partially) pagan monists who have succeeded in translating spiritual theory into physical reality.[87]

Joseph Campbell, Guru to George Lucas

By mentoring George Lucas, producer of Star Wars,[88] Joseph Campbell exercised an immense influence upon modern spirituality and mythology. An apostate Roman Catholic, Campbell sought wisdom in the pagan myths and delivered much of it on public television.[89] Campbell stated his thoughts on sexuality—and their implication—explicitly: "We always think in terms of opposites... [but we must] 'transcend' duality."[90] We must realize that we are "both mortal and immortal, both male and female."[91]

This is a socially explosive message in a time of sexual and religious chaos. How explosive? We have some idea of its power by measuring the worldwide success of the Lucas movies—though this is just a drop in a bucket. As our modern world joins Western material success to Eastern spirituality and unites the globe around the twin notions of economic ease and the spiritual unity of all religions, we begin to see that the next great opponent of Christian truth will be triumphant, global paganism—in both its spiritual and sexual forms.

Mircea Eliade, World Religions Scholar

Mircea Eliade, a respected world religions scholar, explains the religious function of the asexual priest-shamans: "true hermaphrodites, who dress and behave like women." They can function as priests because "they combine the two cosmological planes—earth and sky—and also from the fact that they combine in their own person the feminine element (earth) and the masculine element (sky)." We have here ritual androgyny, a well-known formula for the *coincidentia oppositorum*, that is, "the joining of opposites."[92] Again, radical sexual egalitarianism takes us to the heart of pagan spirituality.

THE MECHANISM

"Sexual energy is a physical expression of spiritual power," says Margo Anand in *The Art of Sexual Ecstasy*.[93] Androgynous people, whether homosexual or bisexual, express within themselves both sexual identities.[94] In the sex act they engage *both* as male and female, the "hard" and the "soft"[95]—and thus taste both physical and spiritual androgyny.[96] On the physical plane they become classic monists, joining the opposites, experiencing a world without distinctions. As we will see, distinctions in heterosexuality reflect the fundamental theistic notion of the Creator-creature distinction. Androgyny erases distinctions, including that between the human and the divine.[97]

According to Eliade, the androgynous being reaches the goal of the mystical, monistic quest:

> In mystical love and at death, one completely integrates the spirit world: all contraries are collapsed. The distinctions between the sexes are erased: the two merge into an androgynous whole. In short, at the center one knows oneself, is known, and knows the nature of reality.[98]

The elimination of sexual distinctions is not an incidental footnote of pagan religious history but represents one of its fundamental ideological commitments. That the pagan *priesthood* would so often and so universally blur sexual identity indicates the priority paganism has always given to undermining God-ordained, monogamous heterosexuality, and explains paganism's enthusiastic promotion of androgyny.

Spiritual Model: American-Indian Shaman

The idealization of androgyny makes sense theologically and theoretically and is confirmed by gay thinkers. Says J. Michael Clark, professor at Emory University and Georgia State University, "Something in our gay/lesbian being as an all-encompassing existential standpoint...appears to heighten our spiritual capacities."[99] Clark claims gays share the same sentiments as radical feminist theologians whose "religious impulses are being killed by [traditional] Judeo-Christianity."[100] The real problem, Clark implies, is not "hateful" Christians but the hated biblical worldview and its theological paradigm.[101] Clark turned away from the Bible and his Christian roots to the paganism of Native American animism for an acceptable spiritual model.

We must understand the radical move away from Christian spirituality to the spirituality of the androgynous, homosexual shaman. For Clark, an excellent spiritual model is the *berdache*, an American Indian shaman, born male but choosing to live as a female. The *berdache* achieves "the reunion of the cosmic, sexual and moral polarities"[102] (the "joining of the opposites"). The *berdaches* were known as "Sacred Balancers," unifying the polarities to "nurture wholeness."[103]

Anakin

Most parents would not encourage their children to become "sacred balancers," yet the great destiny of Anakin Skywalker (*Star*

Wars), a model hero for today's youth, is to be "the balancer" of the two sides of the Force. Do our kids—even those raised in Christian homes—have any idea of what they are absorbing from George Lucas? Of course, there is no *direct* relationship between religious homosexuality and sci-fi movies. However, little by little the pagan worldview subtly imposes itself on the global community, gradually becoming the norm rather than the exception.

Our sophisticated age turns to the *berdache,* an expression of ancient pagan animism, for a moral warrant to deny distinctions, mystically join the opposites, assume our contradictions, and reign supreme over the creational distortions and moral failings. All this gives spiritual support so that homosexuals can declare the normal abnormal and the abnormal normal.[104]

Behind this view of sex is great optimism. "Queer theory" and pansexuality, it is claimed, will liberate us from the "false and calcified notions of masculinity and femininity."[105] Christian de la Huerta expresses the exhilarating hope that "perhaps gay men will be able to reinterpret and model for straight men a more compassionate, open-hearted, humor-filled, and tolerant masculinity,... [and that] lesbians will continue to stretch the boundaries of what it means to be a woman [in terms of the issues of] emancipation and empowerment."[106]

The reality is that homosexuality is surely the final taboo of sexual transgression that *must* be celebrated if the pagan worldview is to be normalized. The two rise or fall together. It is optimism for paganism but bad news for theism. For, as homosexuality rises the God of the Bible and the biblical worldview are banished to the margins. During times of Christian dominance, homosexuality was alluded to in hushed tones as "the love that has no name." If the Christian worldview is fully undermined then homosexuality as the sexual sacrament of the new spirituality must and will be publicly celebrated and socially supported. As paganism begins to dominate the planet in the years to come, homosexuality will be a no-compromise issue for the sexual utopia. If the tiny homosexual lobby of the late twentieth century managed to gain such influence over education and politics in a country where the vast majority still claimed to be Christian, what will hold back its control if paganism dominates the globe?[107]

A powerful spiritual-sexual agenda exists in our neopagan culture. "Progressives" call it the "new consciousness."[108] The optimism of the 1960s sexual revolution remains intact, even after a generation of experimentation that brought devastating social and human consequences. We have naively crossed the bridge into the third millennium to the tune of Lennon's "Imagine,"[109] full of hope for a new world order of unity and love, respect and democracy. At the front of the procession, leading the way across that bridge is the androgynous, sexually unfettered new human of pagan spirituality. Just as the new age gurus declared the arrival of the Age of Aquarius, so the prophecy of theosophist Franz von Baader (1765–1841) concerning the reappearance of the original androgyne at the end of time[110] seems about to be fulfilled. Are we on the verge of a final, global Sodom and Gomorrah as the title of a recent progay book, *Reclaiming Sodom*, proposes?[111] Most of us are unaware of the danger this would pose—sluggish, spiritual couch potatoes, overfed by a Hollywood-concocted diet of sexual degradation and calmly reassured by the spiritual and moral liberation of modern pagan priests and priestesses who have never been more optimistic that they are now. Recognizing the setbacks of the past of the countless human failures to change the world, they believe that this time it will be different. Why? Global consciousness is causing us to create "one unified species [through] a global consciousness/super-consciousness...[a] human species so united in love and goodwill that there [will] be some kind of spiritual center."[112] As if by magic the perfect new man will arise from the failed old man.

It is important to see homosexuality in the context of its pagan worldview for two reasons. One, there is a movement afoot to make opposition to homosexuality a treatable illness.[113] A number of mental health professionals now see those who are repulsed by homosexual practice as suffering from a pathological neurosis—"homophobia." In other words, a person who views the legitimization of homosexuality as sinful, immoral, or destructive to society may well have a mental disorder! To show that this flows logically from a worldview as ancient as the Bible might be an important defense in the days to come. Two, in spite of the optimism, the free practice of this sexuality does not bode well for the future of the race. The "liberated" view of sex hardly promises a human utopia. Seeing the worldview implications clearly indicates that the breech in the levees of our biblical protection will mean the inundation of our culture by a pagan flood that will lead to personal, social, and sexual self-destruction.

Chapter 5

Unintended Destructive Consequences

₪

Psychological Dangers of "Liberated" Sex

Our culture has shoved away from its creational moorings and has launched into an adventure on the wild seas of sexual deconstruction and androgynous reconstruction. Like a child in a small boat on a big lake, we glide into the uncharted waters of the twenty-first century lured by irrational hopes of human progress, ignorant of the costly experiments of the past, and perilously unaware of the tsunami of human evil just off the horizon.[1]

The new sexuality has sought a place for all forms of deviancy and has made the nonconformist few feel accepted in society at large. The price is high. The whole culture is held hostage because of the confused state of a miniscule number of transvestites, homosexuals, and transsexuals. A case in point: Virginia Mollenkott is happy to disrupt the "normality of heterosexuality" (for the millions of people who are normal) in order that a few transvestites can "be themselves" without stigma in a "new reality"—"a society in which men, women and all people in between are respected as being made in the image of a God who is neither male nor female and yet is inclusive of every degree of 'masculinity' or 'femininity.'"[2] Mollenkott idealizes a "spiritual" world, the "ultimate community...of the planet"[3] where the "oppressive" notion of sexual normality, like the term "deviancy,"[4] no longer has meaning.[5] She is driven by this vision. "Where there is no vision," she says, reprising a biblical text, "the people perish."[6]

THE GOD OF SEX

THE LOSS OF SELFHOOD

This vision of a pansexual utopia fails to see the perishing victims all around us—and it must surely get worse, as some of the revolutionaries seem to admit. Mark C. Taylor, whom I cited above, sees the social and religious implications of his pagan program with astonishing clarity. His full comment is worth re-citing. "The death of God [is] the disappearance of self and the end of history. [It] unleashes the aberrant levity of free play...purposelessness."[7] Taylor develops the implications of this new freedom: "The lawless land of erring, which is forever beyond good and evil, is the world of Dionysus, the Antichrist, who calls every wander[er] to carnival, comedy and carnality."[8] Human beings with no purpose save mere levity and animalistic urges do not constitute a humane and just society. This vision of the coming sexual utopia fills me with dread. "The lawless land of erring...beyond good and evil" may well turn out to be history's most fearful nightmare. When you mix the ingredients of human selfishness, no moral restraints, and a false sense of one's own divinity, the mixture can only produce a social and moral Molotov cocktail of unimaginably destructive power.

In spite of his own pagan persuasions, Eliade, one of the contemporary proponents of the "new humanism,"[9] felt obliged to sound a warning before he died in 1986. In speaking about "ritual androgyny" as a "source of power" but also a fearsome possibility of great loss, Eliade offered this sobering admonition:

> Every attempt to transcend the opposites carries with it a certain danger. This is why the ideas of a *coincidentia oppositorum* (joining of the opposites) always arouse ambivalent feelings: on the one side, man is haunted by the desire to escape from his particular situation and regain a transpersonal mode of life; on the other, he is paralyzed by the fear of losing his "identity" and forgetting himself.[10]

Most people have been hoodwinked by the elite's appeals to self-expression, individual liberty, democracy, and the promise of a global utopia. But these values will never come about if the radical program succeeds in taking us into "the lawless land of erring." The identity Eliade feared losing, what Taylor calls "the disappearance of self,"[11] is what it means to be human, what the Bible calls "the image of God."

Christian writer Philip Yancey states:

> I might feel more attraction towards a reductionistic approach to sex if...I sensed that the sexual revolution had increased respect between the genders, created a more loving environment for children, relieved the ache of personal loneliness, and fostered intimacy. I have seen no such evidence.[12]

Yancey senses what we all sense. Deconstruction and pagan reconstruction have hurled us instead into a maelstrom of social decay and psychological destruction. Lesbian literary and social critic Camille Paglia observes that "history shows that male homosexuality...always tends toward decadence."[13]

The reality if far from utopist! It is a nightmare. The spiritual nature of the movement often blinds its followers to its destructive consequences, but one young author is not duped. He calls his generation the "Porn Generation."[14] Psychologically, this oversexed generation is "jaded," incapable of real love and genuine affection, capable only of "hooking up" and one night stands.[15] Physically, this generation is threatened not only by the risks of promiscuous heterosexual sex, but by the even riskier exposure to promiscuous homosexual sex. The title of one article recognizes the deception: "Medical Downside of Homosexual Behavior: A Political Agenda Is Trumping Science."[16] It attempts to show how the political goals of the homosexual movement deliberately obscure the scientifically established life-threatening implications of the gay lifestyle. This is the generation that will take our place.

MENTAL ILLNESS

One sign gives the program away. Though the American Psychiatric Association in 1973 removed homosexuality from its list of psychopathologies, a stubborn, scientific fact has remained—homosexuals have unusually high rates of suicide and of emotional and mental illnesses such as major depression, drug abuse, bipolar disorder, panic disorder, agoraphobia, and obsessive-compulsive disorder.[17] Liberation was supposed to bring psychological release. But we must recognize the facts. If the emerging society of sexual inclusion promises an increase of spiritual contentment why are its cutting-edge proponents so dissatisfied with themselves and their lifestyle? The homosexual community does not deny the high incidence of mental disorder. It simply attributes such problems to social rejection and homophobia on the part of heterosexuals.[18] However, even in countries such as the Netherlands where gay, lesbian, and bisexual relationships have been normalized for a long time, the rates of mental and psychological problems remain the same.

J. Michael Bailey, in his commentary on the professional research on homosexuality and mental illness, concludes, "These studies contain arguably the best published data on the association between homosexuality and psychopathology, and both converge on the same unhappy conclusion: homosexual people are at a substantially higher risk for some forms of emotional problems, including suicidal tendencies, major depression and anxiety disorder."[19] Violence is another sign of instability. In their book *Men Who Beat the Men Who Love Them: Battered Gay Men and Domestic Violence*, Island and Letellier show that "the incidence of domestic violence among gay men is nearly double that in the heterosexual population."[20] Such violence also marks the lesbian community.[21] Bailey goes on to warn his prohomosexual colleagues: "It would be a shame if sociopolitical concerns prevented researchers from conscientious consideration of any reasonable hypothesis regarding homosexuality."[22] In other words, in the debate on the mental health of homosexuals, politics (an ideological cover-up) should not trump science (well-established facts about the homosexual lifestyle).[23]

And the point I am making? This is a poor start for the "new, pansexual utopian society" of love and goodwill. Homosexuals are exposed to great physical danger and may also be unusually anxious because of the instability that typically characterizes their relationships. Rarely are these long-term, faithful arrangements. The dominant homosexual pattern is promiscuity. Gay author Gabriel Rotello notes the perspective of many gays that "Gay liberation was founded on a 'sexual brotherhood of promiscuity,' and any abandonment of that promiscuity would amount to a 'communal betrayal of gargantuan proportions.'"[24] Neale Donald Walsch's ideal sexual society—"a world where we can make love to anyone, any way we wish to, at anytime, anywhere"[25]—is not merely a dream but a present reality in the contemporary world of homosexual practice. The most extensive survey of sexual behavior in the United States found:

> 94 percent of married people and 75 percent of cohabiting people [heterosexual] had only one partner in the prior year. In contrast, long-term sexual fidelity is rare among Gay/Lesbian/Bisexual (GLB) couples, particularly among gay males. Even during the coupling period, many gay men do not expect monogamy. For gay men, sex outside the primary relationship is ubiquitous even during the first year. Gay men reportedly have sex with someone other than their partner in 66 percent of relationships within the first year, rising to approximately 90 percent if the relationship endures over five years.[26]

The average gay or lesbian relationship is thus short-lived. In one study only 15 percent of gay men and 17.3 percent of lesbians had relationships that lasted more than three years.[27] Our present society reels from the destabilizing effects of heterosexual divorce, presently occurring in 50 percent of marriages. We rightly think this is bad and wonder how a culture can survive such fickle decision making, but in the gay population an astonishing 85 percent of all relationships do not last beyond three years! And this is the trendsetting sexuality of the glorious omnigendered future? How can this not be a factor in societal and mental instability? A far-ranging study of homosexual men published in 1978 revealed that 75 percent of self-identified, white, gay men admitted to having sex with more than 100 different males in their lifetime: 15 percent claimed 100–249 sex partners; 17 percent claimed 250–499; 15 percent claimed 500–999; and 28 percent claimed more than 1,000 lifetime male sex partners.[28] This is decadence. Is there any wonder that the result is emotional and mental disorder?

These figures also explain a second cause of anxiety: the physical risks of such a lifestyle.

PHYSICAL DANGERS

Is the gay lifestyle hazardous to your health? "The only epidemiological study to date on the life span of gay men concludes that gay and bisexual men lose up to twenty years of life expectancy."[29] In other words, the probability of a 20-year-old gay or bisexual man living to 65 years is only 32 percent, compared to 78 percent for men in general.

Gays die sooner in part because promiscuity is an efficient way to spread disease. Common sexual practices among gay men lead to numerous STDs and physical injuries, "some of which are virtually unknown in the heterosexual population."[30] While syphilis is found in heterosexuals, a study in King County, Washington, in 1999 found that "85 percent of syphilis cases were among self-identified homosexual practitioners."[31] A similar result is found for hepatitis A, B, and C, as well as anal cancer and the sexual transmission of typhoid. Incidentally, the risk of anal cancer soars by as much as 4,000 percent for men who engage in anal intercourse with other men. The list of medical diseases found with extraordinary frequency among male homosexual practitioners as a result of abnormal homosexual behavior also includes chlamydia trachomatis, cryptosporidium, giardia lamblia, herpes simplex virus, human immunodeficiency virus (HIV), human papilloma virus

(HPV or genital warts), isospora belli, microsporidia, gonorrhea, and syphilis.

Some in the gay community are lucid, seeing themselves "as under siege by a powerful external threat, the most dangerous virus humanity has yet encountered," namely AIDS. Two well-known lesbians recognize where the blame lies. Tammy Bruce cites Camille Paglia with approval: "Everyone who preached free love in the 1960s is responsible for AIDS. This idea that it was somehow an accident, a microbe that sort of fell from heaven—absurd. We must face what we did."[32]

Gay sex is dangerous. Physical injuries of the intestines and the rectum come not from extremist behavior but from the actual regular practices associated with gay sex, for which the body was not designed—rimming, fisting, anal intercourse, barebacking, plus "golden showers," and direct contact with fecal matter. Such practices often lead to sadomasochism.[33] All this has given rise to the creation of a specialized term, "Gay Bowel Syndrome," now commonly used in the medical literature.

In 2003 the prestigious and progay *Journal of the American Public Health Association* devoted substantial space to the risks associated with homosexual practices.[34] The journal, containing articles by many progay therapists and scholars, "reads like a litany of bad news, one article following another," according to a respected therapist.[35] Mary E. Northbridge, PhD, MPH, editor-in-chief, introduces the devastating studies on the numerous risk behaviors of gays by saying, "Having struggled to come to terms with the catastrophic HIV epidemic among MSM (Men who have Sex with Men) in the 1980s, by addressing the pointed issues of sexuality and heterosexism, *are we set to backslide a mere 20 years later* as HIV incidence rates move steadily upward, especially among MSM?"[36] Another editorial is titled "When Plagues Don't End" and again places the focus on the resurgence of HIV/AIDS among homosexual men.[37] This editor's other contribution is titled "The Second

Wave Will Drown Us."[38] The incredible fact is that despite all the evidence and all the scientific studies that clearly demonstrate the medical and psychological risks of such behavior, most medical groups and professional associations embrace the validity of the homosexual agenda and advocate that lifestyle.[39] Says Charles Colson about the recent decision of the American Psychiatric Association's decision to endorse same-sex marriage for "health reasons": "It seems the politically correct, but destructive homosexual agenda is trumping science and fooling the general population."[40]

SOCIAL DANGERS

Marriage under Attack

One devastating result of the sexual revolution is the explosion of the divorce rate—now over 50 percent—and the resulting destruction of marriage and of the two-parent family. Barbara Dafoe Whitehead, a writer based in Amherst, Massachusetts, who specializes in issues concerning children and the family, wrote a book about marriage in America whose title says it all—*The Divorce Culture*.[41] Professor Lawrence Stone of Princeton made this stunning observation about the state of divorce in the modern West: "The scale of marital breakdowns in the West since 1960 has no historical precedence that I know of. There has been nothing like it for the last 2,000 years and probably longer."[42] What more proof do we need of the determined, deconstructive and effective character of the social revolution we have experienced in this last generation? And we are supposed to construct a human utopia on this agenda? Countless lives have felt the destructive effect, and no one more so than the children who now must shoulder the burden of building the next stage of civilization.

With marriages breaking down in vast numbers many do not even bother to marry but choose instead the easy road of cohabitation. The University of Chicago issued a report (November

24, 1999) showing that in 1972, 46 percent of Americans lived in traditional families (two parents plus children). Today, only 26 percent do. Cohabiting couples have increased 700 percent since 1970.[43] Presently, one third of all babies are born out of wedlock. In Europe, cohabitation is almost the norm. In Norway, 49 percent of births are to unwed parents; in Iceland, 62 percent; in the United Kingdom, 38 percent; and in France, 41 percent. Leading European politicians appear with their mistresses. The British government recently removed a section on marriage as the most desirable family structure from its recent position paper on family.[44]

According to the "Report to Congress on Out-Of-Wedlock Childbearing" by the National Center for Health Statistics, 68.7 percent of African American babies are now born illegitimate. Thus, just under a third of African American babies are legitimate. The Department of Health and Human Services released a report titled "Family Income in the 1970s: The Demographics of Black/White Differences." It says that...illegitimacy among African Americans was only 25 percent in 1965. According to that report, 29.7 percent of illegitimate children must repeat at least one grade in school—compared to the average rate of 11.6 percent. By their thirties, those born illegitimate have an average income of $11,500 less than those from two-parent families; the illegitimate child is seven times more likely to be poor as the child in a two-parent family. Seventy percent of children in long-term juvenile jails did not live with their fathers while growing up.[45]

An anecdote confirms this. A friend who worked for the Los Angeles Police Department told me that in the 1960s a police officer found cohabiting was discharged without appeal. By the 1980s, half the police academy cadets were cohabiting. By the end of the century, no one even cared. A 1969 Gallup found that 21 percent of the population supported premarital sex; in May 2001, 60 percent favored it (and 67 percent of young adults).[46]

How successfully this agenda has deconstructed the old culture can be measured by the hard evidence of the Census Bureau. In

August, 2005—for the first time in American history—single-adult households displaced two-parent families with children as the most common kind of US household. As recently as 1990, nuclear-family households were the most common, but by 2000, they had moved to second place. Children are both the victims and the present focus of this destructive agenda.

Children under Attack

Someone has said, "Children are the last bastion of the old sexual morality."[47] Proof of the determined deconstructive agenda of the "progressives" is the fact that they want your children. The "last bastion" must go. The revolutionaries want to gain control of the future; thus they want to recruit as many youthful adherents as possible. Both hetero and homo excess is now on the agenda of our schools. GLSEN (Gay, Lesbian, Straight Educational Network) claims there are Gay-Straight Alliance clubs in 3,000 high schools across the land.[48] The National Education Association was among the first national organizations to actively promote a gay-lesbian pride month and to endorse homosexual and "transgendered" teachers. Tammy Bruce again has the right words: "Conditioning children into sex addiction *guarantees* the Left Elite control of your culture for generations."[49]

Destruction of a Child's Sexual Identity

The attempts to co-opt the next generation for the revolution are overt and constant.[50] According to the view of modern mental health "experts," it is a positive use of the school's time to include graphic discussions about sex, coital positions, homosexuality, and even bestiality in the classroom setting.[51]

My daughter is a counselor for troubled teenagers in a public school system in a major city on the East Coast. A few weeks ago, she sent me this note:

Dear Dad,

I was quite saddened and frustrated to know that Planned Parenthood was coming to speak to an already disturbed and troubled group of youth, but even more disturbed when the presenter began using some of the most graphic sexual language as she described ways to have "safe sex." She pulled out her "bag of tricks," split the group up into two teams, and handed them each a kit of contraceptive devices. Many kids giggled and sneered as she described in detail how to use plastic wrap as a way to prevent STDs when giving oral sex to a partner (whether on the genitals or the anus). I was appalled and shocked to watch a thirteen-year-old boy handling a diaphragm and describing in detail how to use it to prevent pregnancy.

On her second visit, she presented a video on HIV/AIDS. After the video one girl made the comment that she thought it was wrong that a thirteen-year-old girl in the video had six partners. She said, "She's a slut for sleeping with so many boys at such a young age." The presenter reprimanded her for her comment and instead redirected her to consider what was worse, a girl having unprotected sex with two partners or protected sex with six. The class chimed in and responded that the better of the two options was the protected sex with six.

Today the presenter reprimanded the kids for making fun of anal sex and the "rainbow room" specially designed for gays and lesbians within the Planned Parenthood centers.

I am sickened by this. I plan to go to my boss and request that a prolife group be allowed to come present to our kids. What a loaded agenda! Even some of the kids came to me and felt very strange about the way she presented sexuality. Having become pregnant on the Pill soon after my marriage, I know that sex ultimately is not "safe." And what of all the ramifications of sex on the young adult's psyche and soul?

"An already disturbed and troubled group of youth," as my daughter characterized them, is now deeply disturbed by teachers who prod them to question their gender and to experiment with another. Questioning one's gender is a recognized psychological condition: Gender Identity Disorder (GID), which appears in the *Diagnostic and Statistical Manual of the American Psychiatric Association*. Warren Throckmorton, past president of the American Mental Health Counselors Association, believes in keeping with psychiatric wisdom that it is inappropriate to engage in discussions about homosexuality in K–12 institutions. He asserts that "it is very early in life to make a definition about one's sexual identity. Educators should give kids options to wait awhile, to consider a straight identity if they would rather [have] that."[52] Dr. Melvin Anchell, the eminent Los Angeles-based expert who was repeatedly called upon by the government in court cases involving sex crimes in the 1970s and 1980s, wrote in his 1983 book *Sex and Insanity* that early sex education bypasses the well-established "latency period" of childhood development, where children learn compassion before they learn "passion."[53] This process is short-circuited in the rush to early sexualization. As a case in point, a new sex-education pilot program in Montgomery County, Maryland, insists that children seriously ponder their gender identity. In plain English this means "Boys should examine whether they really want to be boys, and girls should wonder if they should be girls."[54]

Destruction of a Child's Moral Sense

As my daughter indicates, when the subject is raised only one side is heard. Ideological brainwashing in the strict sense of that term—meaning there is no place for the other side to make an opposing case—is beginning to characterize the teaching of sex in school. Moral standards are abolished. There is no right and wrong in sex anymore. Any attempt to interject the moral question is silenced. For instance, at the National Education Association's annual convention in 2005, the Ex-Gay Educators Caucus positioned itself in the convention's exhibit hall. The larger, prohomosexual contingent was "offended" and challenged the NEA's new policy of allowing an ex-gay faction to market its wares under the emblem of "democracy" and "diversity." "You might as well set up a Ku Klux Klan booth," remarked one delegate. Kevin Jennings, founder of Gay Lesbian Straight Education Network (GLSEN) actually said,

"Ex-gay messages have no place in our nation's public schools." He went on: "There is no 'other side' when you're talking about lesbian, gay, and bisexual students."[55] Recently, Jennings was honored with the NEA's coveted "creative leadership" award at the convention! With leaders/educators like this, any notions of sexual morality become unthinkable.

When one puts together the essentially pornographic suggestions and images in modern sex-education classes with the inevitable exposure to Internet and television pornography, the results are depressing. Values about relationships, sex, intimacy, love, and marriage are now often absent. In their place photographs, videos, magazines, virtual games, and Internet pornography that depict rape and the dehumanization of females in sexual scenes constitute powerful but deforming tools of sex education. Deviancy has been normalized. There are no longer any moral categories in the realm of sexuality. Sociologist Anne Hendershott writes about the politics of deviancy and shows how deviancy is now justified. She mentions an example in Conyers, Georgia, where a large number of very young teenagers were engaging in promiscuous sexual behaviors—some with more than one hundred partners, a behavior that led to a syphilis epidemic in the upscale suburb. The response from some women's groups and sociologists was, to say the least, shocking. Deborah Tolman, a research scientist and director of the Adolescent Sexuality Project at Wellesley College, suggested that "girls are entitled to their own sexual desire or sexual pleasure and that 'good' girls or 'nice' girls are depriving themselves of a full life."[56]

This "full life," which includes syphilis, is also a new, liberating day for pornography—with equally disastrous results. Many studies have demonstrated that exposure to significant amounts of increasingly graphic forms of pornography has a dramatic effect on how adult consumers view women, and on sexual abuse, sexual relationships, and sex in general.

These studies are virtually unanimous in their conclusions: When male subjects were exposed to as little as six weeks' worth of standard hard-core pornography, they developed an increased sexual callousness toward women; began to trivialize rape as a criminal offense or no longer considered it a crime at all; developed distorted perceptions about sexuality; developed an appetite for more deviant, bizarre, or violent types of pornography (normal sex no longer seemed to do the job); devalued the importance of monogamy and lacked confidence in marriage as either a viable or lasting institution; viewed non-monogamous relationships as normal and natural behavior."[57]

What kind of world is being prepared for us, with this kind of understanding of sex? It is worse than we think. One of my books was once published under the title, *Pagans in the Pews*.[58] The other day I saw a newspaper article with the phrase "elephant in the pews." They may be the same thing, since we are not seeing this proverbial sexual-spiritual elephant. Someone has called pornographic Web sites the "crack cocaine of sex addiction." The article was about the 25 percent to 50 percent of Christian pastors with a pornography addiction.[59] With "men of God" like that, salt and light are getting thin on the ground.

Destruction of the Child's Sense of Cultural Achievement

Since the divorce rate has skyrocketed in our country and pansexuality is normalized, the signs of social collapse since the 1960s are proof that the agenda to destroy the family has succeeded. But not just the family is destroyed.

- ₪ SAT scores: down 10 percent (College Entrance Exam Board)
- ₪ Child abuse: up 2,300 percent (Health and Human Services)
- ₪ Criminal arrests of teens: up 150 percent
- ₪ Violent crime rate: up 550 percent
- ₪ Teen suicide: up 450 percent
- ₪ Illegal drug use: up 6,000 percent (National Institute on Drug Abuse)

₪ Divorce: up 350 percent (Bureau of the Census)

₪ Births to unmarried girls: up 500 percent (Bureau of the Census)

₪ Abortion: up by untold thousands of percentage points.[60]

Note that while some of these categories do not seem related, studies show that the breakdown of marriage and the family have repercussions on the whole network of human relations. These are hardly encouraging figures for the arrival of the sexual and human utopia. One has to wonder if the program of deconstruction/reconstruction does not have as its immediate goal the total meltdown of contemporary society, so that in the chaos they can seize control.

In spite of the facts that children still can be taught abstinence and restraint[61] and heterosexual monogamy has time and again been shown to be the most stable form for human life,[62] the present moral, social, and physical chaos seems to make no dent in the revolutionary optimism.

PROSPECTIVE

So, despite the devastating social collapse, at which we continue to cast massive sums of money, the revolution continues. Sexual freedom must not be hindered even at the cost of the future of our children and grandchildren and of our civilization. The flower-power people of the 1960s have brought their ideology into power as they have taken positions of leadership in the political, educational, economic, and religious structures. Their dream to give free expression to sexual appetites lives on after their own appetites may have waned. The push for more and more sexual freedom will not be restrained in the new millennium by the forces of "reactionary Puritanism" or "Right Wing extremism," as traditional morality is now described. The genie will not go back into the bottle. The toothpaste will not go back into the tube. The Left Wing intellectuals are now in ideological power, and they have redefined the enemy. In the old days it used to be sinister capitalistic bosses. Now that they *are* the sinister capitalistic bosses, they have chosen another enemy: the patriarchal "Right Wing sex police."

The sexual liberation of the masses has become as big an agenda for the revolutionary elite as was the Marxist liberation of the worker. The dismantling of the great evil of patriarchy (the father as protector and representative of the home) at every level of society makes the communist revolutions pale into insignificance. The true utopia turns out to be not only "buns and butter for the workers" but endless sexual choice—buns unlimited whether you work or not![63] The sexual revolution is eagerly guaranteed not only by the educational theories of the intellectual elite, but by a constant diet of sexual excess offered by the myth-making elite of Hollywood to every consumer in the privacy of his own home.

But nothing is free. Is pornography free? You "pay-per-view," and for viewing sexual mayhem the cost is incalculable. The old communism "had to" sacrifice millions of workers for the sake of "the Worker." The sexual revolution has sacrificed millions of unborn children—generational suicide[64]—and has destroyed the moral order and youthful innocence of several generations of young people for the sake of this so-called "new civilization." This is the price we must now pay for the "noble" cause of prochoice adult and adult-entertained sexual freedom. And pay we will.

Peter G. Peterson, a much-respected counselor of recent presidents from Richard Nixon to Bill Clinton, adds up the bill in the form of an urgent warning to today's Western society, a warning concerning the "graying of the population." He calls it "the gray dawn."[65] In the 1960s, the problem was overpopulation. Not anymore. Because of the changes in sexual thinking and practice in contemporary society, the West is not reproducing itself. This is another form of "generational suicide." Journalists speak of the "infertility time bomb." The rise of sexually transmitted diseases and the postponement of childbearing for the sake of careers and financial independence are producing a population crisis.[66] In this culture we do not make babies, we make old people. Peterson shows that in 2030 one in four people will be sixty-five years old or older. Where there used to be two sets of grandparents, two parents, and a number of children, now out of every four people, one is elderly. Put another way, of all the people in the history of the world who lived to sixty-five, two-thirds are alive today![67] By 2040 there will be more people over eighty than the number of kids entering preschool.[68] Obviously, people are living longer, but this process starts when people have fewer and fewer babies.[69] This phenomenon places an unprecedented financial burden on working people. The increased costs in health care (which in the United States are going through the roof) and Social Security payments will amount to an additional 9 percent to 16 percent tax on working people to pay for the extra 64 trillion dollars it will take to care for older people in the years to come.[70] In Italy, 30 percent of a worker's wages goes to paying the bill for retired workers.[71] Many countries in Europe are in a similar plight. And it will get worse. In addition to the costs, which may lead to "global financial meltdown,"[72] Peterson sees a demise of the family,[73] a threat to the world's free nations, a rise of socialism,[74] a diminution of global peace-keeping, and significant dangerous changes in the geopolitical make-up of the planet.[75] The "new civilization" looks compromised.

Behind the politics and sociology is religion. If you see the pagan paradigm as a perversion of the Truth,[76] then the whole sexual construct flowing from it is built on a false premise and must inevitably lead not to utopia but to dystopia—social chaos and a cultural nightmare. The royal way to sexual excess and human nirvana is disturbingly full of cracks and potholes.[77]

Is there another way? Is there any voice of social and spiritual sanity? Is there a truth, *the* Truth,[78] to which sex should conform, written into the deep structures of creation and confirmed by a trustworthy word of prophetic revelation from God the Creator?

To put it another way, does Christianity have a message for this self-destructing sexual madness?

TWO GOSPELS

Writer Philip Yancey understands the relationship between God and sex. He understands that sex abstracted from its Creator is still religious. "If humanity serves as your religion, then sex becomes an act of worship. On the other hand, if God is the object of your religion, then romantic love becomes an unmistakable pointer, a rumor of transcendence as loud as any we hear on earth."[79] We can say that God is interested in sex. We can say that good sex is part of the good news. But we say this in a particular social context, in the presence of two "gospels," and both have sexual implications.

The pagan gospel preaches that redemption is *liberation from* the Creator and *repudiation of* creation's structures. It offers the "liberation" of sex from its heterosexual complementary essence.

The Christian gospel proclaims that redemption is *reconciliation with* the Creator and the *honoring of* creation's goodness. This gospel celebrates the goodness of sex within its rightful, heterosexual limits.[80] The options cannot be more starkly drawn, and they cannot both be right. If one is good news of the "truth," the other must be bad news, or, as the apostle Paul would say, "the lie."[81]

Perhaps contemporary preaching—in an exaggerated sense of prudishness—has often omitted the sexual element of the gospel. In a pagan world this will no longer do. We cannot afford to preach either a truncated gospel that speaks only of personal salvation ("Jesus raptures me out of here to an asexual mansion in the sky") or a sentimentalized, amorphous "gospel" of theological liberalism that allows for homosexual bishops. Christianity is not a religion of either sexless angels or of "believers" who play fast and loose with their sexuality. The Gnostics tried that and failed.[82] The Bible proves such a message false. Every human being on earth is a sexual being, and the Bible's teaching on sexuality within the context of creation must be announced as an essential part of the good news. Reconciliation with God makes interpersonal relationships and good sex possible.

If paganism could become the religion of our global future, and if the church is ever going to make a convincing case for monogamous heterosexuality, it is of supreme importance that we understand the worldview of the Bible and the place of sexuality within it. Our culture urgently needs to hear not a moralistic of do's and don'ts but a fresh, compelling case for the integral relationship between the personal, life-creating God of the Bible and life-promoting, satisfying, biblical sex.

This is what we will attempt to do in Part 2.

PART TWO

SEXUALITY ACCORDING TO THE BIBLICAL WORLDVIEW

Introduction to the Second Part

Part 2, "Sexuality according to the Biblical Worldview," is an invitation to enter a world other than the one our children are taught in school and see on today's television screens. Those who think I am calling for an old-fashioned worldview must realize that the current upbeat vision of liberation is, in reality, a return to a much more old-fashioned worldview. In fact, the worldview proposed today as cutting edge is the same as that proposed by equally old-fashioned pagan religions of the historical past. Oddly, in the third millennium, we are placed before a choice of two equally "old" worldviews.

There is deep correlation between a theistic, biblical understanding of God and the practical issues of spirituality—particularly, sexuality. As we saw in Part 1, the pagan understanding of God as a spiritual force within nature produces a deconstruction of heterosexual norms. Polytheism produces "polygender."

The Bible's theistic teaching reveals God not as the Spirit within nature but as nature's distinct Creator. Scripture also, therefore, emphasizes the created distinctions of heterosexuality, which the church maintains as a witness to the pagan world. The early church's belief and practice emerged from serious interaction with the implications of a biblical worldview.

We can do no less in our time.

Chapter 6

God and Sex

₪

Introduction to Worldview

In 2003 George Barna interviewed more than two thousand American adults about their worldview. The study produced some startling results. Only 9 percent of born-again Christians, 7 percent of Protestants overall, 2 percent of adults who attend mainline Protestant churches, 4 percent of the general population, and less than one-half of 1 percent of Catholics had a biblical worldview. Among the most prevalent alternative worldviews was postmodernism, which seemed to be the dominant perspective among the two youngest generations."[1] If this survey is even close to reality, its results are staggering, particularly as they apply to the future of sex.

Worldview is the organizing structure that allows us to make sense of all the ideas going around in our heads. The Bible, too, has an overall structure. In the sexual realm, for example, the few texts dealing with homosexuality come within the framework of the Bible's understanding of the nature of reality. Without understanding that framework, we cannot understand individual texts.

The God of Football

My childhood church in Liverpool, England, was once a Welsh Presbyterian chapel. The redbrick building with wooden pews for two hundred people sits nestled between a row of semidetached houses on Spellow Lane, just one block from the mighty six-ty-thousand-seat stadium of the Everton Football Club, a premier professional soccer team. (Football is the game you play with your feet, not your hands!) The church is so close that on prayer-meeting night, as a teenager, I was sometimes swept right past its open doors into the crowded stadium, where the glow of floodlights lit the night sky. Unfortunately, my Christian commitment was still weak and could not compete with the powerful attractions of the "world." The immediate glory of Everton Football Club was blinding for a soccer-mad kid like me.

When I went off to college (the first in my family), the pull of soccer gave way to the temptation of secularism. The Bible verses and emotional piety I had learned as a child in a warm, simple, Bible-believing community could not stand up to the brilliant, broad-ranging arguments of unbelieving teachers. Like many Christians, the cultural revolution of the 1960s took me by surprise because I had no notion of the Bible's worldview. I knew plenty of Bible verses but had no wide biblical lens to help me process, understand, and counter the pagan, Eastern worldview of the hippies. Quoting Bible verses did not seem to be enough.

And then I read Francis Schaeffer.

A Christian missionary in Switzerland, Schaeffer articulated—in an understandable way—the cultural movements that were shaking the foundations of Western society. By exposing the issues behind the headlines and sit-ins and by describing in global terms a biblical view of reality, Schaeffer engaged both the emotions and the intellect. As we try to understand the connection between sex and worldview, we must begin, as did Schaeffer, with our view of God.

THE GOD WHO IS THERE

When I lectured in Brazil I learned that the Portuguese translation of the title of Francis Schaeffer's first book is *The God Who*

Intervenes. It is a genuine attempt to render the somewhat odd English title—*The God Who Is There.*[2] When I first saw that title, I thought it was almost like saying, "Everywhere you go, there you are." If this phrase applies to anyone, it surely applies first to God, so why bother saying it? It is only thirty years later, after studying the coherent system of paganism, that I finally understand the logic of this title. God's objective existence outside of creation is the most appropriate starting point for understanding the way the Bible views reality. If we are to convince ourselves, our children, and our culture of the Bible's view of sex, we must begin with the Bible's view of God.

THE GODDESS WHO IS NOWHERE

The God Who Is There is not a title the pagan worldview would use. Pagans believe that the God(dess) is "nowhere." Says Joseph Campbell, guru to George Lucas, "In religions where the god or creator is the mother, the world is her body. *There is nowhere else*" (emphasis mine).[3] Campbell promotes a religion in which there is no "there" for God. Campbell is not an old-style rationalistic atheist. He is advocating spiritual paganism. *God* is a word for the divinity of all natural things, but s/he has no special place. God is simply everywhere, within everything.[4] Buddhism states this in a comparable way:

> The basic vows that we take as Buddhists remind us that there is no "other." The most basic practices...of Buddhism...point to the fact that there is no "other." The fundamental teachings of the Buddha tell us that there is no "other."[5]

This statement uses studied repetition to insist that there is no God outside of us, no God who is "other," different from us. Campbell, an ex-Roman Catholic, feels that the Bible went wrong in rejecting the goddess of the ancient Canaanites and her consort, the serpent. The serpent, which constantly sheds its skin,[6] symbolizes the rejuvenation of nature and expresses the divine character of natural life.[7] Says Campbell,

> The serpent represents immortal energy and consciousness...life in its most primal quality....In India...the cobra is the sacred animal, and the mythological Serpent King is the next thing to the Buddha....In American Indian traditions [there is] the snake dance of the Hopi.... In the Christian story, the serpent is the seducer. That amounts to a refusal to affirm life...the serpent is the primary god in the Garden of Eden [representative of the goddess]. Jahweh...is just a visitor. The garden is the serpent's place.[8]

Campbell is a radical and as antibiblical as one can get. In this quote he claims that there is no "God who is there" and that the earth belongs to the serpent—which is just a repeat of what the original serpent implied in his seduction of Eve.[9] Knowing Campbell's influence on George Lucas, try watching *Star Wars* with this subject in mind.

In this conflict of truth, who is right? One thing is certain. They cannot both be right.

THEISM

The pagan belief in the divinity of all things is called *monism.* Monism is *Oneism*; that is, humans, animals, trees, rocks, and God are one because all things share the same nature. Think of a big circle. Everything belongs in this circle, including God. According to C. S. Lewis, this god is a "mere zero," a "nonentity," a "featureless generality."[10]

The opposite of monism is *theism* (Twoism), the noble world-view of the Bible, revealing and honoring God as Lord of all. God (*theos* in Greek) and the universe are distinct, like a watch and a watchmaker, or to use a biblical image, like a potter and his clay.[11] Before Schaeffer, C. S. Lewis said it in different terms: "God is a particular Thing."[12] God does not belong in the monistic circle, or the "circle of life," as some kind of diffuse energy. He is outside of it because he created it. He has his own place—"there," his own domain of existence. Describing that specific domain establishes who and what God is.

GOD IS HOLY

When someone uses the word *holy*, you may think of Mother Teresa, of mystics sitting on poles in the desert, or of people with pure lives and an impeccable public record. But such a definition puts the cart before the horse.

When we use the word *holiday* (which we are forced to do more often now that *Christmas* is not a politically correct term), we are using an abbreviation of "*holy day*." Holy days are holy because we have set them apart as special. Thus, when we say God is holy, we mean he is special. In God's case he is uniquely special.

To say "God is there" is to affirm his holiness. To give God a distinct "place" is to sanctify him, or admit him "holy" because the root meaning of holy is "set apart." Things and people have their special places. For instance, in the Old Testament, we learn that no one was to enter the temple of the Lord except the priests and Levites on duty: "They may enter because they are consecrated [made holy, that is, set apart], but all the other men are to guard what the Lord has assigned to them."[13] These priests were holy not because of unusual moral purity, but because God had set them apart for a special, priestly task. Even their robes were holy because the robes had been "set apart."[14]

The command to acknowledge God as holy means to set him apart as unique, that is, not to confuse him with other claimants to deity nor to confuse him with what he has made. The two are not the same. In a certain sense, Joseph Campbell is right. God *is* a visitor in the garden of Eden, but he visits as its caring Creator and wise Sustainer. But Eden is not his true domain. "This is what the Lord says: 'Heaven is my throne, and the earth is my footstool.'"[15] Granting him that special, high location of his own throne, rather than confusing him with the earthly footstool, makes God holy in our eyes, honors him in his unique place, and recognizes his unique being. Says Isaiah,

> For thus says the One who is high and lifted up, who inhabits eternity, whose name is Holy: "I dwell in the high and holy place."[16]

God's holiness has to do with his place, high and lifted up, dwelling in eternity. In other words, God is holy because he is different from his creatures. In Jesus' well-known prayer, known as "The Lord's Prayer," Jesus teaches us that we are to pray, "Hallowed [holy] be your name."[17] We make God's name holy by not misusing it.[18] We are not to pray like the pagans, who, with their mantras, do not address the true, personal God.

What we do on earth, the angels also do in heaven. "In the council of the holy ones God is greatly feared; he is more awesome than all who surround him."[19] In heaven there are particular orders and ranks, and God is distinct from them. Isaiah was granted a vision of the Lord on his heavenly throne. He says,

> I saw the Lord seated on a throne, high and exalted.... Above him were seraphs.... And they were calling to one another: "Holy, holy, holy is the Lord Almighty; the whole earth is full of his glory."[20]

The holy angelic council declares God three-times holy. In this experience, Isaiah also understood, as few do, the Creator-creature distinction. Having seen what angels do, Isaiah declares himself undone: "Woe is me!...I am ruined! For I am a man of unclean lips."[21] Even to be near such a holy, transcendent Lord without protection means destruction.[22] Whatever or whoever fails to recognize God's special place relative to the created order can be defined as unholy or sinful. It is because of God's character as the unique sovereign Creator that we, his creatures, are to worship *him* rather than the *creation*. God reveals to Moses, the leader of Israel,

> You shall have no other gods before Me. You shall not make for yourself a carved image—...you shall not bow down to them nor serve them. For I, the Lord your God, am a jealous God....[23]

Paganism often makes specific images of God to worship, but it also worships the earth, the water, the sun, the sky, and other created things. It is thus guilty of the formidable sin—idolatry, the ultimate insult and ultimate foolishness—which is worshipping the creation rather than the Creator.[24] Wisdom consists of the very opposite. "The fear of the Lord is the beginning of wisdom, and knowledge of the Holy One is understanding."[25]

God Is Unique

The Bible insists on God's uniqueness. On Mount Carmel, God puts himself on trial before Elijah, the prophet of Jahweh, before the 450 priests of Baal, the 400 prophetesses of Asherah, and before the assembled people of Israel. As fire falls from heaven, God declares his uniqueness through a demonstration of his power, and the people cry out, "The Lord—he is God! The Lord—he is God."[26]

God is incomparable. "To whom will you compare me or count me equal? To whom will you liken me that we may be compared?"[27] His deeds are incomparable,[28] as is his person.[29] This is why it is such an affront to make images of God.[30] Nothing in the created order is like him. Idols don't show people to be primitive savages so much as they prove them to be sophisticated worshippers of nature. God is "jealous," not because he is insecure, but because he is jealous that the true nature of things be known. The first commandment is based on that claim ("You shall have no gods before me") and gives rise to the great confession of Israel, known as the *Shema*, still repeated today in many Jewish homes: "Hear, O Israel: The Lord our God, the Lord is one."[31]

In speaking of the "living God"[32] or the "true and living God," the Bible further affirms God's uniqueness and his special place.[33] Over against the false gods and their idols, there is only one true God who has his own life and is the source of all created life. Paul reminds the recently converted pagans in the church of Thessalonica, "You turned to God from idols to serve the living and true God."[34]

Since God is truly unique and unlike anything else, we call him "transcendent" or "other" because he exists far beyond anything we know. This is the kind of God I can honor and worship, a real God of absolute mystery, and in no sense a human clone.

Lloyd Geering does not agree with me.

God Is Transcendent

Geering, whose radical ideas we met in a previous chapter, proposes that the major problem with the Bible is the transcendence of God, that is, that God is radically different from us. "We humans," he affirms, "have come forth from the earth as from a cosmic womb."[35] Geering hopes to redefine Christianity along these goddess-worshipping, pagan lines. But you cannot get away from the fact that from the beginning of the Bible until the end, biblical faith maintains separateness between God and his creation. If you alter this, you are no longer faithful to the Bible.

J. Gresham Machen, a stalwart defender of Christian orthodoxy, writing in the 1920s, saw the beginning of the radical, apostate movement of which Geering is a most recent expression. Machen saw liberalism as paganism—in Christian dress[36]—entering the mainline churches, and he adeptly put his finger on the essence of this apostasy at a time when it was not so obvious:

> The truth is that liberalism has lost sight of the very centre and core of the Christian teaching. In the Christian view of god as set forth in the Bible, there are many elements. But one attribute of God is absolutely fundamental in the Bible; one attribute is absolutely necessary in order to render intelligible all the rest. That attribute is the awful transcendence of God.[37]

From the truth about God's transcendence flows what theologians call God's "incommunicable" attributes. This does not mean that God is not good at communicating. He created communication. It means there are some things in his divine nature he does not share with us. Here is a sample list:

₪ God had no beginning (his *eternity*); creation did.

₪ God is independent (his *aseity*); we are dependent.

₪ God is all-powerful (*omnipotent*); we clearly are not.

₪ God is all-knowing (*omniscient*); we are not.

₪ God knows the future; we do not.

₪ God's presence is felt everywhere (*omnipresent*); we are limited in space and time.[38]

₪ God is absolute; we are relative.

₪ God is changeless (*immutable*); we are changeable.

I read this list to a group of cool Southern California yuppies. To get their attention I promised a copy of one of my books to anyone who had just one of these attributes of God. At the end, a man in his early forties came to me and claimed a book. He said, "My wife says I never change." I gave him a book for creativity but not for accuracy.

In spite of this yuppie husband's sense of humor, none of these attributes of God can ever be attributed to creatures. It is obvious, in light of the Bible's revelation of God, that no creature can ever become God. To claim divinity fails to recognize who God is and fails to "hallow his name." God will never be anything other than the Lord over all. God says to Israel, "You thought I was altogether like you,"[39] and reminds them, "My thoughts are not your thoughts, neither are your ways my ways."[40] To honor God we must maintain the difference between his nature and ours. We must respect his formidable transcendence and his consuming holiness, which is the essence of worship. The psalmist says, "Worship the Lord in the splendor of his holiness; tremble before him, all the earth."[41] Holiness is God's separateness or transcendence about which the created earth trembles.

God Is Personal

How could such a formidable God be also personal? He is, says Paul, the "one God, the Father, from whom all things came and for whom we live."[42] In associating "Father" with "Creator" Paul is not innovating. He found this notion in the Old Testament. Moses declares to Israel, "Is he not your Father, your Creator, who made you and formed you?"[43] The prophet Malachi repeats what Moses said with equal clarity: "Have we not all one Father? Did not one God create us?"[44] The Creator is not an impersonal force, but the Father.

George Barna notes the decline in the belief in the doctrine of the Trinity. He recounts that "On Trinity Sunday I was in an Episcopal church, where the rector averred that this was only something for pastors to think about. Ordinary people did not have to bother with it."[45] Certainly the doctrine of the Trinity is mysterious and no human can really explain it, but it is nevertheless essential for a Christian understanding of God and the world.

Many have no understanding whatsoever of this important doctrine. June Singer, the Jungian psychologist who was raised a Jew and converted to Gnosticism, shows a total ignorance for the God of her fathers when she says, "The creator god is in a state of utter Loneliness...in the midst of endless emptiness."[46] Similar is the Hindu notion of the creator who feels lonely and lacking any sense of pleasure.[47]

The Trinity reveals that God is *transcendently* personal. That is, he does not need you or me to get personal. The gospel of John begins, as does Genesis, describing divine creation: "In the beginning was the Word, and the Word was with God, and the Word was God.... through [the Word] all things were made."[48] We learn clearly from this text and others in the New Testament what is already discernable in the Old: The God behind the created world is a self-contained union of three divine persons—Father, Son, and Spirit.

> [Since] God is already, "in advance" of creation, a communion of persons existing in loving relations, it becomes possible to say that he does not need the world.[49]

In the Trinity there is quite enough love and personal communion to go around forever. God was not cosmically lonely or in need of human friends or personal affirmation. Says Gunton,

> God is able to will the existence of something else simply for its own sake. Creation is the outcome of God's love indeed, but of his unconstrained love.... The world is given value as a realm of being in its own right. It is, in the words of Genesis, "very good," not only partly good or as a means to an end, but simply as and for what it is: the created order.[50]

While God is transcendently personal, the fact that he creates male and female in his own image forges a personal connection between the Creator and created human beings. Unlike monism, the Christian faith explains why human beings are people and not rocks; why we can sing, love, paint, and write poetry. The personal God made men and women to reflect his personal nature. God's written Word of revelation reveals the path he opens for us to become united to him in eternal love.

Monism (Oneism) renders God diffuse. It makes the world whatever you would like it to be, like the *chi* lines of energy that, according to Eastern medicine, supposedly run through our bodies. No one quite knows where they are or even whether they exist. In paganism the one circle of pagan unity turns out to be a foreboding black hole of impersonal nothingness.

The Bible proposes a personal relationship with the Maker of heaven and earth. That relationship is already seen in the Old Testament but comes to its pinnacle in Jesus Christ and in his gift of the Holy Spirit. God's presence is intimate, comforting, and real. Creatures can know the joy of deep personal intimacy with their Maker. Only this definition of God allows the personal relationship associated with prayer, as Machen also saw:

> True prayer always conceives of God as personal, whereas much of modern religious thinking conceives of God as only another name for the world.... The personal distinction between man and God is absolutely essential in prayer.[51]

Christians pray, while pagans chant or meditate. Christians address the personal Creator who truly is "there" and answers the door when they knock.[52]

God Is Creator

God's holiness, uniqueness, transcendence, and incomparability come to observable expression in his role as Creator, as God himself says:

> "To whom will you compare me? Or who is my equal?" says the Holy One. "Lift your eyes and look to the heavens: Who created these?"[53]

There is not just one circle enveloping reality, as the monists claim. The Bible insists that Christians draw two circles. There are *two* kinds of reality: the reality of the divine Creator and the reality of the created order. This Twoism between heaven and earth, between God and creation—so vilified by pagan thinkers—is the very essence of the biblical revelation.[54] For this reason, the very first line of the Bible contains the stunning statement "In the beginning, God created the heavens and the earth."[55] One might even say that everything else the Bible reveals is commentary, a consequence of that first programmatic statement. First there was God and nothing else, and then God made the universe.

Christians do not believe that God *is* the creation or that God is a sort of impersonal spirit within all things. While the imprint of his creative hand is truly on everything,[56] God is nevertheless different from what he made, just as the watchmaker is not a watch.

This claim of the Bible—that the God who inspired the Bible is the Creator of heaven and earth—stands in stark contrast to paganism. A choice must be made, as Colin Gunton affirms:

> There are, probably, ultimately only two possible answers to the question of origins, and they recur at different places in all ages: that the universe is the result of creation by a free personal agency, and that in some way or other it creates itself. The two answers are not finally compatible, and require a choice, either between them or an attitude of agnostic refusal to decide.[57]

Critical scholars sometimes admit that the Christian message is unique in this claim. After treating Genesis as one more primitive myth of origins comparable to the many similar myths of ancient paganism, some now admit to the particularity and distinctiveness of Genesis. Far from being one ancient myth among many, the Bible lays out a message not found in any other ancient text. The Bible is different and brings a unique message.[58] Klaus Westermann, the critical German Old Testament scholar contrasts the Genesis account with the Babylonian creation myths in the following way:

> What distinguishes the [Genesis] account of creation among the many creation stories of the Ancient Near East is that for Genesis there can be only one creator and that all else that is or can be, can never be anything but a creature.[59]

Not all scholars are willing to give Genesis such treatment. Lloyd Geering dismisses it as a "myth recounting noogenesis [the birth of consciousness]," an imaginary story about how the primates emerged from self-consciousness to self-transcendence.[60] Amazingly, modern Judaism is doing the same and now confesses:

> In order for Judaism to survive, it must divest itself of traditional views of God, and the spiritual dimension of the faith must be reformulated in humanistic terms.[61]

Another leading Jewish scholar contends that if Israel is to move forward, it must expect "the eclipse of Jewish theism."[62] Many contemporary Jewish leaders are ready to ditch this unique jewel of their tradition for a bowl of global pagan porridge, as are many apostate Christians. Sadly, the gem they are throwing into the dust is the very heart of what makes the Jewish Bible unique. According to Gunton, the biblical account says things that have not been said elsewhere in the history of human thought. Biblical faith in this regard is unparalleled. "In general," says Gunton, "Greek thought held that matter was both eternal and inferior to mind or spirit. The Bible teaches that matter both had a beginning and, for that reason, was not inferior but intended by a good creator."[63] Gunton goes on to make the point about the uniqueness of this scriptural teaching:

> What does this revolutionary doctrine of creation distinctively say?—creation was "out of nothing." This teaching is fundamental and makes the Christian teaching unique. It affirms that God in creating the world relied on nothing outside himself, so that creation is an act of divine sovereignty and freedom, an act of personal willing that there be something other. It further implies that the universe had a beginning in time and is limited in space: it is neither eternal nor infinite.[64]

PRACTICAL IMPLICATIONS FROM THE BIBLE'S REVELATION OF GOD

Having examined the Bible's revelation of God, two essential, fundamental notions emerge that define God, without which there is no biblical God:

1. God is holy, separate from what he made. The foundational stone of biblical faith is the Creator-creature distinction. Because he is God, only he can reveal truth about the universe, hence our need of Scripture; because he is God, only he can save.

2. God is personal. Though God is separate from us, intimacy with the Creator is possible. Indeed, without personal distinction there is no genuine intimacy.

These characteristics about God determine our view about the world and, in particular, about sex.

Once you accept this biblical understanding of God, Christianity makes a lot of sense. Theism is not the faith of bigoted people who refuse to fit in or get along. It is the truth about who we are as finite creatures in an amazing, beautifully designed universe that we did not make, face-to-face with the personal God who did. Why am I a theist? Because only God could be the author of the event that radically determines my entire existence, past, present, and future, over which I have absolutely no control—namely, my creation. I do not—I cannot—claim this power. I merely recognize and praise Another's transcendent power and amazing skill.

We are in the presence of two radically opposite, religious world notions. John Shelby Spong, a retired, apostate Episcopal Bishop of Newark, New Jersey, states without nuance in a manner similar to the Jewish leaders cited previously, "If Christianity depends on the theistic definition of God, then we must face the fact that we are watching this noble religious system enter the rigor mortis of its own death."[65] While our time seems a propitious moment for toxic heresy, such heresy can be traced far back into the history of the church, which has always had its radical dissenters. The first discernable gnostic,[66] Marcion (ca. AD 150), rejected the God of the Bible and preached "the Alien God"— above, beyond, and within—who was everywhere and nowhere.[67]

The lines are drawn. The conflict is not over details, nor is the disagreement of recent date. If we are having trouble with sex, it is because we are having trouble with God. We need to ask ourselves a few questions:

- ₪ How does the biblical doctrine of God affect the Bible's teaching on sexuality?
- ₪ If the biblical view of God as transcendent Creator is locked in such a no-holds-barred conflict with the protagonists of neopaganism, is it any wonder that biblical sexuality is under such all-out attack from the proponents of the pagan sexual utopia?
- ₪ If God is "there" in his own "holy" place, what is our holy place, and what is the holy place of sexuality?

The answer to these questions is the subject of the next chapter.

Chapter 7

THE BIRTH OF SEX

₪

I hardly know anyone more different from me than my wife. She likes sweet breakfasts; I like savory. She relies on maps; I guess. She looks at the details; I look at the big picture. She plays music by sight; I play music by ear. She hates to eat outside; I love to eat outside. She is a night owl; I am a morning bird. She loves Home Depot; I love Sports Authority. We have been married thirty-five years!

VIVE LA DIFFÉRENCE

With a marriage like ours, it is good to know that, according to the Bible, God's design for marriage is "difference." As any couple does, we've struggled with our differences from time to time. But we have also grown both personally and as a couple because of them. As the say in France, where we lived for more than seventeen years, "Vive la différence."

Eve was created as a helper *different from Adam*.[1] She complemented him in every way—equally valuable but crucially and essentially different. Essential because the human task—as the Bible describes it—was (and still is until further notice) to make the earth habitable and fill it with offspring. From this perspective, homosexuality is a creational dysfunction, and homosexual marriage an oxymoron.

A pagan priestess recently found my Web site and wrote, "I am a woman, and according to the bible [sic] I am evil and the temptation of man. Well I am proud to be able to bring forth life. This is a great joy to me." Her misunderstanding of the Christian position about sexuality is echoed by apostate bishop John Shelby Spong, who sees "'sexlessness' and the connection [between]... pervasive human guilt...and...sexual desire...[as] a largely Christian achievement."[2]

Whatever strange things certain Christians in the history of the church might have said about sex, the evidence of Scripture renders the above judgments wrong and misleading. Consider the following phrases used in the Old Testament:

> *How beautiful you are, my darling.... Your lips are like a scarlet ribbon....*
> *Your neck is like the tower of David, built with elegance.... Your two breasts are like two fawns....*[3]
>
> *May you rejoice in the wife of your youth.*
> *A loving doe, a graceful deer—may her breasts satisfy you always, may you ever be captivated by her love.*
>
> *Why be captivated, my son, by an adulteress?*
> *Why embrace the bosom of another man's wife?*[4]

In one biblical book, there is even an exhortation to "be drunk with love!"[5]

Any religion that contains in its canonical scriptures such an erotic yet holy expression of sexuality can hardly be accused of guilt-ridden sexlessness. Reflect for a moment on the New Testament notions about a man's love for his wife and the comparison made to Christ's love for the church.[6] Consider the biblical commands that spouses must give themselves sexually to each other.[7] Such statements do not denigrate human sexuality. Such ignorance may be expected of pagan priestesses but not of an Episcopal bishop. Both the priestess and the bishop fail to understand the biblical notions of holiness and sex because they fail to understand the biblical revelation of God the Creator.

The Bible gives great honor to the woman.[8] As opposed to the ancient pagan Greeks who speak of the "foul tribe of women" (Menander),[9] the Bible celebrates Eve as "the mother of all the living."[10] The idealization of woman found in the Bible[11] stands in contrast to the Greek dismissal of woman as "the greatest evil" or the "plague." Socrates began each morning thanking the gods that he was born a man, not a woman. Aristotle dismisses women as "irrational."[12] Scripture, however, describes the woman as "clothed with strength and dignity...[who] speaks with wisdom... [and gives] faithful instruction."[13] She is "far beyond the price of pearls."[14]

Spong's charge of "sexlessness" does not fit the Bible. Nowhere, of course, does the Bible approve of sex as an appetite-satisfying meat market. Nor is it an animalistic urge or an evolutionary mechanism by which the fittest survive. Sex, according to the Bible, is a beautiful creation from the mind of God, covered in his moral perfection. How do we know that?

FINGERPRINTS

When my children were little, I could tell where they had been by looking at the white doorframes or the sliding glass door. It didn't take a team of detectives to follow their fingerprints.

God's fingerprints are all over the world he created, but they don't ruin its beauty and they can't be wiped off. Those prints *are* the world's beauty. "God's...qualities," says Paul, "have been clearly seen...from what he has made."[15] The prophet Isaiah says, "The whole earth is full of his glory."[16] God has invested himself in a fabulous piece of divine creativity. The earth reflects the good and holy character of its Maker. Thus God exhorts his people: "Be holy, because I am holy."[17] But what does it mean to be holy?

Creation as Separation-Sanctification

As we saw, the root meaning of holiness is intentional "thereness"—being in a specific place for a particular function. This is how God is holy. From that unique position God created the world. But God is not the only one to have a place. We, his creatures, also have a distinct, holy, and significant place where we rightfully belong.

The first two chapters of the Bible tell the story of how God created. The terms and structure in this account make God's intentions for his creation clear.

Separation

The Creator-creature distinction determined the way God creates. God brought forth cosmic matter from nothing, from the original "chaos"[18] or unformed matter. God's work of creation turned chaos into ordered cosmos. Like a skilled craftsman carefully honing every detail of his masterpiece, God created by establishing distinctions, by separating things out, and giving each thing its place and function. This is the essence of what the Bible means by the act of creation. This is why separation is immediately associated with "goodness." Paganism believes separation is evil; God states that it is good. "And God saw that the light was *good*. And God separated the light from the darkness."[19] God *separated* the waters above from the waters below.[20]

Kinds

Another phrase seems equally important in the Scriptures' insistence on distinctiveness and separation. The phrase "according to its kind" is a programmatic theme used ten times in the first twenty-five verses of the Bible. Each type of vegetation,[21] every living creature is created "according to its kind."[22] Thus the distinction of "kinds" is also declared "good."[23]

Names

Everything must be named so that it can be clearly distinguished.

God called the light "day." He called the darkness "night."[24] Significantly, God names the first human being by a specific name, "Adam." Not surprisingly, Adam functions in the created world in an analogous way. God brings all the animals "to the man," says the Scripture, "to see what he would name them."[25] The Bible affirms real, identifiable, created distinctions—things with clear labels (names).

Adam's task of naming the animals indicates the special role of man in the created cosmos.[26] In comparable ways, God and Adam uniquely share "dominion" and "glory."[27] Paganism rejects the idea that man has a special place. Man is rather a blight on nature, the cause of all our woes. Certainly, man is responsible (that is his glory) and often sinful (that is his shame), but the Bible will not give up on its notion of human nobility.

Holiness

God's acts of creative "separation" are related to the notion of holiness. God commands Israel, "You are to set the Levites apart from the other Israelites" in order that they might maintain the service of the Temple.[28] Moses uses the same verb, "to separate," here in Numbers as he does in the creation account of Genesis. These Levites may enter the Temple "because they are consecrated" (made holy, set apart).[29] To separate and to make holy are synonymous terms.[30]

Naming is also closely tied to holiness. This deep connection is clear with regard to special feasts. In Leviticus, God says to Moses, "Speak to the Israelites and say to them: 'These are my appointed [or called/named] feasts, the appointed [named] feasts of the Lord, which you are to proclaim as sacred assemblies.'"[31] These special assemblies are set apart by God, called "holy" by God. As we shall see, the difference between male and female is an essential part of cosmic holiness.

It is fair to say that in creation, the separation and naming of its elements as being recognizably different constitutes the sanctification of the cosmos. By separating things out and giving each one a specific name and different function, God is "sanctifying" and declaring holy what he makes. They reflect in some creaturely way the holiness of God.

An ordered, personal cosmos also appears in the notion of "covenant."

COVENANT

Difference and intimacy are essential to the biblical notion of knowing God, described in the Bible as a *covenant*. A covenant is constituted by two parties sealed in a personal, legal relationship for the sake of a significant goal. God's covenant defines a holy, that is, structured life, with goals and prohibitions. Perhaps the best known is God's covenant with Abraham.[32] A similar arrangement is established with Adam in Eden.[33] God gives Adam a function and the terms of a faithful relationship. To keep that covenant, the text immediately says, "It is not good that the man should be alone; I will make him a helper fit for him."[34] In other words, marriage and sexual intimacy are first introduced within the larger context of God's covenant with humanity and, by extension, with the whole of creation.

The Witness of Subsequent Old Testament Scripture

The first two chapters of Genesis are not all the Bible says about the original creation.

Psalm 8

Psalm 8 is a majestic declaration of the Old Testament understanding of the glory of the original creation:

> O Lord, our Lord, how majestic is your name in all the earth!
>> You have set your glory above the heavens...When I look at your heavens, the work of your fingers,
>> the moon and the stars, which you have set in place,
> what is man that you are mindful of him,...Yet you have made him a little

lower than the heavenly beings
and crowned him with glory and honor.
　You have given him dominion over the works of your hands;
you have put all things under his feet...

The soaring vision of human dignity is, to my knowledge, without parallel in the literature of the ancient world. God is the sovereign Creator; humans, both male and female—with all things submitted to them—are God's viceroys, and everything else has its designated and rightful place, as a great symphony of praise. Here is God's original intention for the cosmos.

Israel's Life of Holiness

The witness of Scripture to this created order is not limited to a few "proof texts." Even after the fall, creation serves as a blueprint for Israel. The term "holy" (*qodesh*) occurs 468 times in the Old Testament, indicating it is a most significant theme. The life of Israel, as light and witness to the nations,[35] must reflect the holy character of the life God creates as Maker of heaven and earth at the beginning.[36] The nation serves as a microcosm of what the original created cosmos should look like. By setting Israel apart, the holy God makes her holy. "You are to be holy to me because I, the Lord, am holy, and I have set you apart from the nations to be my own."[37]

As a theocracy, a state ruled directly by God, Israel reflected his holy character down to the minutest detail. All of life is regulated according to the following principle: "You must distinguish [separate] between the holy and the common, between the unclean and the clean."[38] Note that separation (what God does in creation) and holiness are tied together here. Life is given meaning and direction as Israel is told how she

₪　may eat:[39] "You must distinguish between the unclean and the clean, between living creatures that may be eaten and those that may not be eaten"[40]

131

₪ makes fabric for clothing: "Do not wear clothing woven of two kinds of material"[41]

₪ raises livestock: "Do not mate different kinds of animals"[42]

₪ farms: "Do not plant your field with two kinds of seed"[43]

While we moderns may find these commands bizarre, the rules about seeds and animals refer back to Genesis 1 when God creates and distinguishes plants according to their kind, and animals according to their kind. And there is more. Israel's offerings to the Lord are described as "that which is separated for him."[44] Her Sabbaths proclaim the same reality. One day is separated out as "holy" to recall the worship owed to God—the Creator.[45] These many details indicate how Israel's everyday life is connected to God's original creative acts, as a witness to the pagan nations of her faith in and knowledge of God the Creator.[46]

The Witness of New Testament Scripture

A popular misconception is to think of the Old Testament God as the God of creation (and Law), and the God of the New Testament as the God of salvation, love, and radical freedom. A closer examination indicates that the God of creation is everywhere in the New.

The Savior Is the Creator

The New Testament makes an amazing claim. You can take it or leave it, but its implications are immense. Jesus Christ—born of the virgin Mary, crucified under Pontius Pilate—is the Creator. The apostle John, who was closer to Jesus than anyone during his earthly ministry, begins his gospel with this stunning declaration:

In the beginning was the Word.... All things came into being through him.[47]

Such a surprising claim concerning Christ as Creator is not unique to John. In the epistle to the Hebrews, Jesus Christ, the eternal Son, is described as "sustaining all things by his powerful word."[48] The apostle Paul speaks of "one Lord, Jesus Christ, through whom are all things and through whom we exist"[49] and "in whom all things hold together."[50] In other words, it is Christ who separated all things out and sanctified them, giving them form and significance, and who, since then, maintains them that way.

Christians who love their Savior cannot avoid identifying with God the Creator.

The Goodness of Creation

It would be wrong to think of the earthly Jesus as the St. Francis of Assisi of Palestine, with birds landing on his arms in a bucolic, pastel-colored scene worthy of modern-day Tuscany. He was a "man of sorrows" who met a violent death, but he understood the beauty of creation. His appreciation for "the lilies of the field," the sparrows, and the sunshine and rain indicate that Jesus was no earth-denying gnostic guru, awaiting death as the liberation of his spirit from matter. On the contrary, Jesus prayed to and worshipped the heavenly Father as the good Creator of all earthly things.

The Importance of the Body

God is in the body business. To be holy in body is to use the body in the correct way in accordance with God's creational design. Modern feminists reject the feminine body. "Biology," they say, "does not equal destiny."[51] New Testament Scripture says, "God gives...a body [to everyone] as he has determined."[52] Being in the right place at the right time is ultimately what makes things morally right. In ancient Israel the body's physical state symbolized God's demand for moral purity, both of the individual and of the nation.[53] But while the ritual symbolism falls away with the end of the theocracy, God's demand for bodily holiness in the new covenant does not exist.

Here is the program from the apostle's pen: "For God did not call us to be impure, but to live a holy life."[54] "The body is...for the Lord, and the Lord for the body."[55] The place where believers are to serve and honor God in holiness is not in some angelic spirit, but in their body. Living a holy life involves not just thinking pious thoughts or doing loving actions but actually using one's body in God's prescribed way. Sin is misusing the body, as Paul says:

> Just as you used to offer the parts of your body in slavery to impurity... so now offer them in slavery to righteousness leading to holiness.[56]... each of you should learn to control his own body in a way that is holy and honorable.[57]

Here "honorable" and "holy," and by logical extension "dishonorable" and "unholy," are synonyms as is indicated elsewhere.[58] Obviously, doing *honorable* things *honors* the Creator. What false worshippers do not do—honor God[59]—true believers do.[60] "You were bought at a price. Therefore honor God with your body."[61]

This role for the body gives it great dignity. While many forms of paganism dismiss the physical body as worthless illusion, the New Testament places the body in the center of Christian discipleship. Notice Paul's logic: Since "the life of Jesus...[is] revealed in our body...,"[62] "now as always Christ will be exalted in my body."[63] The exaltation of Christ is what the Christian faith is all about— and it is done in the body! Because this is true, the body is given the noble title, the "temple of the Holy Spirit."[64] Once more the body is associated with holiness (Holy Spirit), and holiness is understood as God's designated, special use. So, how does sexuality fit in?

SEX IN THE BIBLE

The Bible's statements about sexuality cannot be isolated from this overall understanding of the nature of the created order, of which sexuality is a fundamental element. Indeed, the second thing the Bible says about humanity, after its momentous declaration about man's being made in God's image, is a ringing declaration of human heterosexuality.[65]

Vive la Différence

As I mentioned earlier, my family and I lived in France for more than seventeen years. The French invented the phrase *"Vive la différence"* for many reasons. France produces four hundred different kinds of cheese. One night as I sat at a beautifully laid table in a high-class restaurant overlooking the historic Marseille harbor, the tuxedoed *maître d'* informed me that each of those four hundred French cheeses requires a different French wine! I gulped in amazement. How could anyone be so discerning?

Difference is the spice of life—in cooking, in sex, and in the great issues of the meaning and significance of life itself. In the pseudo world of pagan imagination, all the cheeses taste the same, and the four hundred wines match one cheese as well as another. This is a church potluck gone wild and the French, at least, define it as Hades, not utopia. What is true of cheese and wine is also true of spirituality. Thomas Molnar says about Buddhist pantheism, "The dissolution of god [into all things] leads directly to the dissolution of the self and all the attributes that make the individual a multifaceted human being."[66]

A Worldview for the Body—and for Cheese

"Speaking the truth in love" is an essential Christian calling.[67] But Christianity is not just talk. Embodying the truth in one's physical body is an essential part of Christian discipleship.

In the land of the four hundred cheeses, theologians speak of the danger of *angélisme*, the error of thinking that once one becomes a follower of Christ, one becomes an angel. Things concerning the body—like cheese and sex—no longer matter. This, of course, goes against everything the Bible stands for. For if God is the Creator then, as we have noted, *everything* God created is good. From one perspective the gospel is the revelation of what God does with flesh-and-blood bodies—and what he thinks about cheese! Physical things are indispensable to the Creator's present and future intentions. This is why the "spiritual" Paul urges Christians to "offer your *bodies* as living sacrifices, holy and pleasing to God—this is your spiritual act of worship."[68] Not spirits, but bodies too.[69] As we await the coming of Christ, we are to learn about the sanctification of the body.

Here is where sex fits in.

MALE AND FEMALE

Creation is brought to its culmination in the further and final distinction within humanity—between male and female.[70] The implicit distinction in this creative act is made clear by the fact that Adam distinguished Eve by naming her. Adam declared about his wife, "She shall be called 'woman,' for she was taken out of man."[71] This name declares the woman's fundamental equality with the man. Unlike the animals, she is "from man"[72] and "suitable for man."[73] But she is also different. This might shock the modern feminist reader raised on a diet of egalitarian sameness, but the *Los Angeles Times* had a whole section on the fundamental biological differences between men and women. Sherry Marts, vice president of the Society for Women's Health Research, states, "Women aren't just small men with different plumbing...there are differences in all the psychological systems of the body."[74] In Genesis just as light and darkness have different names, so does the original human pair. In an act of naming, Adam renamed his wife "Eve, because she would become the mother of all the living."[75] The creation distinctions are essential for the realization of the redemptive project and thus of the significance of creation. In an unusual though telling way, Paul reaffirms this when he says, "Women will be saved in childbirth."[76] With Paul, we are in a totally different, creation-affirming world from that of the ancient gnostics who in the name of "Christ" exhorted their women to "destroy the works of femaleness."[77] If the reader had any doubt that gnostic notions of spirituality and sexuality had returned to our shores,[78] then note the statement of feminist Shulamith Firestone: "The heart of a woman's oppression is her childbearing and childrearing roles."[79]

In Genesis the last divine act of separation in the original creation is when God makes humans, male and female.[80] God emphasizes this distinguishing, creative act four chapters later at the beginning of the history of the line of Adam to Noah: "He created them male and female."[81] Through Moses, God reveals that heterosexuality is the only model for human sexuality. The statement has a programmatic ring about it.[82] Consistently, the fundamental male-female distinction is maintained in the civil code in Israel as the only sexual form acceptable to the Lord.[83] The male-female distinction is thus spelled out as normative in the Old Testament, and the same is true of the New Testament.

Jesus, schooled in the Scriptures, takes the Genesis statement as programmatic. In his endorsement of permanent heterosexual marriage, he replies to the trick questions of the Pharisees, "Haven't you read...that at the beginning the Creator 'made them male and female'?"[84] Our Lord here simply assumes without question the normative status of heterosexuality as taught in the creation account. Similarly, the apostle Paul in describing humanity via three different binary categories sees "male and female" as one of them. In this much-disputed passage, Paul is not calling for an end of male and female genders.[85] Otherwise, everything else he says about sexuality would be blatantly contradictory. On the contrary, he affirms that these two possibilities—male and female—are all there are. He is making a normative statement about gender, deliberately employing this striking, technical language—*male and female*—which everyone knew came from the creation account. This is why he calls homosexual relations "unnatural."[86]

The apostle Paul endorses this worldview as he teaches the ex-pagan Corinthians about the resurrection. "But God gives... bod[ies] as he has determined, and to each kind of seed he gives its own body. All flesh is not the same: Men have one kind of flesh, animals have another, birds another and fish another."[87] The obvious implication is that what God has given in such varied splendor should not be mixed. This is true on the sexual level. We are sexually holy by observing the original God-ordained distinctions of sex and gender.

DIFFERENCE WITH INTIMACY

Difference does not keep God from his creation nor people from each other. Rather distinction is an essential element of biblical intimacy.

Exclusive Communion: God as Person

In a surprising way, God's *otherness* is no insurmountable obstacle to his *nearness*. Though the "awful transcendence of God" (Machen's phrase cited previously) might imply an unbridgeable distance, as a matter of fact, God can only be truly *near* if he is *other*. To put it another way, God's holiness or otherness is the essential requisite of his personhood. In his statement referenced earlier, Thomas Molnar captures what happens when God is reduced to pantheism: "The dissolution of God [into all things] leads directly to the dissolution of the self and all the attributes that make the individual a multifaceted human being."[88] According to pantheism, though God is all things and thus apparently very close, he ends up nowhere and so not close at all. He only shows up when I look inside and see myself.

This is not the God Paul declared to the very religious Athenians,"The God who made the world...is not far from each one of us."[89] The God of the Bible is a personal God who can be sought, found, and known. J. Gresham Machen, who defended "the awful transcendence of God" against liberalism in the 1920s, saw what would happen to prayer if this were lost. Bishop Spong is a living result of that liberal theology. He says about prayer:

The definition of God implicit in the Lord's Prayer cannot be the operative definition for us today.... I do not begin [praying] by saying, "Our Father who art in heaven." The deity I worship is rather part of who I am individually and corporately.[90]

The truth is that Spong prays no more, or as Jesus says in introducing the Lord's Prayer, prays like the heathen. Spong is a disciple not of Jesus but of Tillich, who did not pray either.[91]

Exclusive Communion: God as Faithful Husband

The personal God of theism proposes himself as a faithful husband and lover of his people. "For your Maker is your husband."[92] This is the high point of Israel's hopes: "'In that day,' declares the Lord, 'you will call me "my husband"; you will no longer call me "my master."'"[93] This hope is taken up in the New Testament as a partly fulfilled reality, inasmuch as the church is now betrothed as the fiancée of the Messiah. So Paul says to the Corinthians, "I promised you to one husband, to Christ, so that I might present you as a pure virgin to him."[94] The full realization is still future. The love story contains a majestic climax, as do all great romances. The happy ending is recounted in the prophecy of Revelation, which seeing into the future declares, "I saw the Holy City, the new Jerusalem, coming down out of heaven from God, prepared as a bride beautifully dressed for her husband."[95]

This story also contains pathos and disappointment. Spiritual unfaithfulness to the Lord is also presented in marital terms.[96] Religious idolatry of paganism is described as adultery and prostitution.[97] This is why sex is not only to be heterosexual; it must also be exclusive, for in this way it reflects God's great project for the universe. The obvious should not be missed. Exclusive heterosexuality is the *only* sexual vehicle the Bible uses to describe God's relationship with his people. There are no alternative lifestyles that qualify.

When God created the world and sanctified it by making distinctions, he imprinted his own person on the way things are. God's own mysterious person gives ultimate expression to the notion of exclusive, faithful communion between separate beings. For the God of theism is a Trinity. God the Father, God the Son, and God the Holy Spirit are three distinct persons bound in eternal communion. Together they collaborated to create the material universe, and it is that divine image that the universe reflects.

Christians know God in a union comparable to marriage. As in marriage—a relationship in which neither partner abandons his or her identity but both are nevertheless united in deep intimacy—so, too, we human creatures can maintain our differences with God and still have a true and living union with the Creator.

THE POWER OF ONE

My children tease me for being a mathematical zero. Naturally, I hesitate to get into theological mathematics, but here goes. The deep intimacy between two sexually different human beings united in marriage is expressed in the biblical notion of "the two becoming one." The implication of this affirmation seems to be this: that one is greater than two, or to change the metaphor, that the sum is greater than the parts. This statement—"[the two] shall become one flesh"—is made once in the Creation account[98] and repeated twice both by Jesus[99] and by Paul[100] as they teach with divine authority about the nature of marriage.

Becoming "one" is the *main* idea of paganism. Monism, you will recall, is the theory of "mono," that is, "oneness." When we try to compare the way monism sees "one" and the way theism sees "one," we meet another unbridgeable chasm. In paganism, oneness involves the destruction of distinctions, the radical autonomy of the individual, and the ultimate annihilation of personhood. In theism, oneness nurtures, encourages, and celebrates distinctions and brings them together in a rich, God-ordained tapestry of endlessly varied complementarity.

Biblical Oneness

Oneness is not just a New Testament notion. As in all things the Old Testament is a prophecy of the New. Terms such as "respond[ing] with one voice,"[101] or God "giv[ing] them one heart,"[102] suggest conformity to God's will. Conformity to the holiness God lays down for his people in the Law is the essence of oneness. Such conformity underlies the vision for national unity. Note the theme of "the two becoming one" in the following citation as God promises through Ezekiel, "I will make them one nation in the land, on the mountains of Israel. There will be one king over all of them and they will never again be two nations or be divided into two kingdoms."[103]

The promise of one king over one nation is fulfilled in King Jesus in the New Israel, the church. "You are all one in Christ"[104] is the great statement of Christian unity. There are no longer two, but one. Paul affirms this four times in the same passage.[105] This oneness is achieved by Christ, who by his blood has brought near those who were far away (the pagans) into communion with those who are near (Israel). Notice how the creational marriage structure provides the categories for redemption. Just as God creates humans male and female in order that they become "one flesh" to carry out the creational mandate of filling the earth,[106] so God's "purpose," says Paul about redemption, "was to create in himself one new man out of the two, thus making peace."[107] This new, singular body made up of two fulfills God's saving, re-creational plan for the universe: "Through the church the manifold wisdom of God is made known to the rulers and authorities in the heavenly realms, according to his eternal purpose."[108]

Often—particularly in reference to sports—we call this notion of oneness "teamwork." The same teamwork is present in the work of the gospel. "He who plants and he who waters have one purpose, and each will be rewarded according to his own labor."[109] Each has a separate role; each will receive a different wage, but both are one in purpose because they combine their different efforts to achieve a common, sanctified goal.

Marital Oneness

This oneness is true in sexuality. It is right at the beginning of the Bible: "Therefore a man shall leave his father and his mother and hold fast to his wife, and they shall become *one flesh*."[110] At the beginning of the Bible we encounter this programmatic statement about heterosexuality. In these verses is stated (1) the deep human equality of the human pair—"bone of my bone"; (2) their sexual distinction—she is "woman," he is "man"; (3) their complementary oneness—"they shall become one flesh."

Clearly, Paul means for us to see marriage as a picture of redemption. This "two becoming one" principle in marriage is even used to express the very essence of "the mystery," that is, the gospel. Not only do Jew and pagan become one as a consequence of Christ's redeeming work on the cross, but also human sinners become united to their divine Savior to become "members of his body"[111] so that these "two" form "one new man"[112] or "one flesh."[113]

Redemption does not annihilate creation but rather builds on it. Christian marriage takes up creation's structure for life in the flesh— as both Jesus and Paul insist—but it is also the symbol of incredible cosmic redemption because it holds within it the very secret of the universe—personal identity in selfless intimacy with the other. The two do not become two androgynous, autonomous individuals as in the pagan notion of the joining of the opposites. Rather each spouse becomes one in project and communion. Oneness for a project is true of marriage as it is true of the church. The divinely sanctioned male-female distinction within marriage, like everything else God sanctifies, is created for a purpose, namely:

₪ procreation (children are a gift from the Lord and essential for the maintenance of civilization);

₪ personal communion (marriage sanctifies);

₪ prophecy (marriage expresses the ultimate and final meaning of existence).

What more could I ask from sex and from life? Such a structure holds the secret of genuine happiness—a project that brings me into deep communion with another who is different and yet complementary to me without destroying my own identity; a life project that is life-giving and fundamentally unselfish, that mirrors the meaning of the cosmos. In effect, heterosexual monogamy is not just the subject of a few Bible verses but rather expresses the major tectonic plates of the Bible's essential structures.

The power of one means a commitment to lifelong faithfulness, *monogamy*, as well as commitment to the generations to come. It means for a man the occasion to discover the joy of maleness: the joy of being a father and grandfather, of learning to be a provider, a knight in shining armor, a courageous leader, a spiritual model, a sensitive lover, and finally the joy of discovering through all these aspects of sex that one's life is a life for others.[114]

HEALTHY SEX

This is not male chauvinism. It is mainline psychiatry. It is health-giving therapy. Well-known psychiatrist Richard J. Stoller states with disarming simplicity, "The first order of business in being a man is: don't be a woman."[115] Recognized therapists speak of the process of discovering one's male or female identity as essential for mental health and personal maturation. The task of a boy, says psychiatrist Joseph Nicolosi, is to "identify with his dad and the masculinity he represents...incorporating a masculine sense of self."[116] Gender distinctions are imprinted in the simplest of things. "While learning language ('he and she,' 'his and hers')," says Nicolosi, "the child discovers that the world is divided into natural opposites of boys and girls, men and women."[117] In this light, Mollenkott's desire to eliminate "he" and "she" would be disastrous for mental health. Since such distinctive identities are absolutely crucial for personal health, it is equally essential that the church maintain those distinctives. Specifically, the church must affirm different male and female roles in its life and ministry. If, as Nicolosi claims, "Masculinity is an achievement...[that] requires good parenting...and family support,"[118] it also requires church support.[119] Those who defend the biblical teaching of male pastors are not male chauvinists interested in conserving masculine power. Those that I know are concerned that the church also reflect the truth that the God of the Bible is both Creator and Redeemer, and that the sexual differences of creation are maintained even in redemption. This is so, both for the sake of Christian witness to God, the good Creator, and for the sake of raising healthy people.[120] But I digress!

For a woman, commitment to monogamous heterosexuality means the discovery of maternity (if God so blesses), being a mother and grandmother, learning to be the lover of a man so different from herself, being the emotional center of a family, finding her identity and true liberation in the common project of a family and her spouse's calling, the creative development of the nesting instinct in a stable and welcoming home, the joy of seeing her children "rise up and call her blessed."[121]

This God-designated and created sexual relationship is thus invested with part of the meaning and significance of cosmic history. It reflects God's intentions for humanity. It fits the worldview of the Bible and is written into the warp and woof of existence. God will be Lover and Lord of what he has made.[122] In this divine project, the creature will know personal union with the covenant-keeping Creator. Christ will faithfully love his church the way a husband loves his wife.[123] The meaningful "God who is there" gives meaning to everything he makes and sets apart. Heterosexuality mirrors the character of a divinely created universe in which oneness is that of the communion of differences.

7: The Birth of Sex

SEX IS GOOD

The Bible begins with a wonderful statement about creation. The appearance of blinding, warming, life-giving light is "good." Creation of the ocean's boundaries and the formation of land masses of *terra firma* are "good." From God's rich imagination mangos and sequoias and sweet-smelling roses adorn the earth and make it "good." In the heavens appear the music of the stars and the mind-bending vastness of untold galaxies, all under God's control and bearing the mark of "goodness." The teeming animal kingdoms of sea, air, and land, intriguing in both their number and endless diversity, are also declared "good." Six times God looked at his creation and pronounced it "good." The seventh time—after God had created humans (male and female), the crowning touch of his work—he pronounced the whole of creation "exceedingly good." It might be easy to miss why when God looks at the whole interlocking, pulsating cosmos for the seventh time with a sense of delightful achievement he pronounces the whole creation "exceedingly good."[124] But notice. Between the sixth "good" and the seventh "exceedingly good" there is but one more addition to God's masterpiece—sex. This is sex in its full human dimension as God creates the crowning touch of his entire work, namely, humans—male and female—made in God's image. This final addition of humanity—which includes gender roles and sexuality—makes God's work "exceedingly good." The Bible bubbles over with childlike astonishment at the beauty and goodness of creation. "The heavens declare the glory of God; the skies proclaim the work of his hands." "O Lord, our Lord, how majestic is your name in all the earth!"[125]

At the other end of the Bible, in the New Testament, Paul gives his "amen" to this praise of creation. With virtually identical words to those found in Genesis, Paul solemnly declares to Christians living in pagan Ephesus, "Everything God created is *good*."[126]

If everything is good, the sex is good too.

THE GOD OF SEX

THE PURPOSE OF CREATION

In 1993 I sat for seven days as an observer at the Parliament of the World's Religions in Chicago. This massive event brought together some 8,000 representatives of 125 religions and produced in me the strangest emotional reaction. In spite of the endless variety of gurus, priestly garments, languages, and religious traditions, I was bored! Not once did I see this vast audience moved to genuine praise. The truth is that pagan religion is strictly about the self. To be sure, some can be moved by nature, but if nature is divine and we are part of nature, then we are divine, so it is all about us. Then praise for nature becomes praise of the self. This is self-praise, not praise, and we all have problems with people who praise themselves.

The biblical revelation of God and the goal of his creation meet one of the deepest needs of the human heart. We were made to praise God. This is what you find in the Bible from the beginning to the end of which Psalm 148 is a notable example, for it cannot stop praising God and his works. Only a Creator separate from the creation can evoke this kind of praise.

We were also made to be witnesses, that is, to point to someone beyond ourselves. If God the Creator is distinguished from the things he made, then maintaining the differences—in life in general and sexuality in particular—is an essential part of the truth about the world. To say that there is no separation between us and God, to say that everything is the same, to say that all sexual permutations are good is to express a falsehood about reality.[127] It is not good for God; it is not good for the world. All our judgments about what is right and wrong, true and false, good and bad, holy and unholy, and all our declarations of what is meaningful and significant depend upon this basic Creator-creature distinction. The drama of humanity's affair with the personal Creator is found in the interplay of sexual differences, the drama of courtship, and the beauty of marriage and family. Monogamous heterosexuality is a witness to the glorious mystery of the relationship between the Creator and creation.

> *Praise God, from whom all blessings flow;*
> *Praise Him, all creatures here below;*
> *Praise Him, above ye heavenly host;*
> *Praise Father, Son, and Holy Ghost.*[128]

The purpose of sex is to help bring the physical cosmos to its consummation. Thus Eve is called "the mother of all the living," and with Adam, this heterosexual, monogamous couple pursues the cultural mandate to have dominion over, multiply, and fill the earth. In a marital relationship comprised of difference, intimacy, and vocational significance, they also witness and bring praise to God, the distinct, transcendent Trinitarian Lord.

This, as we shall see, is not God's last word about his "good" creation. In the meantime, however, the Serpent and sin have something to say.

Chapter 8

THE DEATH OF SEX

₪

As I write this chapter New Orleans is staggering under the destructive blow of Hurricane Katrina. But the reactions of people are equally destructive, as in the case of the young man who shot his sister in the head as they fought over a bag of ice. Both "Mother Nature" and human nature here show evident signs of the fall. But you need not look any further than your own relationship with family and friends to realize that we all fall short of the creational ideal described in the previous chapter. We treat people like objects for our own pleasure, even though most of us wish we didn't. Our failings accuse us; our deepest desires show the need for personal significance only a personal Creator can satisfy. Though made to praise God, we spend our time praising ourselves.

Our practice of sex is messed up. Some who are married wish they could get free. Some seemingly perfect couples struggle with pornography, violence, or boredom when in the privacy of their home. Many of those who have chosen homosexuality are deeply dissatisfied with what their lives have become. The list could go on.

The Bible says creation is groaning.[1] We groan too.[2] Jesus himself groaned at the death of his friend,[3] and at the evil of the crucifixion the earth itself reacted with seismic convulsions.[4] Something is profoundly wrong, and we need to know why. According to the Bible, creation is fallen and in the process of dying. A fascinating text from Paul, Romans 1:18–32, demonstrates how this is so. There are good reasons for listening to what Paul has to say:

₪ Since this book seeks to clarify, from an unself-consciously Christian starting point, the fundamental relationship between worldview and sexuality, between one's view of God and one's sexual practice, it is important to test the book's thesis against the norm of Scripture.

₪ Looking at this ancient text brings clarity to the contemporary debate, for while homosexuality is now presented as the cutting-edge agenda of twenty-first century civil liberties, it was present in Paul's day, two thousand years ago, when he denounced it as an inevitable expression of pagan religion. At this profound level the question of civil liberties is not really the significant issue.

Seeing the relevance of ancient Scripture applied to a burning contemporary debate only confirms the faith that Christian believers have in the truthfulness and dependability of God's Inspired Word.

TWO VERY DIFFERENT SERMONS ON HOMOSEXUALITY

1.   THE SERMON OF THE PRESIDING BISHOP, FRANK GRISWOLD, which closed the proceedings of the 74th General Convention of the Episcopal Church USA in August 2003, is a perfect example of pagan spirituality masquerading as the Christian gospel. By a 2-to-1 ratio the assembly voted to ordain as bishop a divorced father of two who lived with his male lover. "This Convention," said Griswold, "has been about love...something has happened that is larger than any one perspective." Notice the moral positions have become "perspectives." To underline his major point, Griswold does not cite the Bible. He cites the Sufi poet Rumi: "Out beyond ideas of wrong doing and right doing there is a field. I'll meet you there." "The field," continued Griswold, "is the field of the divine compassion where all things are reconciled in ways that we can only dimly comprehend."[5]

This is coded language. Sufism, a pagan Muslim sect, rejects, like many leading "Christian" bishops, the notion of God the Creator distinct from creation. This means that God and the world are one, and all distinctions are eliminated, including that between right and wrong. Think of the yin and the yang or the two sides of the Force. Griswold's main point affirms in subtle, "Christianized" language the pagan joining of the opposites. The real justification for homosexuality in the church is not Christian "love" or the gospel. It is the rehabilitation of a pagan worldview antithetical to the Bible. The presiding bishop's sermon makes no appeal to Genesis nor to the Bible's clear teaching on creation nor to the church's historic creeds. "I believe in God, the Father almighty, Maker of heaven and earth." This first phase of the Apostle's Creed has long ago been dismissed as primitive myth.

Canadian Senator Marilyn Trenholme Counsell, a self-proclaimed Anglican Christian, made the public statement that Jesus Christ would have voted as she did in Parliament, in favor of the gay marriage.[6] "As a Christian," she said, "I often ask myself 'What would Jesus do?' In this case, in this time, I believe he would say yes." Her reason: "We have come a long way in our understanding of human sexuality."[7] Short of mere subjective sentimentality, how does one know what Jesus would do in such cases? Lesbian Episcopal priestess, Susan Russell, believes she knows. She is convinced that what matters to God is not "sexual orientation but theological orientation."[8] How does she know what God thinks? This ex-wife and mother who says, "[I] still sometimes think of myself as a soccer mom," also states, "I heard in my head the voice of God saying 'This is how I made you.'"

Senator Counsell and Reverend Russell make no attempt at understanding the biblical worldview of Jesus as revealed in Holy Scripture. Their thinking is determined by personal feelings, not by the objectivity of Scripture, though Scripture was the reference for the first Christians and even for Jesus himself. When tempted by the Devil, Jesus did not go within to seek subjective illumination. He cited Old Testament Scripture.[9] This is how Christians know what God thinks. Such an approach is no more clearly shown, especially in relation to the connectedness of God and sex, than by Paul, Christ's apostle, in his Scripture-based sermon in Romans 1.

2.   "BISHOP" PAUL'S "SERMON" TO THE FIRST-CENTURY Roman church is quite different. Here we have an entire world-view based on an understanding of God as Creator, a theme so evident in the warp and woof of every Bible text that you can only miss it, says Paul, if you are spiritually "blind." In Romans 1:18-32 Paul describes a religious process, classically described as the fall, that moves out from theory to practice, from belief to action, as in "ideas have consequences." Specifically, he describes how false theology (thinking about God) leads to false spiritual-ity (idolatry) and then to unnatural sexuality (homosexuality). He understands very well that "the passion of lust" is typical of the "pagans who do not know God."[10] In other words, though all are capable of lust, "lust" and "paganism" are part of a system of thinking.

ROMANS 1:18–32: PAUL'S TEACHING ON HOMOSEXUALITY

Paul addresses three essential areas of human religious life, mentioning three exchanges that drive his point home. Paul's choice of three repetitions follows, no doubt, the biblical pattern of three, signifying totality and completeness. (For example, the cherubim say of God, "Holy, holy, holy," proclaiming the absolute state of holiness.)

Paul lists three exchanges in three critical domains:

1. Theology (Rom. 1:23): "They exchanged the glory of the immortal God for images made to look like mortal man and

birds and animals and reptiles."

2. Spirituality (Rom. 1:25): "They exchanged the truth for the lie and worshipped and served the creature rather than the creator."

3. Sexuality (Rom. 1:26): "They exchanged natural sexual relations for unnatural ones."

This exchanging turns creation on its head. The exchange is radical apostasy in the essential areas of theology, spirituality, and sexuality. Pagans clearly make this exchange, as Paul reminds the Ephesian Christians.[12] But it is also a woeful possibility for God's special people according to Psalm 106:19–20 to which Paul alludes in verse 25. The psalm reads, "They made a calf in Horeb and worshipped a metal image. They exchanged the glory of God for the image of an ox that eats grass." A similar notion is to be found in Jeremiah 2:11 (NJB): "Does a nation change its gods?—and these are not gods at all! Yet my people have exchanged their Glory for the Useless One!" Problems ensue when the true view of God is exchanged for a false view.

Theology: Who Is God?

> The wrath of God is being revealed from heaven against all the godlessness and wickedness of men who suppress the truth by their wickedness.... For although they knew God, they neither glorified him as God nor gave thanks to him, but their thinking became futile and their foolish hearts were darkened.[13]

Paul begins with a powerful statement about the person of God (theology proper) and about humanity's false thinking about God. God's *divine nature* precedes all created reality, and his *eternal power* determines what things exist and how they relate to him. (The whole of chapter 6 was devoted to such a view of God.) Bishop Griswold's sermon has no place for that view, whereas it is Paul's starting point from which everything else flows. This fact of

God's separate, divine, powerful, and prior existence establishes who we are as dependent, created human beings. For creatures a right relationship with God thus involves recognizing the essential distinction that must be preserved between the sovereign Creator and the dependent creature, often referred to as the Creator-creature distinction.

The essence of human sin is the refusal to honor that distinction. "Men...suppress the [plain] truth by their wickedness."[14] What is the plain truth? It is what may be known about God as the sovereign Creator. It is written into the fabric of creation and is part of the image of God that every human being bears. Later in Romans, Paul describes the sin of Adam as "disobedience,"[15] and from Genesis we know that the disobedience was Adam's refusal to recognize God's right to lay down the terms for life in the garden.[16] This is the quintessential, primordial sin, the paradigm for all the rest. In principle, what happened when Adam and Eve transgressed the Creator-creature distinction had become, by Paul's time, a flood of pagan religions that suppressed this truth and turned nature into God. The rebellion of Adam and Eve is the seedling that comes to mature fruition in the full-fledged systems of God-denying paganism.

The human problem is a theological one, knowing (but rejecting) the truth about God's identity. The acute sense of disorder in the cosmos comes from rejecting the God of biblical revelation. According to Romans 2:8 there is an ultimate and woeful consequence for such disobedience.

The effects of this theological shift are seen in man's focus on this worldly, idolatrous spirituality.

Spirituality: You've Got to Serve Somebody

Claiming to be wise, they became fools, and exchanged the glory of the immortal God for images resembling mortal man and birds and animals and reptiles.... they exchanged the truth about God for a lie and worshipped and served the creature rather than the Creator, who is blessed forever! Amen.[17]

Human beings, created in God's image, are spiritual. That is the way God made us. The real divide, both then and now, is not between atheists and "people of faith" but between two antithetical kinds of "faith."

Total Commitment

How spiritual are those whom Paul describes? He states that those who reject God nevertheless "worship and serve" other objects of religious veneration.[18] Those are strong terms. His expression "worship" reoccurs in Acts describing "the goddess Artemis, who [was] worshiped throughout the province of Asia and the world."[19] This term for worship is sometimes translated as religious "fear."[20]

The second term, "serve," is used in the Old Testament to describe the service of the Levites in the Temple. Their role is to "minister," or literally "to serve."[21] The same term occurs in Romans 12, where Paul speaks of the believer's "spiritual worship."[22] Notice that the combined phrase "worship...serve" occurs elsewhere in the Bible as a statement of total devotion.[23]

Regardless of whether you're talking about true or false worship, the point is that this kind of true worship is total and exclusive. In both cases, it is worship of the heart. In their devotion and commitment both groups are disconcertingly the same; in the objects of their veneration the two are in complete contradiction. One is "the lie" or "deception";[24] the other is "the truth." One worships the creation; the other worships the Creator who is blessed forever.

Bishop Griswold would not appreciate being called a pagan, but compare his statement with the words of a priestess of the goddess Sophia. Caìtlin Matthews, a self-professed pagan, says that Sophia (another name for Isis) is the divine savior who "will lead us out of the delusion of duality."[25] Matthews and Griswold agree on the pagan definition of God—he is to be found within, is beyond right

155

and wrong, the truth and the lie.

The Truth and the Lie

To deny the Creator-creature distinction is the essence of the pagan lie. Into the fallen world comes the notion of truth and error. At the heart of biblical faith is the choice between them. Joshua confronts Israel with these memorable words: "Choose for yourselves this day whom you will serve."[26]

This is the same courageous disobedience evidenced in the decisions of Shadrach, Meshach, and Abednego who refused to worship the pagan king Nebuchadnezzar because they could not "serve and worship any god except their own."[27] The exclusivity of the Christian claims is as old as the Bible, and Jesus made a clear distinction between God and mammon (earthly things),[28] the kingdom of God and the kingdom of Satan,[29] the narrow way to life and the broad way to destruction.[30]

Paul's mission to the pagan world draws out the antithetical divide between the religions of his day and the gospel of Christ. Paul affirms the antithesis, not to be obnoxious but to be lucid and unambiguous so that people might believe the truth and be saved. He sets in stark contrast two opposing systems that he calls the truth or the lie,[31] righteousness or wickedness, light or darkness.[32]

The logical result of pagan spirituality is worship of the creation and of the self. Paul says as much in language that could have been penned today: "Although they claimed to be wise, they became fools and exchanged the glory of the immortal God for images made to look like mortal man and birds and animals and reptiles."[33]

Graven Images Then and Now

The thinking is foolish because it begins from a flawed premise, but moving from that premise, the logic is implacable. Belief in the transcendent Creator implies a specific kind of spirituality. Because God is separate from the created order, it follows that "you shall not make for yourself a carved image, or any likeness of anything that is in heaven above, or that is in the earth beneath, or that is in the water under the earth."[34]

Belief in nature as divine has its own spiritual expression. Belief in the divinity of nature means that paganism is awash in images of created things. Graven images are found on the altars of Baal, the god of fertility.[35] Whenever Israel is tempted by paganism, she makes "abominable images."[36] The move is as inevitable as it is ultimately foolish.

Graven images are making a comeback. Paul's words on this subject have a remarkably contemporary application. Ancient history is our history as the spirituality of the past is rediscovered in our present. Thomas Berry, an apostate Roman Catholic priest and one of the leaders of the revival of paganism in our day, believes that the task of contemporary humanity is to reconnect with the spirituality of the ancient times. "Earlier human traditions," he says, "experienced a profound intimacy with the natural world.... We have moved from this intimacy.[37] This relationship found visible expression in the totemic carvings."[38] In plain English this is idol worship. Like Berry, more and more twenty-first-century sophisticated intellectuals are worshipping "totemic carvings," that is, man-made idols.

It goes even deeper. In contemporary transpersonal (occultist) psychology, seekers of deep spirituality experience a "connection with animals, plants and elemental forces of nature."[39]

All this indicates that the two spiritual worldviews offered—paganism and theism—are as old as the hills and that the theological struggles of the past are now our struggles today. These two "timeless" worldviews oppose each other in the present as they have in the past because they are the only two, mutually exclusive, pure ways of conceiving of spirituality—the worship of creation or the worship of the Creator.[40]

Nowhere is this clearer than in the debate over sexuality.

Sexuality: Male and Female

> For this reason God gave them up to dishonorable passions. For their women exchanged natural relations for those that are contrary to nature; and the men likewise gave up natural relations with women and were consumed with passion for one another, men committing shameless acts with men and receiving in themselves the due penalty for their error.[41]

A leading New Testament scholar says, "If...there is a single major New Testament text which unambiguously portrays homosexual practice as a sign of humanity's alienation from God the Creator, [it is this]."[42] The "theologic" is impeccable. This is not an "irrational" opposition to the homosexual agenda. It is the rationality of a theistic universe. Those who reject the Creator also reject the notion of the created "natural" order. If there is no Creator there are no norms or boundaries. Everything is evolving, including sex. People are free to follow their own passions and lusts. Homosexuality destroys the heterosexual separation that God has placed between male and female, muddying the boundaries. The joining together of the opposites that God has separated is both a radical rejection of creational norms and a powerful spiritual expression of pagan monistic rebellion.

Professor Richard Hayes sees the deliberate reference in Romans to the original heterosexual pair of Genesis 1, and comments: "By way of sharp contrast,...Paul portrays homosexual behavior as a 'sacrament' [so to speak] of the antireligion of human beings who refuse to honor God as creator: it is an outward and visible sign of an inward and spiritual reality, [declaring] through the 'dishonoring of their bodies' the spiritual condition of those who 'have exchanged the truth of God for a lie.'"[43]

From the way Paul argues in Romans 1:18ff., it seems evident that these questions about God and the world, about idol worship and perverted physical sexual activity are timeless questions. Paul incorporates the whole worldview of the Old Testament as he develops this theological argument. And he is not unique in doing so. The rabbis, of which he was one, had already made this deep connection between the hardwired created order and pagan perversion. In the *Testament of Levi* we read:

> Sun, moon and stars do not alter their order; thus you should not alter the law of God by the disorder of your actions. The Gentiles, because they wandered astray and forsook the Lord, have changed the order and devoted themselves to stones and sticks, patterning themselves after wandering spirits. But you, my children, shall not be like that: in the firmament, in the earth, and in the sea, in all the products of his workmanship discern the Lord who made all things, so that you do not become like Sodom, which changed the order of nature.[44]

Paul describes homosexual and lesbian sexual relations as being "against nature";[45] Jude speaks of "strange flesh."[46] They find no place for the unnatural and strange in God's ordered creation. Both biblical authors predict ruinous consequences.[47]

Paul, as a Jewish Christian theologian, is making general statements about the person of the Creator and the nature of the creation. Like the rabbis cited previously, Paul identifies the intersection of perverted sexuality, false theology, and idolatrous spirituality. His text reads, *"For this reason* God gave them up to dishonorable passions."[48] The immediate *reason for* sexual perversion is the worship of the creation rather than the Creator.[49] For Paul, it follows logically that once you worship creation anything is possible, even practices that go "against nature." Once the creature becomes god, he gets to define what is normal.

This reference to creation is doubtless why Paul uses the terms "male" and "female" rather than "man" and "woman."[50] Paul implicitly sends us back to the beginning when everything—including sexual distinctions—was made "good." The Genesis text reads, "So God created man in his own image, in the image of God he created him; *male and female* he created them."[51] The Old Testament prohibitions against male homosexuality also use the term "male."[52] Jesus cites this foundational Genesis text, including the technical terms "male" and "female," to establish the God-ordained character of marriage—"from the beginning."[53] It is the only time these terms are found on Jesus' lips. Paul uses "male" and "female" only one other time: when he declares that nothing—not even created gender—can be used to obstruct a person from incorporation into the body of Christ.[54] Here he explicitly compares "natural" male-female sex with "unnatural" male-male and female-female sex.[55]

An interesting parallel occurs between Romans 1, verses 25 and 26. In verse 25, Paul speaks about "exchanging" "the truth" for "the lie." In verse 26, he speaks about "exchanging" "the natural" for "that which is against nature." This verb occurs only four times in the entire Bible: twice in the Old Testament and twice here in the New.[56] We thus have an unusual verb and technical terms for male and female, set in a kind of literary parallelism. The *truth* exchanged for the *lie* represents the overturning of the essential notion of the way things really are: the creation taking the place of the Creator. On the sexual plane the *natural*, created order is overturned, and the *unnatural* and perverted is put in its place. Once again sexuality mirrors theology.

IS PAUL A HOMOPHOBE?

Why does Paul single out homosexuality? In his thought, homosexuality is deeply connected to pagan religion. (See chapter 4.) All disloyalty to God, he argues here, produces human sin (Rom. 1:28–32), including, in the sexual domain, heterosexual adultery and fornication. No one is off the hook. "All have sinned and fall short of the glory of God."[57] All, including the moralizers who judge others from positions of moral superiority, are "without excuse."[58] Among sinners, God has no favorites. God's wrath falls powerfully on hypocrites, who in their outward lifestyle appear to be good but inside are deeply flawed.[59] "Just as sin entered the world through one man, and death through sin, and in this way death came to all."[60]

However, the radical "exchange" of pagan religion, which denies the Creator altogether and elevates his created handiwork in the place of God, results in the extreme sexual disorder of homosexuality and produces "a culture of death." In this text, Paul is not talking about individual sinners but about worldview, about the implications of sexuality for theology and vice versa. Implicit here is the argument that heterosexual fornication, while equally sinful, *misuses* the divinely ordered structure of sexual difference. Homosexuality, on the other hand, treats that order with complete disregard and denies, at a principal level, the significance of the difference and place of the Creator. It is thus the absolute refusal of creational life.

In our day, convinced of the inevitable progress of human and civic freedoms, state courts declare gay marriage a constitutional right. From a biblical point of view such an action overturns one of the essential building blocks of creation. Such an action—though no doubt motivated in part by noble intentions—tears down the biblical cosmology. Since heterosexual marriage reflects the character of the triune God, both as Creator[61] and Redeemer,[62] the legalization of gay marriage will effectively annihilate one more sign of God's handiwork from the memory banks of contemporary culture. If the new spirituality promises to "reinvent the human at the species level"[63] (which in the past was believed to be God's prerogative alone), the normalization of homosexuality would effectively contribute to the project—the new man as androgyne.[64]

The correctness of Paul's analysis has once more been proved right in our day with the simultaneous rise of pagan spirituality and militant, spiritual homosexuality. This connection did not escape Paul. It should not escape us. If, as Paul argues, homosexuality reflects on the sexual plane the spirituality and religion of paganism, it surely follows that monogamous heterosexuality on the sexual plane would reflect something of the image of God in humanity and thus the religion of biblical theism.[65]

The Fall of Heterosexuality

Alas, heterosexuality is also fallen. The beautiful stained-glass window of human sexuality has been smashed almost beyond repair. If the creation is an interlocking network of separate but organically related spiritual and physical elements, anything discordant will skew the whole system. Man is the crown of God's creation and male-female intimacy in marriage reflects the very intimacy of God with man. The best place to start dismantling the creation is its most beautiful element: human sexuality. The death of sex begins with heterosexual disorder.

At the beginning there is no sexual deviance: "The man and his wife were both naked and were not ashamed."[66] It was neither the Bible nor orthodox Christians who associated physical sex with the fall. On the contrary, the Bible affirms the noble character of motherhood and childbearing.[67]

The fall of sex begins not with "unnatural" sex, but with the refusal of sexual gender roles.[68] Adam, who is the divinely appointed "head" of his wife[69] as well as her protector and provider, stands passively by, observing as Eve falls for the Serpent's temptation.[70] Eve, created *from* Adam's side, to be *at* his side as "helper," autonomously makes her own woeful decision to change the condition of Eden.

Part of the fall is the fall of sex itself. Male and female were created for oneness.[71] The two sexes mutually support one another in the divine vocation to fill the earth. This heterosexual oneness has roots in God's very nature. For just as God wants exclusivity in our communion with him, he creates a reflection of that exclusivity in the human sexual relationship of marriage. Sin breaks the pattern, and the relationship begins to fall apart. Eve seduces her husband into disobedience.[72] Adam blames his wife.[73] Eve blames the Serpent.[74] The rest is fallen human history.

In the Old Testament following the Fall, adultery, prostitution, the taking of concubines, and polygamy mark even the sexual life

162

of Israel. Paul refers to the Gentile nations as those who have "given themselves over to sensuality so as to indulge in every kind of impurity, with a continual lust for more."[75] God's goal for humankind is "holiness," not "uncleanness,"[76] but his own people in both the Old and the New Testaments suffer from the fall of sex.

A lot of sexual counseling awaits Paul in the churches he starts. He deals with a Christian who is proudly sleeping with his father's wife[77] and with believers who are having sex with prostitutes.[78] (How many seminary students imagine that they may minister in a church like this?) "Do you not know that he who united himself with a prostitute is one with her in body? For it is said, 'The two will become one flesh.'"[79] For Paul, sexual communion with a prostitute so distorts heterosexual marriage that we can no longer recognize God's good and satisfying gift. It joins what God commanded to be kept separate—a man with a woman other than his wife. Such distortions are common in our world. We experience unrestrained sexual obsession, sex as fast food, life as a constant physical orgasm, and sex extracted from its rightful place of holistic personal integration and employed for individual pleasure. Such obsessive imbalance surely sows the seeds of moral disintegration.

Paul would disavow the sentiments of the Buddhist poet Saraha: "Enjoying the world of sense, one is undefiled by the world of sense. One plucks the lotus without touching the water."[80] Actually, you cannot have your lotus without getting wet. Sexual union does not leave you untouched, but engages you in a common project and a common worldview. Dreadful is the state of a Christian who fools around with prostitution, pornography, or other sexual perversions. Paul warns against the power of sexual sins—"sins against [the] body"[81]—as being a particularly potent combination where "spirit, soul and body"[82] are fully engaged in the project of disobedience.[83] Paul is not one to underestimate the power of bodily union, whether for good or for bad.[84] The fruits of this lifestyle are evident: rampant divorce, a refusal of marriage, and commitmentless cohabitation. As a culture we are playing with fire—moral and eternal.

GOD GAVE THEM OVER—AGAIN

Those who follow their own rebellion against God's structures will suffer the effects. Again, Paul offers a set of three terms in Romans 1:18–27. Three times, God "gave them over":

1. Rom. 1:24: God gave them over to sinful desires.

2. Rom. 1:26: God gave them over to shameful lusts.

3. Rom. 1:28: God gave them over to a depraved mind.

This threefold biblical declaration is a solemn warning of physical death, ultimate judgment, and final spiritual death.[85] Entertaining apostasy leads a soul to the dangerous place beyond God's mercy. Making these three exchanges is an insistent affirmation of unbelief, inviting three dreadful declarations of final judgment. According to the Bible, idolaters will stand one day before the Creator as Judge,[86] when the holiness God requires will be the only standard for eternal life with him.

God could have brought down final judgment as soon as Adam and Eve sinned, but he withheld his wrath and promised redemption. The so-called curses of Genesis[87] were actually merciful provisions for the maintenance of human life. Adam was cursed in his role as protector and provider, but the earth would produce nourishment for the first human couple. Eve was cursed in her role as helper and mother of the race, but life did go on. Because of sin, the roles would be difficult, but in the midst of the curses came the first faint call of the gospel trumpet: "I will put enmity between you and the woman, and between your offspring and her offspring; he shall bruise your head, and you shall bruise his heel."[88] Immediately following the curses, Adam, in hope, named his wife, Eve, "the mother of all the living."[89]

I have both good news and bad. The bad news is because of the fall, in the maintenance of created life, "one flesh" heterosexual marriage is difficult like life in general. All our difficulties ultimately stem from the "impossibility" of the oneness and union of sinful, selfish human beings with the God of burning holiness. Our pretended autonomy from the God who made us leaves that most fundamental relationship in tatters, so that all other relationships, especially marriage, tend to disintegrate as well. Two egotistical sinners do not make good candidates for the full range of one-flesh intimacy.

The good news is there is life after the fall. Holy sex is meant to draw us to our holy Creator. The death knell will be transformed into marriage bells. For though we, like sex, face disintegration, the Creator is also the Redeemer. So just as Christ the Redeemer brings reconciliation to two irreconcilable peoples, Jews and pagans, and makes them one in the church, so Christ reconciles male and female sinners and makes them "one flesh" in the holy institution of matrimony. In other words, biblical sex has a future.

Chapter 9

BORN-AGAIN SEX AND THE FUTURE

₪

SOCKS STILL IN THE SHOES

Colored bunnies, chocolate eggs, and greeting cards are the only version of Easter that some people ever know. But these symbols have nothing to do with the truth of the resurrection.

There was no egg in the nest, so to speak. The original Easter hunt was unsuccessful—there was no body in the tomb. Three days after Jesus expired at the hands of Roman executioners, an inexplicable crack appeared in the otherwise predictable physical universe, and the Christian movement began with an incredibly good, though disturbing, message. For the first and only time in history, a corpse came back to life with a new kind of body.

Around the supper table my family and I came in our reading to John chapter 20, the amazing account of the resurrection. I explained that the miracle of the empty tomb was actually the miracle of the empty grave clothes, because of the way John describes the event. The two disciples see two pieces of grave clothing lying in the place where the body had been lying. They see the shroud in the place of the body and the head scarf still in the shape of a circle lying where the head had been. To illustrate, I suggested the picture of a dead Mafia don lying on a slab in a city morgue, dressed in his black suit, black hat, and black-and-white shoes. The body had gone through the clothes without disturbing them—the suit in its place and the hat in its place where the head had been. My young son, Toby, seeing the point immediately, threw in, "and the socks were still in the shoes." That's it! Jesus did not get up and neatly fold his grave clothes. By the incredible power of the resurrection, his new body went *through* them, socks and all!

A BORN-AGAIN JESUS

The early Christians understood that a unique, "cosmic" miracle had taken place in that garden tomb on Sunday morning. The new man, the resurrected Jesus, by an act of God had become a prototype of bigger and better things to come—not just for them but for all of creation.

Alas, the Christian message has been dumbed down. We have swallowed a "gos-pill"—a truncated, personalized version of the gospel in which Jesus dies for *me* and will rapture *me* out of this earthly mess. We talk about being born again and think little of what that means for the universe. The truth is that the gospel is good news not just for our personal salvation, but for the future cleansing and spectacular transformation of the entire cosmos, comparable in scope to the original cataclysmic event of creation itself. If the Redeemer is the Creator of all things material, then resurrection *must* be physical and the tomb *must* be empty. At the resurrection of his physical body, Jesus was born again. This is perhaps an unusual formulation but entirely biblical.[1] While the blood of Christ cleanses from sin, his physical resurrection ensures a renewed physical cosmos.[2]

Religions have a broad, optimistic vision of the future. The desire for a "happy ending," as the French say, seems innate within the human breast. Even the Beatles "imagined" they could "work it out." Many thinkers hope for "utopia," an idyllic society in which everything is perfect. But Hitler's extermination of the Jews or the wanton destruction of life caused by terrorists crashing commercial planes into the World Trade Center sends a reality shock throughout the world. In the context of World War II, C. S. Lewis said:

> If we had foolish hopes about human culture, they are now shattered. If we thought we were building up a heaven on earth, if we looked for something that would turn the present world from a place of pilgrimage into a permanent city satisfying the soul of man, we are disillusioned, and not a moment too soon. In ordinary times only the wise realize it. Now [in wartime] the stupidest of us knows it.[3]

When peace returns, how quickly we forget such reminders of humankind's inability to fix things.

UTOPIA—THE GREAT TEMPTATION

Thomas Molnar, a Roman Catholic theologian, proposes that "utopianism is the original temptation."[4] He means, if I understand him correctly, that sinful humans always believe they can fix their own mess. As to the original temptation, the Serpent plays on the fact that creation, even prior to sin, is not the ultimate state God intends for the universe. Endless probation for Adam and Eve is hardly eternal bliss. Perhaps part of the power and subtlety of this temptation was to encourage our first parents, who had all things placed under their feet,[5] to believe that they, in their created strength, could bring about a utopian consummation (a good thing in itself) independently of God (which is the essence of sin). Satan deploys the same technique in his wilderness temptation of Jesus, the last Adam. If it worked once, use it again! Pressing the desirable goal of end-time consummation, the Tempter proposes that Jesus take possession of all the kingdoms of the earth and bring about a fulfilled and unified earthly utopia. The only minor (!) requirement is that the second Adam must bow down before him the way the first Adam did. Jesus refuses. He knows that going to the cross is the only way of removing that original Adamic sin and of successfully bringing about God's utopia *God's* way.

169

Rebirth—The Last Act of God the Creator, Bringing Utopia

Everyone senses that creation is not the way it should be—even pagan monists who claim to believe that the yin and yang each has its place. But the temptation is still strong to believe that we can redeem our messy world rather than to rely upon God, the only one who can. Friedrich Nietzsche, a nineteenth-century Christian apostate philosopher, exhorted his contemporaries: "I entreat you, my brothers, *remain true to the earth,* and do not believe those of you who speak of super-terrestrial hopes."[6] The apostle Paul disagrees: "If only for this life we have hope in Christ, we are to be pitied more than all men."[7] Paul is not a pie-in-the-sky escapist. He knows that only God, the transcendent Creator, is capable of producing a cosmic utopia in which death is defeated and creation is transformed. Only a future vision of these proportions is worthy of our highest human aspirations.

The God Who Creates Is the God Who Re-creates

Both the ancient Gnostics and their modern counterparts believe that God the Creator is a bumbler and that rebirth will be achieved by "the god behind God." The Bible insists that the only God—the God of creation—undertakes the mission of redemption. The difference between paganism and the Bible resides here. According to Scripture, Christ the Redeemer is he by whom "all things were created."[8] The Redeemer is the Creator, so the project of redemption emanates from the Creator. Paul's calling is "to make plain to everyone the...mystery [the gospel], which for ages past was kept hidden in God, who created all things."[9] What we know about the new creation comes from the wisdom and plan of the God who created all things in the first place. This is good news. You would not buy a refurbished computer from an auto repair shop. Only the Creator of the cosmos can be trusted with its final transformation.

We recoil from death in a natural instinct of fear, revulsion, and anger. Our search for youth-producing drugs and cloning possibilities evidences our deep longing for the good news that death is vanquished. But eternal life can only be accomplished through redemption by the only one capable of doing the job. Our problem is not in the organization of our lives but in our mortality. This is why the "reconciliation of all things must come by [Christ] making peace through his blood, shed on the cross."[10]

The Bible presents God as the author of the two defining events of cosmic history: (1) the past event of creation and (2) the future event of a new, redeemed creation.[11] We are used to thinking not just of creation but also of redemption as a past event, and in one important sense this is correct. "Christ *died* [past tense] for our sins";[12] "you *were* washed, you *were* sanctified, you *were* justified in the name of the Lord Jesus Christ."[13] Verses such as these constitute the solid rock of our salvation secured by Christ. In him we meet the Creator as loving Redeemer, and by grace and by his Spirit come home to the "natural" universe. But, the resurrected Christ is a prototype of what is to come, and so redemption is also and supremely a *future phenomenon* that concerns the still-to-come transformation of the entire cosmos.

REBIRTH—A FUTURE EVENT

A professor at the University of Oxford makes a startling statement about the meaning of Christ's resurrection:

> It might have been possible, we could say, before Christ rose from the dead, for someone to wonder whether creation was a lost cause. If the creature consistently acted to uncreate itself, and with itself to uncreate the rest of creation, did this not mean that God's handiwork was flawed beyond hope of repair?..."But in fact Christ has been raised from the dead...." That fact rules out those other possibilities, for in the second Adam the first is rescued. The deviance of his will...has not been allowed to uncreate what God created.[14]

If the resurrection of Jesus shows that God has not given up on the physical world, then biblical commands to honor God with our bodies similarly show that God has not given up on our physical bodies. Redemption was achieved through a physical body. As Hebrews says, "When Christ came into the world, he said: 'Sacrifice and offering you did not desire, but a body you prepared for me.'"[15] With that body, Jesus gave himself for the sins of the world. He "took bread, gave thanks and broke it,...saying, 'Take and eat; this is my body given for you.'"[16] Redemption procured by a body *redeems the body* and regales it with present and future significance. Redemption is not just present forgiveness of sins and future disincarnated, spiritual bliss. It is the transfiguration of the body, similar to the transfigured body of the earthly Jesus.[17] In redemption, God reclaims what is rightly his and gloriously transforms it, producing a butterfly from a slug, so to speak. This is why, one day, God will call us to account for "the things done while *in the body*, whether good or bad."[18]

Let me repeat—the bodily resurrection of Jesus declares one earth-shaking truth: that God has not given up on creation. This physical world has a glorious future, and the gospel contains God's good word that he has not forgotten his creation.[19]

God Will Re-create the Same Way He Created

A leopard does not change his spots, nor does God change his nature. God re-creates the way he originally created.

God Created and Will Re-create Miraculously

The original creation out of nothing was just as miraculous as the creation's ultimate transformation. The same miracle-working God of the beginning will work miracles at the end. The resurrection of the body is certainly the greatest miracle to take place within our history. But the miracle of creation to begin history was just as enormous. Perhaps this is why the "science of origins" has so much difficulty even now in giving a rational account of the beginnings of physical life. Miracle connects these two great cosmic events. The Bible places these two miraculous creative divine acts on the same level of grandeur. One act miraculously makes creation; the other miraculously transfigures it.

God Created and Will Re-create in an Orderly Fashion

Creation always includes the order and coherence in which it was first composed. We noted previously that in creating, God separated things, producing an orderly structure. He turns chaos into cosmos, distinguishing between light and darkness, land and sea, male and female. This, I argued, was how God sanctified his work, by setting things apart each in its own place. Essential for human life in this holy order is the male-female distinction. In redemption, God does not change. According to the New Testament, God is still a God of order,[20] and in this same order ultimate redemption will be achieved. God as Re-creator of the cosmos still maintains his nature as God. As we speak of the Creator-creature distinction, we must also speak of the Re-creator-transformed-creature distinction. What a contrast against the nirvana of paganism. New Age physicist Fritjof Capra describes the state of consciousness "in which all boundaries and dualisms have been transcended and all individuality dissolves into universal undifferentiated oneness."[21] According to Scripture, there will be differentiation. God as Creator will always be recognized in heaven as distinct and worthy of praise.[22]

As Paul describes the resurrection body in the great chapter on the resurrection, he compares the created order to the new, resurrected reality. Just as there are different kinds of bodies and many kinds of "flesh" in the created order—"men have one kind of flesh, animals have another, birds another, fish another,"[23] and "there are heavenly bodies and there are earthly bodies and different kinds of splendor"[24]—so there is a comparable order in the resurrected universe. In the poetic language of Job, God the Creator "sets the sand [in its place] as a boundary for the sea"[25] and "shows the dawn its place."[26] In the transformation of the cosmos, God sets each element in its "place" or rank: "In Christ all will be made alive. But each in his own turn:[27] Christ, the firstfruits; then, when he comes, those who belong to him."[28]

Inquisitive minds will already be asking the question: Will the order of male and female survive the resurrection? All I can say is read on!

REBIRTH—GOD REESTABLISHES OWNERSHIP OF THE COSMOS

We need to think structurally in order to make sound, biblical judgments about the nature of sexuality within the context of redemption-rebirth. Just what takes place at the resurrection of Jesus? Does the universe have structure? Are there norms for sexual expression?

Here is my answer: The resurrection of Christ is the first evidence that God is reestablishing direct ownership of the cosmos, taking back what is rightfully his but was lost through the fall. Even in the fall, though, God remained in control. God subjected (the same verb that means "to set in its right place")[29] the fallen world to *vanity*.[30] The curse of Genesis 3, this subjection to vanity, was God's action to limit the effect of sin in a world that he still controlled. In a sense, Christ's redemptive work is to participate in this vain subjection to vanity, for he bears the curse,[31] is subject to sin, and is placed "under the law."[32] But the hope remains of a renewed creation, subjected to the will of God, without vanity, where God is everywhere recognized Lord of all.

The First Creation—All Things under Adam's Feet

God owns the creation, for he is its source and he causes it to reflect his character of order and distinction. Within this order is that of the male-female distinction. The God who originally set all created things in their particular places also set humans in place as viceroys with all things under their feet. Humanity is male

174

and female, reflecting God's image. Of Adam and humankind in general the psalmist says, "You made him ruler over the works of your hands; you put [or placed] everything under his feet."[33] Adam shares something of the lordship of his maker, of whom it is said, "He parted the heavens and came down; dark clouds were under his feet."[34] The psalmist David also sees Adam's place as an anticipation of Messiah's lordship within the reality of the fall: "The Lord says to my Lord: 'Sit at my right hand until I make your enemies a footstool for your feet.'"[35]

In the New Creation—All Things under the Last Adam's Feet

In redemption Christ is re-identified as Lord of the created universe. The structure of the old creation is restored and transformed—here is the proof. The statement about Adam's and humanity's place in the first creation is used on three different occasions in the New Testament to describe the new creation and the lordship of the last Adam.[36] There is a great irony to gospel logic: The one who fulfills prophecy by having his feet pierced[37] is now elevated from the cross through the resurrection to universal lordship, and all things are in submission to those pierced feet. Jesus reigned in weakness from the cross, but now he reigns in power as the resurrected Lord. In the great chapter on the resurrection, 1 Corinthians 15, Paul works out the implications of the resurrection for the future of the cosmos by citing the same Psalm 8: "For he 'has put everything under his feet.' Now when it says that 'everything' has been put under him, it is clear that this does not include God himself, who put everything under Christ."[38] Naturally, this lordship is more glorious than that granted to Adam, just as the re-created heavens and earth are more glorious than the old. God's second work improves the first. Thus Paul states:

> He [God] raised him [Christ] from the dead and seated him at his right hand in the heavenly realms, far above all principality, and power, and might, and dominion, and every name that is named, not only in this

world, but also in that which is to come: and God placed all things under his feet and appointed him to be head over everything...who fills everything in every way.[39]

As in many things the apostle Peter agrees:

[Christ] who has gone into heaven and is at God's right hand—with angels, authorities and powers in submission to him [set in their rightful place under him].[40]

These amazing texts apply the reality of universal lordship not to Christ as second person of the divine Trinity, but to Christ, the last Adam, the true prototypical human being of the coming new order. With the dominion and rule originally granted to Adam and Eve,[41] Christ, the last Adam in his kingly role, submits all things to God's holy order.

But it is equally amazing that the new order is the old transformed. "When we describe the saving work of Christ by the term 'redemption,'" observes Oliver O'Donovan:

We stress the fact that it presupposes the created order. "Redemption" suggests the recovery of something given and lost. When we ask what it is that was given and lost, and must now be recovered, the answer is not just "mankind," but mankind in his context as the ruler of the ordered creation that God has made; for the created order, too, cannot be itself while it lacks the authoritative and beneficent rule that man was to give it.[42]

In other words, the saving act of God is the retrieval or restoration of fallen creation from the clutches of evil and death and its final transformation.

This interpretation has the strong support of Scripture. The letter to the Hebrews says, "It is not to angels that he has subjected [set in its rightful place] the world to come, about which we are speaking."[43] It is Christ as *the last Adam,* for the Hebrews text immediately adds, "But there is a place where someone has testified: 'What is man that you are mindful of him, the son of man that you care for him?'"[44] This, of course, is the introduction to Psalm 8, which is then further cited: "You made him a little lower than the angels; you crowned him with glory and honor and put everything under his feet."[45]

Again, Oliver O'Donovan finds the right words:

> The resurrection carries with it the promise that "all shall be made alive"...[this] directs us back also to the message of the incarnation, by which we learn how, through a unique presence of God to his creation, the whole created order is taken up into the fate of this particular representative man at this particular moment of history, on whose one fate turns the redemption of all. And it directs us forward to the end of history when that particular and representative fate is universalized in the resurrection of mankind from the dead. "Each of his own order: Christ the first fruits, then at his coming those who belong to Christ" (15:23). The sign that God has stood by his created order implies that this order, with mankind in its proper place within it, is to be totally restored at the last.[46]

How "All" Is "All Things"?

The phrase "all things" makes the same point. In redemption Christ achieves "the reconciliation of all things."[47] "All things" should be taken here as a reference to the created universe, not totally new things created from nothing. According to Paul, God is the Creator of "all things,"[48] and the first verse of the Bible makes clear what that is: "God created the heavens and the earth."[49] "All things" *is* "the heavens and the earth." As to the future, God's redemptive plan is to "bring all things in heaven and on earth together under one head, even Christ."[50] In this text, "all things" and "heaven and earth" are brought together to show that the object of redemption is still the fullness and vast expanse of the original, ordered, holy creation.

When Paul says that Christ "fills all things," he is saying that Christ, in God's name, has in principle retaken possession of the cosmos. This is not some newly created space known only to God. It is the original heavens and earth that God created from nothing.

The new creation is not "from nothing." It is the redemption and transformation of the old.

The fact that Christ now holds together all things in the created order shows that the cosmos is in his future plans.

> Its plurality of hierarchical grades, its distinctions between heaven and earth, between spiritual and material reality, are held under control. The community of all natures is not permitted to explode in fragments.[51]

Nor is it permitted to implode into the oneness of a monistic black hole. In Christ as the divine Son and Creator, all things in the present in spite of sin, hold together, keep their identities and distinctions, and function the way God the Creator meant them to function. But in redemption, Christ the last Adam delivers all things from the vanity of the fall and in him they are reconciled, that is, brought back to God in a new and glorified form.

Christ as the true man, the last Adam, is our present and future model. When the cosmos is renewed, we will fully share in that universal lordship, as the prophet Daniel announced long ago:

> Then the sovereignty, power and greatness of the kingdoms under the whole heaven will be handed over to the saints, the people of the Most High. His kingdom will be an everlasting kingdom, and all rulers will worship and obey [or be given their rightful place beneath] him.[52]

Says O'Donovan, "[A]s the Redeemer, as the visible presence of the invisible God who is creation's end, he must be, even as creature, 'the preeminent one'...the 'head' of the renewed creation taking shape in the church, the 'firstborn.'"[53]

The picture of creation reoccupied and renewed with things in their rightful place is finally complete when the Son, as true man and true God, sets himself in his rightful place in relation to God the Father. "When he has done this," says Paul, "then the Son himself will be made subject to him who put everything under him, so that God may be all in all."[54] Placed before this majestic statement of completeness, one cannot avoid the sense that all will be right, all will be holy.

On the basis of this truth, it follows that to be in Christ is to take part in the dominion of creation, but how?

REBIRTH AS THE ULTIMATE SANCTIFICATION OF CREATION

God takes back what is his by resanctifying creation. Christ's redemptive work on the cross and in the resurrection places him as head over all things. As head, he resubjects all things, resets all things in their rightful, reconciled places. In other words, as head over all things he sanctifies, or rather resanctifies, the cosmos into its rightful place of "submission" to the will and design of God from which it has fallen. Thus, the general resurrection and final transformation represent the complete sanctification of the cosmos, in which everything finds its rightful and ultimate place. The biblical utopia is a holy place.

The Bible uses *hupotassw*, the verb meaning "set under," to describe both creation and redemption in identical fashion.[55] The psalmist says that God "*set* all things *under* his [Adam's] feet," which is one more expression of God's sanctifying activity to "set things apart in their appropriate places." So when the New Testament employs "set under" to describe the place of the resurrected last Adam, one should conclude that God's final act of re-creation is also a work of holiness, of sanctification. There are good reasons to support this:

₪ The resurrection of Christ is the work of the *Holy* Spirit. The Spirit *of holiness* raises Jesus from the dead, as Paul clearly states: "[Christ] through the Spirit of holiness was declared with power to be the Son of God by his resurrection from the dead: Jesus Christ our Lord."[56] The resurrection is thus the resanctification of created matter.

179

₪ The resurrection of Christ as the last Adam, that is, as a human being, is the moment of Christ's definitive sanctification. It is true that Christ was always holy, always the "Holy One of God," recognized as such by the demonic world.[57] So we cannot take sanctification in its common meaning of moral progress. But we can in its sense of being set apart. For there is a sense in which, at his resurrection, Christ is lifted out of the world of sin and death to be fully and finally set apart for God. As Paul states, "the death he died, he died to sin once for all."[58] Richard Gaffin explains what Paul is arguing:

> The controlling question of this passage...is...are believers to continue to live in sin?...[the answer] is that believers have died and been raised with Christ...[have been given definitive sanctification because] Christ's resurrection is his sanctification.[59]

In the case of Christ who was made to be sin for us[60] as a result of his resurrection, he would never again have to face death and sin. But the Paul adds, "But the life he [now] lives, he lives to God."[61] The present life Christ lives is the life of the resurrection. Set apart for the new life with God, Christ now lives in a new place, the place he is preparing for us.[62]

Because Christ has become holy in the definitive sense, he has become our holiness or the paradigm for holiness. "It is because of him that you are in Christ Jesus, who has become for us wisdom from God—that is, our righteousness, holiness, and redemption."[63] Thus the believer must "put on the new self, created to be like God in true righteousness and holiness,"[64] and is exhorted: "for it is written: 'Be holy, because I am holy.'"[65] Christ, who now lives the re-created, holy life, imparts his life to us.

The present work of Christ through his Holy Spirit is to prepare us for a future new life of holiness, as the following text makes clear: "To the end he may establish your hearts unblameable in *holiness* before God, even our Father, at the coming of our Lord Jesus Christ with all his *saints*."[66] Pursuing holiness now leads to eternal life: "But now that you have been set free from sin and have become slaves to God, the benefit you reap leads to holiness, and the result is eternal life."[67]

The future is for "holy ones," saints. See Colossians 1:12: "giving thanks to our Father, who has qualified you to share in the inheritance of the saints in the kingdom of light."[68] Present discipline is for a future goal: "God disciplines us for our good, that we may share in his holiness."[69]

In the biblical universe of distinctions, after the fall there is holiness and there is unholiness. So in the future kingdom of light, there will be no place for the unholy, for "without holiness no one will see the Lord."[70] This also applies to the unrepentant, sexually unholy.[71] The old earthly Jerusalem was called "the mountain of holiness."[72] "Now we await the coming down of the Holy City."[73]

This emphasis on future holiness surely means that just as the original creation was holy in the sense of each part having its rightful, God-intended place and function, so also the renewed creation will be holy in the same way. To be sure, sin and death will be ended so that *moral* perfection is certainly intended. Nevertheless, this idea of holiness also implies the new life of service to God where redeemed creatures—an imitation of Christ, who himself now lives for God—serve the Lord in ways and structures that honor him as Creator and Redeemer.

Everything will be made new, everything will be holy. You can count on it—"these words are trustworthy and true." But does this promise about everything include sex?

THE REBIRTH OF SEX

What will happen to sex in the coming new heavens and new earth? We must ask this question of the Bible because we asked it of paganism. In paganism, the reader will recall, the future of sex is both a this-worldly, orgiastic paradise of free love and free expression with no boundaries or norms, followed by a postmortem, bodiless, androgynous spirituality of absorption into impersonal spirit. The Christian answer is both more restrained and yet breathtakingly more radical.

The Future Is off Our Charts

Thomas Molnar makes an interesting remark about human futurist visions: "The future is essentially incalculable, [so human] utopia would be a frozen present, if ever carried out."[74] What he means it that man is incapable of a truly transformed, transcendent view of the future, so his imagined ideal world would inevitably be limited to a this-worldly perception and be transcendently boring. Paul would call this kind of thinking "the wisdom of this age,"[75] a wisdom that never gets beyond the present human predicament and is totally unable to understand "the world to come." This is why the Christian view of the future is so sparse. It is not sparse because we know some awful truth and are unwilling to reveal it. Rather it is discreet because God's ultimate future must go beyond all that we earthlings could ever comprehend or even imagine here on earth with our limited and sinful earthly minds. The refusal of the Bible to give us such details is a sign of its very authenticity. It says without embarrassment, "No eye has seen, no ear has heard, no man has conceived what God has prepared for those who love him."[76]

No Marriage

What will happen to sex in the new heavens and the new earth? The Jewish leaders who rejected the afterlife used just such a question to try to trap Jesus in his teaching about the resurrection. They invented a hypothetical case of a woman who outlived seven husbands and who, after such an outstanding effort, died herself. The punch line was meant to stump Jesus and to silence him once and for all about the unbelievable notion of resurrection. You can just see them rubbing their hands as they triumphantly inquire, "At the resurrection, whose wife will she be?"[77]

In his answer, Jesus reveals a fundamental principle about the relation of creation and new creation. The cultural mandate given to Adam and Eve was to "be fruitful and increase in number; fill the earth and subdue it."[78] In order to carry out the program, God created humans, male and female, and provided the institution of marriage. Jesus endorsed the program and recognized the present normativity of creational sex when he said, "Moses permitted you to divorce your wives because your hearts were hard. But it was not this way from the beginning."[79] Eating and drinking, marrying and giving in marriage,[80] according to Jesus, is typical of this-worldly, creational life whose natural purpose reaches its goal when the earth is filled.

But just as naturally, the old creational mandate no longer applies in eternity. Christ fills the universe in a different way that Adam and Eve filled the earth. So Jesus replies to his gainsayers, who have understood neither biblical eschatology nor the power of God, Creator and Redeemer, "The people of this age marry and are given in marriage. But those who are considered worthy of taking part in that age and in the resurrection from the dead will neither marry nor be given in marriage."[81] Marriage and physical procreation are not appropriate activities in the age to come.

Marriage Everywhere

On the other hand, marriage as such will be the very heart of the new creation. That approaching rendezvous is not the faceless black hole of pagan nirvana,[82] but a marriage feast, the marriage supper of the Lamb[83] and the face-to-face meeting between the Lord, Creator, and Savior and each redeemed creature, each in his own rank. In his major work on heaven, Randy Alcorn relates a conversation he had with a single woman who expressed the sense of great loss if she went to heaven never having had a great romance. His response was "our romance with Christ will far exceed any earthly romance. No romance is perfect, and many end in disappointment. Our romance with Christ will never disappoint."[84] Heterosexual monogamy will find its glorious and ultimate fulfillment in the marriage of the Creator and the creature, of Christ and his bride. "The purpose of marriage is not to replace heaven, but to prepare us for it."[85]

With the fulfillment of marriage, does this mean that in the new heavens and the new earth redeemed human beings will be genderless creatures? While there are few biblical texts that deal with the subject, the theology and logic of the Bible are against such a conclusion.

Like the Angels?

One text from the mouth of Jesus has given rise to much debate. Some have taken our Lord's statement, as recorded in Matthew, to mean that we will be asexual beings "like the angels of God in heaven."[86] It is true that angels never marry or are married. They do not procreate. To be like angels would suggest a final state more like a pagan utopia, where as the Gnostics believed, on entering the kingdom of God we would be stripped of the encumbering burden of a male or a female body and would become a pure, androgynous spirit.[87] Jesus' reply in the Matthew account leaves the question somewhat ambiguous, for he says, "At the resurrection people will neither marry nor be given in marriage; they will be like the angels in heaven."[88] In this text the point in common between angels and men is the fact that they do not marry.[89] Luke's account makes it clearer. It centers the reference to angels around a different issue. Jesus says of those in heaven, "They can no longer die; for they are like the angels."[90] Clearly the reference here to angels concerns their immortality, not just their sexuality. Male and female, as expression of the image of God, is not part of the angelic but of the human order (see Gen. 1:27) and is surely destined to survive, indeed thrive, as long as human creatures survive.

9: Born-Again Sex and the Future

MALE AND FEMALE IN THE AGE TO COME?

When the apostle Paul says that in Christ there is "neither male nor female," is he projecting a gnostic view of the church and of heaven, where sexual distinctions no longer apply and spirit replaces flesh? Certainly he is insisting that one's sex may never be a barrier to inclusion in the church.[91] The category of male and female must never be allowed to function as a principle of sinful exclusion from the body of Christ. However, in the much-debated text of Galatians 3:28, Paul is surely not declaring the end of gender distinctions, as many modern feminists maintain.[92] Otherwise he surely would not insist with such passion on the physicality of the resurrection of Jesus or on heterosexual gender distinctions as an image of the gospel[93] or on the importance of gender for the nature of church office.[94] So, because gender distinction does have a noble and significant function among the redeemed people of God in the present, we must inquire whether the male-female creational reality survives in some form in the redeemed reality of the new creation.[95]

We know one thing for sure about the future because our knowledge is based on something that occurred in the past—the resurrection of Jesus. The resurrected body of Jesus was transformed and yet retained continuity with the earthly form. Though the body of Jesus was profoundly transformed, his disciples could still recognize him.[96] Nowhere is there a hint that Jesus was androgynous. There is profound continuity in his physicality before and after the resurrection. Paul teaches this systematically when he says, "[T]he perishable must clothe itself with the imperishable, and the mortal with immortality."[97] At the resurrection, a radical change occurs, but it does not create *ex nihilo* a new physical being. It transforms an already existing body. The apostle John, who saw the resurrected Jesus, declared, "We know that when he appears, we shall be like him, for we shall see him as he is."[98] Paul says the same thing: Christ "will transform our lowly bodies so that they will be like his glorious body."[99] If our bodies will be like his, then we can expect some kind of continuity with what we are now since this was true in the case of Jesus. We are thus obliged to ask what survives of human "bodily" personality.

Ezekiel's vision of the future temple, though clearly symbolic, as is all our language about the future, has within it the notion of distinction. Actually, in describing the new creation Ezekiel uses the same word ("separate") Moses used to describe the old.[100]

The prophet recounts his vision: "So he measured the area on all four sides. It had a wall around it, five hundred cubits long and five hundred cubits wide, to separate the holy from the common."[101] In the sinless reality of the future state, like that of the garden before the fall into sin, distinctions have a place. Why not sexual distinctions as well? The greatest distinction of all, between God and his creation, is clearly maintained in the great splendor of the final kingdom as John's inspired vision shows:

> Each of the four living creatures had six wings and was covered with eyes all around, even under his wings. Day and night they never stop saying: "Holy, holy, holy is the Lord God Almighty, who was, and is, and is to come."[102]

In spite of the deep communion of the final marriage supper, God will forever remain God, and we will forever remain creatures—redeemed creatures. Just as they were of the old, distinctions will be an essential aspect of the new creation, however gloriously transformed it becomes. If we will never stop being creatures made in the image of God, then why not male and female creatures, originally formed in God's image that way? "Receiving a glorified body... doesn't erase history, it culminates history."[103] If in heaven we will be ourselves as we were meant to be when created, but transformed, then male and female is part of the reality to be transformed—doubtless with many new functions we cannot even imagine.

In the new creation, when the function of procreative marriage will have been fulfilled as Jesus taught, sex will be reborn to have other functions like everything else about our present earthly reality. Can we imagine ourselves in heaven without our rationality, especially as we are promised not present partial knowledge but knowledge by which we shall know as we are known?[104] Knowledge is not annihilated. It is fulfilled. Does that mean we will never use our brains again? Surely not. When we see our Maker and Redeemer "face-to-face,"[105] unlike the nonencounter of impersonal paganism, God will not erase our personality. Essential to our personality is our sexuality as many Christian thinkers have affirmed.[106]

If holy sex, like everything else we do here on earth, has eternal meaning, if right now counts forever, then how do we practice "reborn" sex now? If Christ is presently sanctifying his fiancée, setting her apart for the future heavenly wedding,[107] then what is the meaning and status of reborn sex in the present? This question will be the subject of the next chapter.

Chapter 10

Born-Again Sex and the Present

₪

T he best sex is biblical sex.

How do I know? If God created sex and called it good—and in the resurrection of Christ made it better—who would be foolish enough to go elsewhere for true sexual pleasure?

But I hear an objection. If heterosexual marriage is one day fulfilled in the marriage of Christ and the church (what is called the holy marriage of creatures with their Creator), should we not anticipate that future life and abandon earthly sex and marriage? The New Testament answers with a resounding no!

The Many Warnings against Sexual Immorality

So important is the physical body and bodily sexuality in the service of God *in this life* that Scripture gives great attention to their rightful use. The Bible is aware of the power of sexual desire for good or ill. Because the transgression of sexual boundaries is a common expression of human rebellion against God the Creator, the Bible, while never denigrating human sexuality, nonetheless regulates it in accord with the Creator's design. God warns his people to seek bodily holiness and to avoid sexual license. Twenty-three extended texts denounce sexual immorality.[1]

Some would use these texts as a perfect example of a sexually hung-up worldview. Sex is a trap. Enjoyment is evil. However, we must consider another possibility: that these verses show how important sexuality is in God's plan for humanity—*but not just any sexual permutation.* Exclusive heterosexuality within marriage is what God the Creator desires and requires. Exclusive heterosexuality is not only "good" for the human race but points beyond itself to the very meaning of the cosmos. Heterosexuality reflects, on the sexual level, the imprint of the Creator's own nature and character on the things he made. It is not an incidental but an essential component of the Bible's worldview.

A WORLDVIEW FOR SEX

Christianity is not just talk. *Embodying* the truth is an essential part of Christian discipleship. Remember the French people's love of cheese? Physical things are indispensable to the Creator's present and future intentions. Our bodies as well as our souls are offered to God as pleasing, living sacrifices. It is in these bodies that we live and honor God until his future plan becomes a reality.

This realistic view of life, that accepts our bodies as "set apart" to honor God, is the foundation for our worldview about sex. As we await the coming of Christ, we are to learn about the sanctification of the body.

The Body and Holiness

The first image of bodily holiness that comes to mind—that of a virginal child—is not the right one. Remember that the root meaning of holiness is "set apart" in a special place. Bodily holiness means using your body in accordance with God's creational design. "God gives...a body [to everyone] as he has determined."[2] God is in the body business. Being in the right place at the right time is both an effective formula for winning soccer games and for establishing what makes things morally right. In ancient Israel the body's physical state symbolized God's demand for moral purity, both of the individual and of the nation. So he commands, "Speak to the Israelites and say to them: 'When any man has a bodily discharge, the discharge is unclean.'"[3] The ritual symbol falls away when theocracy ends, but God's demand for bodily holiness in the new covenant remains.

The apostle tells us the program: "For God did not call us to be impure, but to live a holy life."[4] "The body is...for the Lord, and the Lord for the body."[5] Believers do not serve and honor God in some angelic spirit two inches above the ground, but in their flesh-and-blood bodies. Living a "holy life" involves not just thinking pious thoughts or doing loving actions but using your body in God's prescribed way. Part of sin is misusing the body.[6]

"Honorable" and "holy," and by logical extension "dishonorable" and "unholy," are synonyms. "If a man cleanses himself [from dishonorable things], he will be an instrument for honor, made holy, useful to the Master and prepared to do any good work."[7] Obviously, doing *honorable* things *honors* the Creator. What false worshippers do not do—honor God[8]—true believers do.[9] They honor God—in their bodies. "You were bought at a price. Therefore honor God with your body."[10]

This gives the body great dignity. Paganism often dismisses the physical body as worthless illusion. The New Testament places it in the center of Christian discipleship. Notice Paul's logic: Since "the life of Jesus...[is] revealed in our body,"[11] "now as always Christ will be exalted in my body."[12] The exaltation of Christ is what the Christian faith is all about—and it is done in the body! Because this is true, it is given the noble title "the temple of the Holy Spirit."[13] Once more the body is associated with holiness (the Holy Spirit), which is understood as God's designated, special use. How does sexuality fit in?

Christian Holiness

Israel served as a warning light to the ancient pagan world. God called her to demonstrate as vividly as possible in all the aspects of her national reality the theistic, created character of the universe. When the true Israelite—Christ—comes, he fulfills the details of

191

Israel's ritual and social life. Christ is the reality, not the shadow; he is the fulfillment, not the promise. He brings the definitive salvation for which Israel hoped.

But the reality of creation continues in the church, the new Israel, though the structure no longer has any national theocratic identity. After Christ's resurrection, the church is sent into the Greco-Roman Empire to seek and to save pagans. It is under obligation to express the truth about God the Creator, for this is the very truth that pagans deny. The Creator as Redeemer is the essential declaration of the church's gospel.[14]

A Holy Church

One of the defining categories of the church is holiness. We think of holiness in the New Testament as a process of moral development. But holiness, just as it was in the Old Testament, is a state that God confers on people and things. Only when it has been *bestowed* can it be experienced as a *process.* This truth emerges clearly in the case of converted pagans.

In the fifties (of the first century AD), Paul established a Christian community in Corinth, one of the most immoral urban centers of the ancient world. It was like starting a church in Las Vegas, only without two thousand years of "Christian" civilization. Indeed, Corinth became a verb—"corinthianize"—that ancient playwrights used to describe a life of sordid debauchery.[15] When Paul taught the Corinthian Christians "that the wicked will not inherit the kingdom of God," they knew exactly what he meant.[16] He then reminded them that this was "what some of you were."

When Paul wrote to converted pagans, their pagan lifestyle was a thing of the past. That lifestyle *had been* true of them. *Now* a structural change had taken place. God had acted on their behalf to sanctify them. The Corinthian Christians did not clean up their act in order to qualify. "You *have been* sanctified,"[17] says Paul to a church that continued to demonstrate deep connections with its pagan, immoral past.[18] He addresses them as "holy ones" or "saints," though they are far from perfect. Salvation is God's work of sanctification. It makes us holy. It sets sinners apart for a life of good works.[19] The Corinthians are saints because they have been set apart to be included in the new Israel, the people of God. Paul says they are grafted into God's holy people, receiving a *holy* status.[20] The exhortation to the church is a reprise of that given to Israel: "Come out from them and be separate."[21]

Holiness Requires Separation

Paul's exhortation to be separate means to make the distinctions implicit in a biblical worldview. Separation does not mean setting up ghettos, running to the hills, waiting for the rapture, or being social misfits. Holiness is an intellectual, theological, and moral separation. It means understanding the antithetical worldviews that separate pagans from believers. It means comprehending the radical divide between the truth and the lie. It means

₪ not being "yoked together with unbelievers," whether by marriage or by any other spiritual communion;

₪ affirming that "righteousness and wickedness have [nothing] in common";

₪ teaching that there is no fellowship between light and darkness;

₪ making the distinction "between Christ and Belial";

₪ recognizing that at the deep level of worldview, the *believer* has nothing in common with an *unbeliever*;

₪ there is no "agreement...between the temple of God and idols."[22]

The exhortation to separation, once given to Israel, is now laid upon the church because the church faces the same temptations as did ancient Israel. Just as Israel was warned, "When you enter the land the Lord your God is giving you [namely, pagan Canaan], do not learn to imitate the detestable ways of the nations there,"[23] so the church must keep herself from the unholy ways of the pagan nations surrounding her. This does not mean forming Christian ghettos.[24] It means being in the world with a radically different lifestyle.

If you want to be God's child, you must understand this kind of separation. Compromise with paganism is as tempting for us as it was for poor Lot and his family who wanted to blend in with the homosexual culture of his day and make an honest living.[25] Our motivation for separation is that which motivated God's people long ago: "Let us purify ourselves from everything that contaminates body and spirit, perfecting holiness out of reverence for God."[26] "This is the will of God, your sanctification."[27] If you wish to reverence God, you must understand holiness. In other words, you must understand the Bible's worldview. With countercultural boldness, in concert with ancient Israel and the first-century Corinthian church we declare, "The earth is the Lord's, and everything in it."[28]

Because of this holy status, Christians must respond to God's imperative call to holiness as did Israel. The church responds in its own way, but the principle is the same. As the apostle Peter states, "Just as he who called you is holy, so be holy in all you do."[29] The new creation, as well as the old, has been named to a special, identified, holy place. To honor this notion of holiness, we are faithful to Jesus' teaching: "This, then, is how you should pray: 'Our Father in heaven, *hallowed be* your name....'"[30] And radical feminist Christians today no longer want to use the name "Father"! According to Jesus, we sanctify God by addressing him as the "heavenly Father."[31] We cannot make the Lord morally pure, but we *hallow* (sanctify) his name when we recognize its special role and place in our lives.

HOLY SEX FOR PERSONAL SANCTIFICATION

There is a holy place for sex just as there is a holy place for everything, including God. The Bible's requirement of exclusive, permanent, male-female marriage is not arbitrary. It reflects the holiness of the creation as well as that of the Creator. There is a right way to have sex and there is a wrong way. To be "one spirit" with the Lord is, on the sexual level, to observe what the Lord says about God-honoring sex. "Therefore," says Paul, "honor God with your body."[32] Being one with the Lord in the domain of human sexuality is to receive in faith the one-flesh project of monogamous heterosexuality as a gift from the Lord.

"She Will Be Saved through Childbearing"[35]

My wife testifies to the same process in her life. Holy sex is the healing influence both in individual lives and also in a godless, sexually immoral world. As our society pushes for the legitimacy of "gay marriage," it fails to think of the next generation and the maintenance of civilization. Alas, a selfish, glamorized vision of life controls the media and promotes immediate self-fulfillment and career as the only path to success. Women (in significant numbers, I fear) now refuse an essential element of marriage—motherhood. The movie *Mona Lisa Smile*, for example, subtly ridicules motherhood and traditional marriage, while promoting the new, autonomous "Wellesley" woman who wouldn't be caught dead submitting herself to a husband.

My wife is a Wellesley woman, as are my first two daughters, but each in her own way cherishes the Scripture "she shall be saved through childbirth." Paul does not mean by "saved" that a woman gains her eternal salvation by having babies. He uses the term as he will use it two chapters later when he speaks of "the living God who is the *Savior* of all people, especially of those who believe."[36] He is speaking about God as the Creator or "benefactor." Women having children (or for single women, nurturing children in the community) brings blessing because this is an essential part of the Creator's good design. They are "blessed" by having children and are blessed by their children. Children themselves are not a blight on the world, as zero-population folks would have us believe, but a blessing to it.

"Dr. Karim" was a specialist in obstetrics-gynecology with a degree from the University of Missouri-Kansas City School of

Medicine who brought the feminist line that she could do it all. But after two decades in the medical profession she left her lucrative career to be a full-time mom who home schools her three children. She says, "I enjoyed my work so much, and I loved my patients. I enjoyed it so much that I couldn't see doing anything else. But God works on you." She came to the realization that "sub-contracting the child rearing" wasn't for her. Now she understands this text of Paul that the "greatest role in life is to be at home with my children and bring them up in the way that they should be and make sure they are godly children. Why in the world would I entrust that to anyone else?"[37]

I am reminded of a verse from Isaiah: "He shall eat curds and honey when he knows how to refuse the evil and choose the good."[38]

"Your Children...Are Holy"[39]

Holy children are not "little angels," but holy in the sense of knowing and basking in their place in the world.

In spite of the social engineering that pushes sameness as a political and religious agenda, God has made the sexes different but complementary—both for their effectiveness and richness but also for the production of the next generation. The West is committing "generational suicide" as more women refuse to have children for the sake of a career and "personal identity." Christians are never to forget the Bible's view of children: a "gift from the Lord."[40] The morning-after abortion pill, called "Plan B," trivializes the sex act by treating it as a physical need on par with eating, whereas God endowed this very physical expression of love with enormous consequences—the production of other amazing human beings made in the image of God. When you realize the enormity of this, you won't need Plan B. You will have chosen God's Plan A.

The biblical view of marriage and family is good also for society. "One day," says Arthur Hunt, "our divorce culture is going to come back to haunt us...[because] strong families help to guarantee a strong nation. The collapse of the family unit weakens psychological resilience and makes us more vulnerable to demagogic seduction."[41] The family is the carrier of civilization.

Marriage Expresses the "Profound Mystery" of the Universe[42]

On top of all this, marriage has an even higher purpose—to symbolize the mystery of the universe. It states in physical, human terms the deep meaning of life by expressing in itself the notion both of difference and oneness, which is also true about the relationship between the Creator and the creation. If the church fails here, all is lost. Morality is not about being nice. It is a gutsy commitment to preserving the created distinctions God has established as good. According to Jesus, being the salt of the earth only works if you are good salt.[43] Good salt will give to the good Creator glory, prayers, thanksgiving, and "good" works "which are obvious to all."[44]

Such living is not just a deep moral responsibility; it is a high and noble calling to reclaim the fallen cosmos.

Holy Sex Reclaims the Cosmos

Complete fulfillment is yet to come, but the future in one sense is *now*. What we know of the *future* new heavens and earth, we've come to understand from what happened to Christ in the *past*, which enables us to know something profound about the *present*. Such knowledge is freeing. People imagine they are free when they follow their urges and obey their imaginations. But they are actually no freer than the dolphin stranded on the beach. Freedom is finding your footing for life in God's great plan—with an eye to the future.

ASSUME YOUR PART IN THE RECLAIMED COSMOS

Because the resurrected Christ is our prototype and all things have been placed *under his feet*, we, male and female, already participate in his lordship. God's "power...enables him to bring everything under his control."[45] The resurrection power of the Holy Spirit is ours, for we are enjoined to reclaim the cosmos for the Creator. The disciples knew this during the time of Jesus. "The seventy-two returned with joy and said, 'Lord, even the demons submit to us [or take their place under us] in your name.'"[46] This power is all the more present after the resurrection of Christ because Christ, the resurrected Lord, is our freedom to act. We act in this confidence: "The God of peace will soon crush Satan under your feet."[47] The resurrection of Jesus is not the end of creation but its rebirth[48] which fills us with hope. We also act in faith because, as the writer to the Hebrews says, "God left nothing that is not subject to him. Yet at present we do not see everything subject to him."[49] The present is a time of faith, not sight.

Reclaiming Creation by Submitting to its Structures

The present task of the Spirit-empowered Christian is to reclaim the original holy creation as a sign of witness to creation's future destiny. We noted previously that the verb *submit* describes the action of Christ in taking back creation as the transformed world to come.[50] That same verb, *submit*, is also used as an exhortation to Christians in their present lives to be salt and light.[51] We are commanded to take control by actively submitting ourselves to the structures God has placed in the world. In doing this we witness to the fact that God is still in control and that everything God created is good.[52] The result of salvation is first of all to make us good creatures. Doing this, we anticipate the victory of Christ, Creator and Redeemer, who reconciles all things—now and in the age to come—and will one day make us fully transformed creatures.[53] As liberated creatures we also place ourselves obediently and joyfully in structures that promote holiness. This is Christian sanctification. This is the reliving of the probation Adam and Eve failed. We reign and rule and submit all things by first and foremost submitting ourselves to the good structures of the earth. We reign over sin as Cain was exhorted to do,[54] and part of our lordship is a self-conscious, willing submission to the will of God. We reclaim the cosmos and honor the Creator by honoring the goodness of creation's structures, not as an ambitious strategy for taking over the planet but as a humble statement of faithful witness to the one who made it. Some are establishing a political vision to wrest God's world from him by undermining his structures (especially in the area of sexuality). They meet with kings and plan together as Psalm 2 says. That is not the Christian way.

It is perhaps useful to pause for a moment and remember what cutting-edge, intellectual pagans say about the area of sexuality. As Christians seek to weigh the importance of biblical sexuality in their calling as witness to the Lord of creation, it is crucial to understand the neopagan agenda. Leading pagan thinkers are mapping out an extensive blueprint for a new civilization, conscious of the crucial role played by sexuality and gender. Of particular note is the statement by Thomas Berry, an apostate Roman Catholic priest with enormous influence in the halls of geopolitical/religious power. In the goal of reinventing the human being "at the species level... by means of story and shared dream experiences,"[55] according to the design of religious neopaganism, one "reinvention" has priority over all the others. States Berry, "[T]he transformation of men and of western [patriarchal] society is a primary condition for every other change."[56] In other words, for the agenda of pagan transformation to succeed in all the dimensions of human life, our understanding of sex and gender roles must be transformed. Berry throws down the gauntlet before the King of the universe.

Everybody Gets to Submit

This is the context in which Christians hear the exhortations of Scripture regarding submission. The moment is fraught with difficulty but also full of witnessing potential. In a whole series of areas, Christians are required to submit—not in a attitude of craven fear but one of willful, intelligent, Christ-honoring obedience to the order that God provides,[57] in acts that reclaim the creation. Nobody is left out. Nobody is made to submit. It is done self-consciously, intelligently, and willingly.[58] There is no group that does not participate.[59] Christ himself, the prototypical new man, knew the reality of submission. In this he is our model. In his incarnation, Christ was born under the law and submitted himself to it. Specifically, he submitted himself to the law concerning parents,[60] but also to all the other structures of created life. Even as the reigning Lord, head of the new humanity, he submits himself to God the Father.[61] When we are renewed in him, we adopt his model of lordship.

The New Testament uses the various related forms of the verb "submit"[62] seventy-six times. Such extensive use by a variety of New Testament authors (involving all kinds of submission for all kinds of people) puts a lie to the radical feminist contention that the biblical teaching on the submission of women is a male-patriarchal plot to grab and hold power.[63] There is nothing demeaning about submission because it is asked of everyone, including Christ. While we are still in the flesh, the good and holy created structures do not change. They exist for our good—and for the good of our feet! We stand on holy ground, since the place where we stand is a re-sanctified cosmos. Only here can we glorify God as the good Creator.

New Testament directives about marriage and the relationships between a husband and wife must not be seen as first-century, strategic adaptations by Paul to Roman cultural norms of a higher "Christian" egalitarian order (as Christian egalitarian writers claim).[64] Rather, such directives express Paul's majestic biblical theology of the renewal of creation in redemption and of the calling and glory of the New Humanity in Christ.[65]

People like to speak a lot about Christian liberty. Margaret Miles, dean and vice president of Academic Affairs, Graduate Theological Union, Berkeley, California—which has just established a Center for Lesbian and Gay Studies in Religion—states, "If Christianity is about anything, it should be an example of incarnation. How do you live lovingly, in a body, in the world?"[66]

Implied is our liberty to set our own boundaries. Here Christian-sounding buzzwords such as "incarnation" and "loving" are used in a context paradoxical to the Bible's worldview. In the discussion of Christian liberty, it is important to remember that, according to Scripture, Christ does not deliver the creation from subjection but from subjection to vanity. Unbounded liberty is a chimera, fool's gold. It does not exist. One is either in subjection to righteousness or to unrighteousness.[67] One is free to be holy or unholy. A "Center for Lesbian and Gay Studies in Religion," like the pagan system that undergirds it, is what the Bible calls "vanity." It does not lead to life or true freedom. It has no genuine place in God's cosmos. Glorious freedom is actually subjection to God's creational structures, including the male-female distinctions, in anticipation of the renewed, perfected cosmic order.

Submission to Biblical Sex

Human sexuality is submitted to the one-flesh structure of heterosexual marriage, which is the complementary relation of a man and a woman who contribute different but equally important functions. What the Bible reveals as distinction and submission for function, our world denigrates as a male power grab and gender oppression. I do not deny that sinful men have made God's structures into "vanity" by misusing the authority given them in order to oppress women or to enhance their own position and pleasure. But all human structures to which we submit—government, employers, teachers, even pastors or elders—have been distorted and used for evil ends. Indeed, the misuse of God's good structures is the very essence of sin.

Eliminating the structures will not rid us of evil. Getting rid of the biblical view of work, family, and marriage will not wipe out personal evil. In fact, destroying the intermediate authority structures places autonomous sinful individuals face-to-face with an all-powerful, equally sinful, impersonal state. This solution has always led to the worst kinds of abuse and oppression. The cure is worse than the illness. For example, misuse of the legal system should not be the occasion for the dismantling of courts, juries, and due process. It should be the occasion for reform. In the case of gender roles, many believe that the feminist revolution was occasioned by Betty Friedan's best-selling book, *The Feminine Mystique* (1963). In articles following her death on February 4, 2006, it emerges that she suffered greatly from anti-Semitism, was a convinced Marxist, claimed to be a battered wife, and, according to her physician daughter, was a deeply troubled woman.[68] Her husband denied the charge of battery with the words, "I am the innocent victim of a drive-by shooting by a reckless driver savagely aiming at the whole male gender."[69]

To solve these very real problems of female frustration, Friedan engaged in a fundamental assault on the traditional family. So devastating were the results that Friedan herself tried, later in life but to no avail, to rein in the movement. The great revolutionary admitted at the end of her life that feminism "denied that core of women's personhood that is fulfilled through love, nurture and home."[70]

The Bible's answer to the misuse of creational structures is to understand these structures within the light of God's good creation and his project of redemption, and then to respond—as creatures with understanding, repentance, and thanksgiving—within the context of the constant earthly struggle for justice.

Reclaiming Sodom,[71] the ultimate homosexual agenda, necessarily conflicts with the Christian agenda of *reclaiming the cosmos for holiness*, including the holiness of exclusive heterosexuality. These two agendas cannot be reconciled, however much "Christian" homosexuals try.[72] Submission to Christ, who in his victory places all things under his feet, must involve active participation in the resanctifyinging of the cosmos, whatever the social cost. Henry Makow makes a profound statement: "A man cannot be ruled by desire for sex and [narcissistic] love. A man is God's agent, creating a New World, the family. This is his duty, purpose and fulfillment. A woman's fulfillment is as his partner and means to this end."[73]

SEX ROLES IN THE CHURCH

Because of the intimate relationship between creation and redemption, the church reflects in its organization the structure of complementary gender distinctions, deriving them from the biblical accounts of our first parents. Though this subject requires a book to itself,[74] it is important simply to note here the difference of worldview between Christian theism and pagan monism. Male leadership in the church is not a macho grab for power, but an integral part of the church's witness in a time of dominant paganism. The apostles understood that if the church—the first-fruits of the new creation—was to reflect the truth of biblical creation, which paganism denied, she needed to reflect in her organization the creational structures that point to the Creator. As we saw earlier, the androgynous/homosexual priest or shaman often becomes a religious leader in pagan religious organizations. Religious androgyny often, though not always, has the symbolic function of expressing on the sexual plane the essential religious commitments of pagan belief. The people of God are organized very differently in both the Old and New Testaments. In the Bible's worldview, church leaders are heterosexual males, normally married, joined to a wife in a legal, permanent, exclusive, marital covenant. There are deep biblical-theological reasons why this is so.

Christians will not win popularity contests in the present self-absorbed, pro-choice, radically egalitarian climate. Even in the church—even in many parts of the evangelical church—these notions are anathema because even Christians do not understand the nature and importance of the Bible's teaching on creation. Many have unwittingly become modern-day gnostics, full of spirit but rejecting the physical creation.

PERFECT SUBMISSION

Submission has gotten a bad press lately. It went out with the old hymn, "Blessed Assurance" by Fanny J. Crosby, which Bev Shea used to sing at the Billy Graham crusades: "Perfect submission, all is at rest; I in my Savior am happy and blessed." In our postmodern world, democracy has run amok and we are all Chiefs. There are no Indians. No one is willing to accept an overarching authority. God becomes the divine Me. This is not the worldview of the Bible! While our submission will never be perfect, Christians do believe that we are set apart as creatures for a special purpose. Submission is an essential part of biblical theism. We accept the structures God has established and place ourselves in the realm and process of sanctification. Submission is not demeaning. It is the glad acceptance of our sanctification in Christ and our holy, significant, God-honoring place in the universe as redeemed creatures.

That is why the ideal picture of the original creation includes the notion of submission. The psalmist says of Adam, "You made him ruler over the works of your hands; you put [submitted] everything under his feet."[75] As viceroys, Adam and Eve ruled over the structures of creation below them.[76] But, as we saw above, man is also subject—to magistrates,[77] church leaders,[78] husbands,[79] parents,[80] employers,[81] God's law,[82] Christ,[83] and God.[84] Such submission is never onerous or humiliating. It is an alignment of the individual in faith before God to the "good" structures God has created and ordained.[85] We Christians rest in them. This is doubtless why, in a few occurrences in the psalms, the Greek verb for *submit* is translated "find rest," as in "Find rest, O my soul, in God alone; my hope comes from him."[86] Christians—even Gentile pagan Christians—have understood submission and find rest in it. Their very faith is called "the submission...[their] confession of the gospel."[87]

Submission to the love and law of God brings rest and a sense of belonging. German philosopher-theologian Dietrich von

Hildebrand, on becoming a Christian at the beginning of the last century, saw that revealed truth "enables the believer to enter into a world of holiness for which he had unconsciously longed."[88] As in the Old Testament, so in the New, God is a God of peace not disorder.[89] Thus, everything should be done in a fitting, orderly, structured fashion.[90] Paul congratulates the Colossians on their *good order*.[91] There is no holy, God-pleasing order without submission. To please God, Christians submit "for the sake of conscience."[92]

Remember, the sinful mind does *not* submit to God's law.[93] The one who opposes ("does not submit to") God, opposes what God has ordained.[94] Those who oppose work are not simply lazy. They are *disorderly*, without creational structure.[95] Willful sinners are not merely wrongdoers. They are rebels, without a spirit of submission to God.[96]

PERFECT SUBMISSION IS THANKFUL SUBMISSION

Rather than eliminate these structures of submission in obedience to modern secular and pagan theories of democratic and personal freedom, the Bible exhorts Christians to embrace them by giving thanks for them. He tells Timothy that "God created [marriage] to be received with thanksgiving by those who believe and know the truth."[97] Though many pagans reject the biblical sexual norm of heterosexual exclusive marriage, Christians do not have that option. "Marriage should be honored by all."[98] Neither do they have an option to reject submission, which, for Paul is an integral part of biblical one-flesh marriage. To introduce his teaching on submission in the epistle to the Ephesians, Paul exhorts the believers always to "[give] thanks to God the Father [as Creator][99] for everything, in the name of our Lord Jesus Christ."[100] And the very next line reads, "Submit to one another.... Wives, submit to your husbands."[101]

Giving thanks is the sign that one has gained the true spiritual understanding of God's creative and redemptive project. Pagans do not give thanks. They "neither glorify God [as Creator] nor give him thanks." Rather than giving thanks, they choose confusion and bad thinking—"they bec[o]me vain in their imaginations, and their foolish hearts [are] darkened."[102] They must deconstruct the created order. The words on a T-shirt at a gay pride parade say it all: "I can't even *think* straight."[103] On the contrary, giving thanks is essential to the Christian faith and to a sound mind. The Lord's Supper is built around thanksgiving,[104] and it is an essential state of mind of the believer, as Paul says: "And whatever you do, whether in word or deed, do it all in the name of the Lord Jesus, giving thanks to God the Father through him."[105]

We thank God because he created us and he has redeemed and will redeem us. Knowing this helps us actively, willingly, and thankfully submit to and embrace the Bible's view of sex.

HOLY SEX AS WORSHIP

"Nothing [God created] is to be rejected,"[106] but rather "received with thanksgiving." This founding statement of the Christian faith, given to newly converted pagans, shows a thoroughgoing endorsement of creation. It teaches them how to live as Christians in relation to the created order. The command flows from Paul's affirmation of the goodness of creation: "Everything God created is good."[107] The earth is not a mistake, nor is matter the result of sin or of the Fall. Creation is the good product of God's benevolent plan. God, the good Creator, is "the Savior [in this case, meaning benefactor] of all men."[108] Creation is a fabulous and wonderful blessing. This is why the Song of Songs is included in the Bible, a majestic hymn of praise to romantic, physical sexuality.

Chapter 11

AWESOME SEX: FEAR NOT

₪

I took my kids to Disneyland. They insisted I go on a ride, a sort of space capsule visiting other planets hurtling through the cosmos at breakneck speed. The embarrassing thing was that the space capsule never moved, just the seats from time to time. I lurched out of that box of fun, and I spent the next three hours lying on a bench trying to recover from motion sickness. The kids left me there to do the real stuff, specifically Space Mountain. I noted how much they clearly loved the thrill of speed. It was both exhilarating and scary. Isn't it odd that sex, while wonderful and exhilarating and passionate, is also scary? There's something strange about becoming so vulnerable and intimate with another human being. But sex involves the most intimate of relationships between two people because it was created to reflect an even more intimate relationship—the one between God and his bride. So in one way it's normal that sex is scary. The holy relationship between a husband and wife is serious as well as fun. And the relationship between God and his bride is serious as well as fun too. We ought to have a healthy fear of sex, just as we ought to have a healthy fear of our relationship with God.

The pattern of separation, of submission and hierarchy, that we have examined in relation to sexuality and holiness also relates to our understanding of fear.

TO FEAR OR NOT TO FEAR

The Bible defines two kinds of fear—good fear and bad fear. Bad fear means running scared. Good fear means showing awe and respect for God and his works. These two senses occur in one verse: "Do not fear, for God has come to test you, that the fear of him may be before you, that you may not sin."[1]

Rightful fear of God, the transcendent Lord, Creator of heaven and earth, preserves his awesome/fearsome character. Life without good fear is boring. C. S. Lewis catches this idea brilliantly in *The Lion, the Witch, and the Wardrobe* in his description of the great lion, Aslan. The children hear about Aslan and are afraid. Susan asks, "Is he—quite safe? I shall feel rather nervous about meeting a lion." Mrs. Beaver replies, "That you will, dearie, and no mistake,... if there's anyone who can appear before Aslan without their knees knocking, they're either braver than most or else silly." Another child, Lucy, interjects, "Then he isn't safe?" to which Mrs. Beaver gives the memorable response: "Safe? 'Course he isn't safe. But he's good."

To be God is to be "fearsome." Moses asks, "Yahweh, who is like you, majestic in sanctity; who is like you among the holy ones, fearsome of deed, worker of wonders?"[2] Thus "fear" is actually a name of God. He is known as "the Fear of Isaac."[3] In this notion of fear is the very character of God.

The fear of God is referred to in the context of the pagan religions that dominated the culture in which God's people lived. God and the gods are compared—and the gods have nothing to offer! "For the Lord your God is God of gods and Lord of lords, the great, the mighty, and the *awesome* God."[4] The "gods" have no ability to inspire fear because they are nothing. Jeremiah pokes fun at pagan worship: "Their idols are like scarecrows in a cucumber field, and they cannot speak; they have to be carried, for they cannot walk. Do not be afraid of them, for they cannot do evil, neither is it in them to do good."[5]

The Lord, on the other hand, is the holy, transcendent Creator. His presence does inspire fear. As Paul says, "Knowing the fear of the Lord, we try to persuade others."[6] When creatures gain this good "fear of the Lord," scary fear, bad fear is banished once and for all and good things happen. Such believers can organize their lives on a correct and wise footing. "The fear of the Lord is the beginning of knowledge."[7] Holding God in awe and respect, which is what the Bible means by godly fear, characterizes the life of the believer. This is what God "requires": "To fear the Lord your God, to walk in all his ways, to love him, to serve the Lord your God with all your heart and with all your soul, and to keep the commandments and statutes of the Lord."[8]

For the Christian, "fear" is normal. Paul describes the essential character of the New Covenant people as those who "work out [their] own salvation with fear and trembling."[9] In Scripture the good fear and respect of God is an essential element of everything his people do—of praise,[10] of salvation,[11] of friendship,[12] of holiness,[13] of love,[14] of trust,[15] of forgiveness,[16] of humility,[17] and of a life delivered from sin.[18] In this sense of well-placed awe and respect, fear is good for human life.[19]

Fear of God is essential in a theistic worldview that emphasizes the Creator-creature distinction. God is the ruler over all the earth so "all the earth [must] fear the Lord; all the inhabitants of the world [must] stand in awe of him!"[20]

This pattern of awe and respect for the Creator is reflected *within* the created order. The fear of the Lord is also expressed as a fear-awe of his works. (Anyone who has gone through an earthquake, a hurricane, a tornado, or a forest fire or stared into the Grand Canyon understands what it is to fear God's awesome works.) Just as we willingly and joyfully submit to the creation's structures, as noted previously, so we just as joyfully hold them in awe and respect. "Submission" and "fear" are thus parallel biblical notions that characterize God's people. Just as we fear God as the one who places boundaries,[21] so also we hold in awe those very boundaries he sets in place. This notion is found throughout Scripture.

The animal kingdom should fear human beings,[22] the nations should fear God's people,[23] citizens must fear rulers,[24] wives must fear their husbands,[25] and slaves their masters.[26] Here is the general principle: "Pay to all what is owed to them: taxes to whom taxes are owed, revenue to whom revenue is owed, respect to whom respect is owed, honor to whom honor is owed."[27] The respect offered is not necessarily because the person in authority deserves respect. Political rulers can be cruel tyrants. Husbands can be sinful cads and scoundrels. Teachers can be authoritarian control freaks. The respect is offered because of the office and because God has laid down the structure. Thus the apostle Peter exhorts believers: "Show proper respect to everyone: Love the brotherhood of believers, fear God, honor the king."[28]

In many Bible passages, "submission" and "fear" occur together, implying that they are parallel notions expressing a fundamental, overarching biblical theme.[29] This structure of respect, fear, or submission influences our understanding and practice of sex. Biblical sex finds its awesome character as it reflects the awesome character of God. Christians do what pagans refuse to do: They receive with thanksgiving created things and structures as good, trustworthy, and awesome.

HUMBLE SEX

One more biblical thread ties all this together—the notion of "humility."

Often referring to the materially "poor" or "humble," this biblical notion cannot be limited to financial or social deprivation, since it describes the spiritual condition of the king of Israel who obviously lacks little in physical comforts.[30] This kind of poverty refers to a state of mind that recognizes human weakness relative to God's eternal power.[31] God saves the "poor/humble" but not the "haughty."[32] Such people are humble because they are aware of God's holiness, of their sin,[33] and of their deep need for God's law.[34] The Bible calls this kind of poverty or humility "distress of soul."[35] Jesus knew it on the cross[36] and taught that his true followers, for whom he died,[37] are the "poor in spirit."[38]

The term for spiritual poverty or humility is also translated as "meekness" and marks the life of Moses,[39] Jesus,[40] and the true disciple. We must take on the yoke of Jesus and learn from him who is "meek." A rightful "poverty of spirit," says Jesus, actually brings "soul rest"[41] and produces optimism, for these are "the meek [who] will inherit the earth."[42]

Humility is thus another biblical thread that fills out the fabric of the Bible's worldview about sex. The one who has understood biblical sex will "submit" to God's creational structures, and will, with humility and meekness, respect and embrace them. Thus masochism, bondage, and domination have no place in the Bible. Specifically these terms of humility, meekness, and submission are all brought together by the apostle Peter and applied to the particular case of the Christian woman. She *submits* herself to her husband with *fear-respect* and with a *meek spirit*.[43] Such living is done "in God's sight"[44] as a witness to the pagan world.[45] In doing good, she is "not to be frightened," for "who is going to harm you if you are eager to do good?" In the same passage, the husband is to be "considerate" with his wife, treating her "with respect as the weaker partner" and as a "fellow-heir of the gracious gift of life." On this groundwork is laid the foundation for intimacy in sex and in prayer. There is no better motivation for sex—it pleases God and, within the context of the Christian home, serves as a picture of Christ's church, thus sometimes bringing pagans to faith.

In company with ancient Israel,[46] with the cherubim Isaiah saw,[47] and with the living beings in the New Jerusalem we will one day see,[48] Christians worship and serve the Creator who is blessed forever.[49] The good work of the Creator, including sex, is not destroyed by the fall nor undone by redemption, nor is it forever in evolutionary flux. It is, like its Maker, blessed...forever!

CONCLUSION

Christians at the dawn of the twenty-first century live in confusing times. Pagan spirituality is on the rise. Homosexuality seeks acceptance. The nature of Christian witness and the essence of the gospel are being redefined. Our nerve is being tested. To survive, some church leaders pit the gospel against the Bible and propose a new reading of Scripture.[50] Reverend Ronald Rude, a Lutheran pastor from Denver addressing the Evangelical Lutheran Church of America's divided approach to the issue of homosexuality, asks, "Does the gospel override the Bible in this case?"[51] Some think that to survive we must ditch the Bible's worldview in favor of a modern notion of liberation that supposedly reflects the "gospel." But such a truncated version of the gospel is no gospel at all. Compromised Christian "churchmen" who reject the theistic understanding of God may survive, but they will be transformed into pagan priests in bishop's robes, pacifying the globe with sexual diversity and religious unity.

Christians must summon the courage to affirm the Bible's worldview *as* the gospel. Christian witness stands or falls with *worldview*. Knowing Bible verses is not enough. Unless God is Creator, Redeemer, and Consummator, and unless his character structures creation, there is no gospel to preach. Gospel reconciliation is reconciliation to God the Creator. Clearheaded preaching will include God's revelation concerning sexuality. For—to our great surprise, perhaps—the battle for our souls is being fought in the battle for our sexual bodies. Those caught in the addictive clutches of pornography will tell you—in moments of clarity—about the muddy, apostate hellhole their deception led them into. Alas, our culture descends deeper every day into that pit.

Little Danielle Van Dam grew up in a neighborhood of elegant suburban homes in Southern California. While her parents were involved in a hopelessly sordid tangle of sexual relations—apparently with partners of both sexes—this seven-year-old girl was abducted. Drugs and alcohol dulled the couple's already weak consciences, and they seemed to take delight in the shock value of their extreme sexual perversion. Their neighbor, convicted of her murder, had stored thousands of pornographic pictures (some of children) on his computer. Even before she was murdered, this little girl was a victim of "liberated" sex. Her parents' enslavement to sexual perversity, her neighbor's enslavement to pornography, the local soccer coach's enslavement to drug dealing—the accumulated sin of the adults in her life—all left her vulnerable to neglect and to the deadly consequences of evil.

For the sake of our children, will no one stand up and denounce this culture of unbridled narcissism?

Someone did. As Savior of the world, it cost Jesus his life. Hopefully, the horror of such enslavement will cause some to turn to Christ, the one who took the consequences of our evil on himself. Only he, our Creator and Redeemer, can break the chains of egotism that bind us all. Both the church and the world need to understand the nature of holy sex, for it leads us to an understanding of the gospel of the true and living and holy God.

Two conflicting worldviews exist. *Pagan monism* (Oneism) abhors the Creator, hates his creation and creation's structures, and promotes anything-goes "liberated" pansexuality. *Biblical theism* (Twoism) loves the Creator, celebrates the creation he has made, and submits to the structure of heterosexual monogamy, which fills the earth with life and paints a picture of the differences God has put in the world as well as the intimate relationship God has with his people.

Biblical theists will be seen, as were the early Christians in Rome, as a suspicious religious cult. In our culture, sexuality draws battle lines. At its deepest level the debate has nothing to do with

213

civil rights; it forces people to choose between religious paganism and biblical theism.

Both the church and the world need to hear and understand the nature of holy sex, which leads us to a deeper understanding of the nature of a holy God. On the other hand, falling prey to the seduction of unholy sex will leave you in bed with lifeless idols.

The worldview choice we make means that we choose between the following two models for sexual identity.

Pagan Androgyny

The model for androgyny is the *berdache,* an American Indian shaman born male but choosing to live as a female who achieves "the reunion of the cosmic, sexual and moral polarities,"[52] or the "joining of the opposites." This kind of gay spiritual man will model for straight men "a more compassionate, open-hearted, humor-filled, and tolerant masculinity,...[and] lesbians will continue to stretch the boundaries of what it means to be a woman [in terms of the issues of] emancipation and empowerment."[53] This androgynous model will free us from the separated "false and calcified notions of masculinity and femininity."[54]

Biblical Heterosexuality

According to the Bible, the model male is someone

above reproach, the husband of one wife,...his children...believers...not open to the charge of debauchery or insubordination...not...arrogant or quick-tempered or a drunkard or violent or greedy for gain, but hospitable, a lover of the good, self-controlled, upright, holy, and disciplined... hold[ing] firm to the trustworthy word as taught, so that he may be able to give instruction in sound doctrine and also to rebuke those who contradict it.[55]

The model female is

subject to [her] own husband, [having a] respectful and pure conduct... [her] adorning [not] external...but...the hidden person of the heart with the imperishable beauty of a gentle and quiet spirit, which in God's sight

214

is very precious...honored [by her husband] heir with [him] of the grace of life.[56]

Both the androgynous and the biblical models are deeply religious. They are mutually exclusive and will definitely determine the kind of culture our children will one day inherit. The androgynous model leaves no room for children. In the biblical model, children are the "Lord's reward."[57] The androgynous model leaves us in the impersonal lap of the Goddess, Mother Nature. The biblical model points beyond itself to a face-to-face encounter with the personal Lord, Creator, and Redeemer of heaven and earth—and of sex.

The choice is yours.

Epilogue

THE REST OF THE STORY

₪

T he burden of this book has been to sketch out the implications of the two belief systems of paganism and biblical theism and show their inevitable implications for sexual practice. Many, like the man I mentioned in my prologue, are unaware of how their everyday and deeply emotional choices—especially sexual choices—actually imply worldview decisions. Many people do not even know there is such a thing as worldview! They have never thought that there is a series of beliefs about the nature of reality and, in particular, of sex, that determines their behavior. Many appear to make decisions on the basis of instincts, urges, and "common-sense" reasons, perhaps because everyone else is doing it or because they saw it on television.

Certainly many have not thought about how their thinking and feeling about ultimate issues affects their actions, or indeed how their actions affect their thinking and feeling about ultimate issues. And yet we cannot leave people there as mere instinctual brutes, incapable of thought or genuine moral action, merely assuaging their physical and sexual appetites as the need arises. I know of few people who would appreciate or accept that view of themselves.

Of course, their high view of themselves is explained by our much-maligned Bible, which makes an amazing statement about the nobility and dignity of human beings.

> God created man in his own image, in the image of God he created him; male and female he created them. And God blessed them. And God said to them, "Be fruitful and multiply and fill the earth and subdue it and have dominion over the fish of the sea and over the birds of the heavens

and over every living thing that moves on the earth.".…And God saw everything that he had made, and behold, it was very good.[1]

The psalmist picks up this same theme and declares:

What is man that you are mindful of him, and the son of man that you care for him? Yet you have made him a little lower than the heavenly beings and crowned him with glory and honor. You have given him dominion over the works of your hands; you have put all things under his feet.[2]

The Bible declares that all human beings are of noble origin, made in the image of God and destined for dignity, beauty, and significance. And while human disobedience stains us with sin and condemns us to death, God's purposes in creation will ultimately—through the amazing grace of his redemption action in Christ—have the last word. There will be new heavens and a new earth, new bodies, a new name, the ultimate wedding feast, new sexual expressions, and no more death. And the Lord of creation and redemption—Father, Son, and Holy Spirit—will reign in cosmic righteousness and holiness forever. This biblical cosmology is the great news of the gospel that sinners of all kinds need to hear.

Oh, and the Rest of the Story

For a number of years I had told the story with which I began this book, the one about the six-foot-ten gay opera singer who approached me after a lecture, thrust a garbled written note in my hand, and walked away. As I told it, I suggested to numerous audiences that worldview thinking is doubtless the best way to speak to the postmodern mind and to the postmodern homosexual mind in particular.

Eight years later I told that story to a group of Christian students in a major university in another part of the country. After the lecture, a young student came up to me. "I recognize that man," he told me. "He's a good friend of mine." He told me the rest of the story. Some time after that fateful lecture, his friend, whose bass voice was one of the best, gave up his singing career because the world in which he worked and traveled involved a homosexual temptation he could not handle. He took a lowly job serving old people in a retirement home. "Does he not sing anymore?" I asked. My young friend, his face glowing, replied, "You should hear him sing in church."

And one day I trust I will. In the heavenly chorus, I am going to request, if possible, a place next to that brother. I anticipate the sound of that bass voice singing with total abandon:

Worthy are you, our Lord and God, to receive glory and honor and power, for you created all things, and by your will they existed and were created.... Great and amazing are your deeds, O Lord God the Almighty! Just and true are your ways, O King of the nations![3]

READER'S GUIDE

₪ ₪ ₪

The subject of sex is one that fits comfortably on a shelf and often stays hidden in shadows until crisis necessitates that we bring it out into the light again. Our nation—indeed, our world—is in the midst of such a crisis. Normalcy is under fire. God is being stalked. And biblical sex is being supplanted by deviant, destructive, perverse alternatives. This particular crisis will not be ignored. Ignorance may be comfortable, but denial is an outright luxury and one we cannot afford. Though the grittiness of our culture's moral condition is alarming, refusing to look at and deal with the facts is a dangerous, costly tactic. We have no choice but to arm ourselves and face the coming flood. To do otherwise is to risk being swept away with the culture.

The following study guide is intended to help you sort through the information contained in this book, analyze your own ideology, and make whatever changes you feel motivated (through the prompting of the Holy Spirit) to make.

Through prayer and study of God's Word, you *can* prepare yourself to face and answer the skeptic—or pagan—who believes that faith in the biblical God is quaint and antiquated, who voices confidently that "permissiveness is progress," who challenges timeless truths with skillful lies.

We pray that as you work through these questions, individually or as part of a small group, you will find yourself strengthened and motivated to take the knowledge you gain here and use it in defense of the Gospel.

May God bless you—and bless the church worldwide as we seek to further his kingdom.

CHAPTER 1
OUT WITH THE OLD: MAKE LOVE, NOT WAR

1. The description of Alfred C. Kinsey raises the question of objectivity. In your opinion should society have taken direction from a man who was himself so entrapped in sexual excess and deviancy?
2. Think about those who direct and advise you. Do they model godly character?
3. God alone has the ability to advise with perfect objectivity from a position of omniscient wisdom. Take note of how frequently you turn to God's Word for direction compared to how often you take advice from people.
4. What do you think of the statement, "Diversity can be a pretext for introducing perversity"? Do you agree or disagree, and why?
5. When you read about porn stars working the college lecture circuit, college students producing and sharing pornography for credit, and sexually-explicit material being given to children as young as thirteen, do you feel paralyzed or activated? Do you believe anything can be done to reverse this tide? If so, what?

CHAPTER 2
OUT WITH THE OLD: THE DEATH OF GOD

1. What do you think of sociologist Alan Wolfe's statement that "we used to be a Christian nation. Recently we have become a nation tolerant of all religions"?
2. Why do you suppose Christianity is the "last approved prejudice"? What did Jesus say about this is John 15:18–19?
3. Take this quote to its final conclusion: "A curriculum revolution is rewriting American history. At all the top colleges in the United States today, students can graduate without taking a single course in American history—replete as it is with endless references to God." What happens to a culture with "historical amnesia"? When God is removed from our history, what remains?

4. Can the elimination of God from our history block Christians from witnessing?

5. Do you believe America is still a Christian country? If not, what are we?

6. Many believe they can safely dabble in yoga, meditation, and other Eastern disciplines and extract only the "helpful" aspects, discarding the spiritual. Do you agree or disagree? Why or why not?

CHAPTER 3
IN WITH THE NEW: THE COMING SEXUAL UTOPIA

1. Episcopalian Bishop John Spong believes that "the death of the God of theism has removed from our world the traditional basis of ethics." If that basis has been removed, what has moved into its place? What comment does Judges 17:6 make to this subject?

2. Much of the pagan agenda involves erasing distinctions between genders. In your opinion, what specific losses would we incur if the two merged and blended beyond distinction?

3. "Thou shalt not judge" has become, as sociologist Alan Wolfe pointed out, the eleventh commandment. Scripture is clear about the correct place for judgment. What does 1 Corinthians 5 teach about the necessity for judgment?

4. What is at the root of unconstrained sexuality and debauchery according to Romans 1:18–32?

5. The effort to erase God is an effort to cast off all moral restraint. As Dostoyevsky said, "Without God, all things are permissible." How do the following verses counter that thought? See Genesis 2:7; Colossians 1:16–17; Psalm 66:8–9.

CHAPTER 4
HOMOSEXUALITY: THE SEXUAL SACRAMENT
OF RELIGIOUS PAGANISM

1. Homosexuals and Planned Parenthood have a voice in the schools,

but Christians do not. However silenced you feel, how does the truth of Psalm 18:6 comfort you?

2. Dr. Jones restated Ephesians 6:12 when he said, "This is a spiritual war, not a polite exchange of ideas." Read Ephesians 6:10–18. How does this direct you personally?

3. Democracy, civil rights, the Constitution—these are ideals most don't dare touch. At what point does your faith inform your views of these ideals? Where do you part ways with these lofty notions?

4. Can morality be settled by majority vote? Why or why not?

5. In this chapter Dr. Jones raised the specter of pastors being jailed for the "hate crime" of speaking against homosexuality. Read Acts 4:16–20. How does this challenge you?

CHAPTER 5
UNINTENDED DESTRUCTIVE CONSEQUENCES

1. Dr. Jones quoted from research scientist Deborah Tolman who said that "girls are entitled to their own sexual desire or sexual pleasure and that 'good' girls or 'nice' girls are depriving themselves of a full life." What do you think of this view? How does Romans 14:11–14 refute Tolman's position?

2. Paganism—and the politics and sociology inherent to it—is a religion that battles the truth of God's Word and has set itself up against God himself. What hope does such an ideology have? Can anything built on a foundation other than Christ survive? What verses do you know that support your view?

3. Read Romans 1:25. Define "the lie."

4. Dr. Jones suggests that the church's silence on the subject of sex has been due in part to a sense of prudishness. Realizing that silence is no longer a viable option (particularly since pagans so vocally express their lies), are you prepared to speak more candidly about sex—in the context of its scriptural blessing—than you have in the past?

5. If you—and the church at large—do not rise up and speak the truth, what do you think will happen?

6. If paganism is built on a foundation of lies and is doomed to failure in the end, why bother taking a stand against it?

CHAPTER 6
GOD AND SEX

1. In this chapter Dr. Jones defined *worldview* as being "the organizing structure that allows us to make sense of the ideas going around in our heads." What is your worldview?

2. Dr. Jones explained that when the cultural revolution of the 1960s presented itself, he knew a few Bible verses but had no understanding of the Bible's worldview and therefore no biblical lens through which to view events. What keeps us safe from deceptive doctrine and philosophy?

3. What examples do you see of idolatry (the worship of creation rather than the Creator) in our culture?

4. Dr. Jones states that God's jealousy is not based on insecurity but on a desire for the true nature of things to be known. Do you ever find yourself feeling frustrated because the "true nature of things" are not yet known? When do you feel this way?

5. Make a list (from those mentioned in this chapter or your own understanding) of God's attributes. Which of these does paganism seek to strip from God?

6. This chapter defined "honoring God" as "maintaining the difference between his nature and our own." Have you inadvertently appropriated any of God's attributes for your own? Before you answer too hastily, consider this: What are you doing when you lean on your own understanding? When you choose your own logic over stated scriptural truths?

CHAPTER 7
THE BIRTH OF SEX

1. On the subject of separation, paganism believes it to be evil, while God has stated that it is good. What other pagan views are in direct

opposition to God's opinion?

2. In this chapter Dr. Jones proposes that by separating created elements into distinctly different, named entities, God was sanctifying or declaring "holy" his creation. Do you agree or disagree? Why or why not?

3. One element of gnosticism was the belief that all material, including flesh, was evil and that Jesus appeared in spirit form but did not possess a body. They further believed that what happened in and to the body was of little consequence and could not damage a person spiritually. As Dr. Jones points out, "Jesus was no earth-denying Gnostic guru, awaiting death as the liberation of his spirit from matter." If Jesus *had* been an earth-denying Gnostic guru, awaiting death as the liberation of his spirit from matter, how would our discussion on sex differ?

4. How would you describe the difference between the biblical view and the pagan view of "oneness"?

5. What do you see as being the greatest danger in believing there is no separation, no distinction between us and God?

CHAPTER 8
THE DEATH OF SEX

1. Many in our culture view the acceptance of homosexuality as a progressive, twenty-first century movement. How could you use the information in this chapter to counter that opinion?

2. What happens when moral positions begin to be viewed as mere perspectives?

3. In this chapter Dr. Jones states that the justification for homosexuality in the church is not love or the Gospel but instead is an attempt to rehabilitate a pagan worldview. Is this possible? In a quest to meld Christianity and paganism, what happens to truth?

4. Dr. Jones quoted from a Canadian senator who claimed that Jesus would have voted in favor of gay marriage. How do we know what God thinks?

5. The same pagans who scoff at the exclusivity of the Bible try to use

a false view of Jesus to buoy their position. But what does Matthew 7:13–14 tell you about Jesus and the notion of exclusivity?

6. Though it is true, as Dr. Jones states, that "among sinners, God has no favorites," this chapter makes a distinction between heterosexual sin and homosexual sin. What difference does Dr. Jones see? Do you agree or disagree, and why?

CHAPTER 9
BORN-AGAIN SEX AND THE FUTURE

1. How does our culture express its utopian, "fix the earth" desire? Give examples of people or groups who have their hopes fixed on earth.

2. How would you answer the environmentalist who proposes that we must rescue and restore earth? What does Dr. Jones say about the state of creation prior to sin?

3. According to Dr. Jones, what evidence do we have that God has not given up on the creation?

4. Read Daniel 7:27. What will we share in with Christ when the cosmos is renewed? Does this prophecy support your previous conceptions about Christ's second coming—and what that means for you personally—or does it cause you to adjust your thinking?

5. If the resurrection of Christ initiated the sanctification of creation and his final return will culminate in the final transformation and sanctification of the cosmos in which everything "finds its rightful and ultimate place," what words would you use to describe the efforts of the secular, utopian proponents who believe we have the power within ourselves to right the universe?

6. Based on the discussion in this chapter, how would you answer a feminist who argued from Galatians 3:28 that gender distinctions have been eliminated?

CHAPTER 10
BORN-AGAIN SEX AND THE PRESENT

1. The unbelieving world sees biblical warnings and admonitions about sex as casting aspersions on the act itself. They deduce that those texts reflect a worldview that is "sexually hung-up" and that considers sex to be evil. According to Dr. Jones, what other reason might those warnings be included in Scripture?

2. Dr. Jones says we are incorrect when we imagine a virginal child to be representative of bodily holiness. What alternate definition does he offer? Does this challenge you, and if so, how?

3. Paganism often minimizes the importance of the body, but Scripture upholds its value. In your opinion, what dignifies the body?

4. Do you believe that we develop and acquire holiness or receive it?

5. How do you effectively minister to a God-abhorring culture while at the same time maintaining your distance from that culture?

6. What is your definition of freedom?

CHAPTER 11
AWESOME SEX: FEAR NOT

1. What attitude toward God should characterize the life of a believer?

2. What opinion does the unbelieving world hold toward that attitude?

3. According to this chapter, what banishes the "bad" fear?

4. What is your definition of humility?

5. How does Dr. Jones describe "churchmen" who reject the theistic understanding of God?

6. Do you know such "churchmen" in your own sphere of influence?

REFERENCE LIST

𐤔

Albanese, Catherine L. "Religion and the American Experience a Century After." *Church History* 57 (Sept 1988).

Alcorn, Randy. *Heaven*. Wheaton, IL: Tyndale House, 2004.

Anand, Margo. *The Path of Sacred Sexuality for Western Lovers*. New York: Tarcher/ Putnam, 1989.

Bailey, J. Michael. "Homosexuality and Mental Illness." *Archives of General Psychiatry* 56 (1999).

Baue, Frederic. *The Spiritual Society: What Lurks beyond the Postmodern*. Wheaton, IL: Crossway, 2001.

Baugh, Steven M. "Savior of All People–1 Timothy 4:10 in Context." *WTJ* 54 (1992).

Baum, Robert M. "The Traditional Religions of the Americas and Africa." Swidler, Arlene. ed. *Homosexuality and World Religions*. Valley Forge, PA: Trinity Press International, 1993.

Berger, Helen A. *A Community of Witches: Contemporary New-Paganism and Witchcraft in the United States*. Columbia, SC: University of South Carolina Press, 1999.

Bergin, Mark. "Gender Blender." *World* (18 June 2005).

Bernard, Jessie. *The Future of Marriage*. New York: World Publishing, 1972.

Berry, Thomas. *The Great Work: Our Way into the Future*. New York: Bell Tower, 1999.

Brooke, Tal. *Avatar of Night*. Berkeley, CA: End Run Publishing, 1999.

Bruce, Tammy. *The Death of Right and Wrong: Exposing the Left's Assault on Our Culture and Values*. Roseville, CA: Forum/Prima Publishing, 2003.

Bryan, G. McLeod. *Voices in the Wilderness: Twentieth-Century Prophets Speak to the New Millennium*. Macon, GA: Mercer University Press, 1999.

Buchanan, Patrick J. *The Death of the West: How Dying Populations and Immigrant Invasions Imperil Country and Civilization*. New York: Thomas Dunne Books/St. Martin's Press, 2002.

Budziszewski, J. "Human Life, Natural Law, and Pastoral Care." *Theology Matters* 7/1 (Jan/Feb 2001).

Bultmann, Rudolf. *Theology of the New Testament*. New York: Charles Scribner's Sons, 1955.

Campbell, Joseph and Bill Moyers. *The Power of Myth*. New York: Doubleday, 1988.

Campolo, Tony. *Carpe Diem: Seize the Day*. Dallas: Word, 1994.

Capra, Fritjof. *The Turning Point: Science, Society and the Rising Culture*. New York: Simon and Schuster, 1982. reprint New York: Bantam, 1983.

Carpenter, Edward. "On the Connection between Homosexuality and Divination, and the Importance of the Intermediate Sexes Generally in Early Civilizations." *Revue d'ethnographie et de sociologie* 11 (1910).

———. *Intermediate Types among Primitive Folk: A Study in Social Evolution* (London, 1919). Manchester, New Hampshire: Ayer Co. Pub., 1975.

Cave, David. *Mircea Eliade's Vision for a New Humanism*. New York: Oxford, 1993.

Chesterton, G. K. *Orthodoxy*. New York: Mead and Company, 1927.

Christenson, Cornelia. *Kinsey: A Biography*. Bloomington, IN: Indiana University Press, 1971.

Clark, J. Michael. "Gay Spirituality." *Spirituality and the Secular Quest*, ed. Peter H. Van Ness. New York: Crossroads/Herder, 1996.

Cohn-Sherbok, Dan. *The Jewish Messiah: The Future of a Delusion*. London: Dr. Williams' Trust, 1999.

Conze, Edward et al. eds., *Buddhist Texts through the Ages*. San Francisco: Harper Torchbooks, 1964.

Coppock, Marjorie. *Wrestling with Angels: The Sexual Revolution Confronts the Church*. Eugene, OR: ACW Press, 2003.

Culpepper, Emily. "The Spiritual, Political Journey of a Feminist Freethinker." *After Patriarchy: Feminist Transformations of the World Religions*, ed. P. Cooey. Maryknoll: Orbis Books, 1991.

Cutler, Winifred B. *Love Cycles: The Science of Intimacy*. New York: Villard Books, 1991.

Dailey, Timothy J. Senior. "Comparing the Lifestyles of Homosexual Couples to Married Couples." *Family Research Council* (4 June 2005).

Das, Surya. *Awakening the Buddha Within: Tibetan Wisdom for the Western World*. New York: Broadway Books, 1997.

Reference List

de la Huerta, Christian. *Coming Out Spiritually: The Next Step.* New York: Tarcher/ Putnam, 1999.

Dunham, Craig. "A Church that's Too Embarrassed to Talk about Sex and Chastity." *By Faith* (July/August 2005).

Duran, Khalid. "Homosexuality and Islam." Swidler, Arlene. ed. *Homosexuality and World Religions.* Valley Forge, PA: Trinity Press International, 1993.

Edwards, James R. "Earthquake in the Mainline." *Christianity Today* (14 Nov 1994).

Eliade, Mircea. "Androgynes." *The Encyclopedia of Religion,* vol. 1, ed. Mircea Eliade. New York: Macmillan, 1987.

———. *Shamanism: Archaic Techniques of Ecstasy.* Princeton, NJ: Princeton University Press, 1972.

———. *The Two and the One.* New York: Harper, 1969.

Epstein, Robert and Christopher Rosik. "Conversion Therapy Revisited: Parameters and Rationale for Ethical Care." *Journal for Pastoral Care* 55 (Spring 2001).

Fee, Gordon D. "The Cultural Context of Ephesians 5:18–6:9." *Priscilla Papers* 16 (2002).

———. *The First Epistle to the Corinthians.* Grand Rapids: Eerdmans, 1987.

Firestone, Shulamith. *The Dialectic of Sex.* New York: Bantam Books, 1972.

Frame, John. "Men and Women in the Image of God." *Recovering Biblical Manhood and Womanhood: A Response to Evangelical Feminism.* Wheaton, IL: Crossway, 1991.

Gaca, Kathy L. *The Making of Fornication: Eros, Ethics and Political Reform in Greek Philosophy and Early Christianity.* Berkeley, CA: University of California Press, 2003.

Gaffin, Richard. *Redemption and Resurrection: A Study in Pauline Soteriology.* Phillipsburg, NJ: P&R, 1987.

Gathorne-Hardy, Jonathan. *Sex, the Measure of All Things: A Life of Alfred C. Kinsey.* Bloomington, IN: Indiana University Press, 2000.

Geering, Lloyd. *The World to Come: From Christian Past to Global Future.* Santa Rosa, CA: Polebridge Press, 1999.

———. *Tomorrow's God: How We Create Our Worlds.* Santa Rosa, CA: Polebridge, 2000.

Giberson, Karl. "The Real Assault on Marriage." *Science and Theology News* (July/Aug 2005).

Gilder, George. "In Defense of Monogamy." *Commentary* 58 (November 1974).

Goldberg, Jonathan. *Reclaiming Sodom.* New York: Routledge, 1994.

Goldenberg, Naomi. *Changing of the Gods: Feminism and the End of Traditional Religions.* Boston: Beacon Press, 1979.

Gombis, Timothy G. "A Radically New Humanity: The Function of the *Haustafel* in Ephesians." *Journal of the Evangelical Theological Society* 48 (June 2005).

Gomes, Peter J. *The Good Life: Truth that Lasts in Times of Need.* San Francisco: HarperSanFrancisco, 2002.

Goodwin, Mark J. *Paul: Apostle of the Living God.* Harrisburg, PA: Trinity Press International, 2001.

Gorbachev, Mikhail. *The Search for a New Beginning: Developing a New Civilization.* San Francisco: HarperSanFranciso, 1995.

Gottschall, Marilyn. "The Ethical Implications of the Deconstruction of Gender." *Journal of the American Academy of Religion* 70 (2002).

Grant, Linda. *Sexing the Millennium: Women and the Sexual Revolution.* London: HarperCollins, 1993.

David Allyn. *Make Love, Not War: The Sexual Revolution: An Unfettered History.* New York: Little, Brown and Co., 2000.

Greider, William. *One World Ready or Not.* New York: Simon and Schuster, 1997.

Grof, Stanislav. *Future of Psychology: Lessons from Modern Consciousness Research.* New York: State University of New York Press, 2000.

Gross, Michael. "When Plagues Don't End." *Journal of the American Public Health Association* 93 (June 2003).

Gunton, Colin E. *The Triune Creator: A Historical and Systematic Study.* Grand Rapids: Eerdmans, 1998.

Guroian, Vigen. "Dorm Brothel: The New Debauchery, and The Colleges that Let it Happen." *Christianity Today* (Feb 2005).

Halifax, Roshi Joan. "Excerpts from Buddhist Peacework: Creating Cultures of Peace." Boston Research Center for the Twenty-First Century: Newsletter 14 (Winter 2000).

Halperin, David M. "Platonic Eros and What Men Call Love." *Ancient Philosophy* 5 (1985).

———. "Plato and Erotic Reciprocity." *Classical Antiquity* 5 (1985).

Hayes, Richard B. "Relations Natural and Unnatural: A Response to John Boswell's Exegesis of Rom. 1." *Journal of Religious Ethics* 14 (Spring 1986).

Heimbach, Daniel R. *True Sexual Morality: Recovering Biblical Standards for a Culture in Crisis.* Wheaton, IL: Crossway, 2004.

Hendershott, Anne. *The Politics of Deviance.* San Francisco: Encounter Books, 2004.

Hewitt, Hugh. "Exiled Voices." *World* (June 2005).

Hinkle, Chris. "More Than a Matter of Conscience: Homosexuality and Religious Freedom." *AAR* (2000).

hooks, bell. *Teaching to Transgress: Education as the Practice of Freedom.* New York: Routledge, 1994.

Horne, Fiona. *Witch: A Magickal Journey: A Guide to Modern Witchcraft.* London: Thorstons, 2000.

Houston, Jean. "An Open Letter to President Bill Clinton." *Tikkun: The Journal of Noetic Sciences* (1997).

———. *The Passion of Isis and Osiris: A Gateway to Transcendent Love.* New York: Ballantine/Wellspring, 1995.

Hove, Richard. *Equality in Christ: Galatians 3:28 and the Gender Dispute.* Wheaton, IL: Crossway, 1999.

Hubbard, Barbara Marx. *Conscious Evolution: Awakening the Power of Our Social Potential.* Novato, CA: New World Library, 1998.

———. *The Book of Co-Creation Part II.* privately published, 1993.

———. *The Revelation: A Message of Hope for the New Millennium.* Novato, CA: Natara Publishing, 1995.

Hunt, Arthur W. *The Vanishing Word: The Veneration of Visual Imagery in the Postmodern World.* Wheaton, IL: Crossway, 2003.

Island, D. and P. Letellier. *Men Who Beat the Men Who Love Them: Battered Gay Men and Domestic Violence.* New York: Haworth Press, 1991.

Johnson, Elizabeth. "Apocalyptic Family Values." *Interpretation* 56 (2002).

Jonas, Hans. *The Gnostic Religion.* Boston: Beacon, 1963.

Jones, David W. "Egalitarianism and Homosexuality: Connected or Autonomous

Ideologies?" *Journal for Biblical Manhood and Womanhood* VII (Fall 2003).

Jones, E. Michael. *Dionysos Rising: The Birth of Cultural Revolution out of the Spirit of Music*. San Francisco: Ignatius Press, 1994.

———. *Libido Dominandi: Sexual Liberation and Political Control*. South Bend, IN: St. Augustine Press, 2000.

———. *Degenerate Moderns: Modernity as Rationalized Sexual Misbehavior*. San Francisco: Ignatius, 1993.

Jones, James H. *Alfred C. Kinsey: A Public/Private Life*. New York: W. W. Norton, 1997.

Jones, Peter. "Androgyny: The Pagan Sexual Ideal." *Journal of the Evangelical Theological Society* 43 (September 2000.

———. "The TNIV: Gender Accurate or Ideologically Egalitarian." *Journal for Biblical Manhood and Womanhood*, ed. Bruce A. Ware (May 2003) TNIV Special Edition. Louisville, KY: Council on Biblical Manhood and Womanhood.

———. *Capturing the Pagan Mind: Paul's Blueprint for Thinking and Living in the New Global Culture*. Nashville: Broadman and Holman, 2003.

———. *Letter to a Homosexual Friend*. Escondido: CA, Main Entry Editions, 2012.

———. *Spirit Wars: Pagan Revival in Christian America*. Mukilteo, WA: Winepress, 1997. reprint Escondido, CA: Main Entry Editions, 2014.

———. *Stolen Identity*. Colorado Springs: Victor, Cook Communications, 2006.

———. *The Gnostic Empire Strikes Back: An Old Heresy for the New Age*. Phillipsburg, NJ: P&R, 1992.

Jones, Rebecca. *Does Christianity Squash Women? A Christian Looks at Womanhood*. Nashville: Broadman and Holman, 2005.

Jung, C. G. *Mysterium Coniunctionis: An Inquiry into the Separation and Synthesis of Psychic Opposites in Alchemy*: Bollingen Series XX: trans. by R. F. C. Hull. Princeton: Princeton University Press, 1970.

Kassian, Mary. *The Feminist Mistake: The Radical Impact of Feminism on Church and Culture*. Wheaton, IL: Crossway, 2005, reprint of *The Feminine Gospel*.

Lampman, Jane . "Churches confront an 'elephant in the pews,'" *Christian Science Monitor* (25 Aug 2005).

Lane, David H. *The Phenomenon of Teilhard: Prophet for a New Age*. Macon, GA: Mercer University Press, 1996.

Reference List

Leo, John. "Media Groupthink: How Gay 'Household' Numbers Are Distorted." *U.S. News & World Report* (23 July 2001).

Leo, John. "Stealth Language at the U.N. is Dangerously Undemocratic." *Jewish World Review* (11 Sept 2001).

Levine, Judith. *Harmful to Minors: The Perils of Protecting Minors from Sex*. Minneapolis: University of Minnesota Press, 2002.

Levine, Michael P. *Pantheism: A Non-theistic Concept of Deity*. New York: Routledge, 1994.

Lewis, C. S. *Miracles*. New York: Macmillan, 1947.

Lie, Gwat Yong and Sabrina Gentlewarrier. "Intimate Violence in Lesbian Relationships: Discussion of Survey Findings and Practice Implications." *Journal of Social Service Research* 15 (1991).

Machen, J. Gresham. *Christianity and Liberalism*. Grand Rapids: Eerdmans, 1923.

———. *The New Testament: An Introduction to its Literature and History*. Edinburgh: Banner of Truth, reprint 1992.

MacLaine, Shirley. *Going Within: A Guide for Inner Transformation*. New York: Bantam Books, 1989.

Magnuson, Roger. *Are Gay Rights Right?* Portland, OR: Multnomah, 1990.

Martin, Dale B. "Asenokoitês and Malakos: Meaning and Consequences." *Biblical Ethics and Homosexuality: Listening to Scripture*, ed. Robert L. Brawley. Louisville, KY: Westminster/John Knox Press, 1996.

Matthews, Caitlin. *Sophia, Goddess of Wisdom: The Definite Feminine from Black Goddess to World-Soul*. London: The Aquarian Press/Harper Collins, 1992.

McCloskey, Deirdre N. "From Donald to Deirdre: How a Man Became a Woman—And What it Says about Identity." *Reason* (Dec 1999).

McKenna, Terence. *Food for the Gods: The Search for the Original Tree of Knowledge*. New York: Bantam, 1992.

Metzger, Deena. "Revamping the World: On the Return of the Holy Prostitute." *Anima* 12/2 (1986).

Milgrom, Jacob. *Leviticus 1–16: The Anchor Bible*. New York: Doubleday, 1991.

Miller, David. *The New Polytheism: Rebirth of the Gods and Goddesses*. New York: Harper & Row, 1974.

Milton, Joyce. *The First Partner: Hillary Rodham Clinton*. New York: William Morrow, 1999.

Mollenkott, Virginia Ramey. *Omnigender: A Trans-Religious Approach*. Cleveland, OH: The Pilgrim Press, 2001.

———. *Sensuous Spirituality: Out from Fundamentalism*. New York: Crossroad, 1992.

Molnar, Thomas. *Utopia: The Perennial Heresy*. New York: University Press of America, 1990.

Moore, Stephen D. "Que(e)rying Paul: Preliminary Questions." *Auguries: The Jubilee Volume of the Sheffield Department of Biblical Studies*, eds. David J. A. Clines and Stephen D. Moore, in *JSOT*, Supplement Series 269. Sheffield: Sheffield Academic Press, 1998.

Moore, Peter C. *Disarming the Secular Gods: How to Talk So Skeptics Will Listen*. Downers Grove, IL: InterVarsity Press, 1989.

Murray, John C. *We Hold these Truths*. New York: Sheed and Ward, 1960.

Nanda, Serena. *Neither Man nor Woman: The Hijras of India*. Belmont, CA: 1990.

Narrett, Eugene. "Proud Ephemerals: Signs of Self Made Men." *Culture Wars* (Dec 1999).

Naudou, Jean. "Sexualité et Ascèse." *Sexualité et Religions*, ed. Marcel Berrnos. Paris: *Editions du Cerf*, 1988.

Nicolosi, Joseph. *Reparative Therapy of Male Homosexuality*. Northvale, NJ: Jason Aronson, Inc., 1991.

Nicolosi, Joseph and Linda Ames Nicolosi, *A Parent's Guide to Preventing Homosexuality*. Downers Grove, IL: InterVarsity Press, 2002.

Nissinen, Martti. *Homoeroticism in the Biblical World: A Historical Perspective*. Minneapolis: Fortress Press, 1998.

Noll, Richard. *The Jung Cult: Origins of a Charismatic Movement*. Princeton: Princeton University Press, 1994.

Northbridge, Mary E. "HIV Returns." *Journal of the American Public Health Association* 93 (June 2003).

O'Connor, Randy P. *Blossom of Bone: Reclaiming the Connections between Homoeroticism and the Sacred*. San Francisco: HarperSanFrancisco, 1994.

O'Donovan, Oliver. *Resurrection and the Moral Order: An Outline for Evangelical Ethics*.

Reference List

Grand Rapids: Eerdmans, 1994.

O'Flaherty, Wendy Doniger. *Women, Androgynes and Other Mythical Beasts.* Chicago: University of Chicago Press, 1980.

Olasky, Marvin. "From Mental Disorder to Civil-Rights Cause." *World* (19 Feb 2005).

Otis, George Jr. *The Twilight of the Labyrinth: Why Does Spiritual Darkness Linger Where it Does?* Grand Rapids: Chosen Books/Baker, 1997.

Penn, Lee. "Dark Apocalypse, Blood Lust of the Compassionate." *SCP Journal* 24:2–24:3 (2000).

———. "United Religions: Globalists and New Age Plans." *SCP Journal* (Nov 1999).

Peterson, Peter G. *The Gray Dawn: How the Coming Age Wave Will Transform America—and the World.* New York: Random House, 1999.

Pickstone, Charles. *The Divinity of Sex: The Search for Ecstasy in a Secular Age.* New York: St. Martin's Press, 1997.

Piper, John. *What's the Difference?: Manhood and Womanhood Defined according to the Bible.* Wheaton, IL: Crossway, 2001.

Piper, John and Justin Taylor, *Sex and the Supremacy of Christ.* Wheaton, IL: Crossway, 2005.

Popenoe, David. *Life Without Father.* New York: The Free Press, 1996.

Ratzinger, Joseph. *The Ratzinger Report.* San Francisco: Ignatius Press, 1985.

Raul, Alan Charles. "How Legalizing Gay Marriage Undermines Society's Morals." *The Christian Science Monitor* (9 Dec 2003).

Reisman, Judith A. *Kinsey: Crimes and Consequences: The Red Queen and the Grand Scheme.* Crestwood, KY: The Institute for Media Education, 1998.

Ringgren, Helmer. *Religions of the Ancient Near East.* trans. by John Sturdy. Philadelphia: Westminster Press, 1973.

Robinson, James, ed. *Gnostic Gospel of Thomas: The Nag Hammadi Library in English.* San Francisco: Harper & Row, 1977.

Rowe-Finkbeiner, Kristin. *The F-Word: Feminism in Jeopardy: Women, Politics and the Future.* Emeryville, CA: Seal Press, 2004.

Rubenstein, William B. "Since When Is Marriage a Path to Liberation?" *Lesbians, Gay Men, and the Law.* New York: The New Press, 1993.

Rudolph, Kurt. *Gnosis: The Nature and History of an Ancient Religion*. Edinburgh: T&T Clark, 1983.

Ruether, Rosemary Radford "Globalization, Christian Ecofeminism and World Religions." in Charles A. Coulombe, "Truth is Divisive." *Mission* 12 (2003).

———. *Integrating Ecofeminism, Globalization and World Religions*. New York: Rowman and Littlefield, 2005.

———. *Women-Church: Theology and Practice*. San Francisco: Harper & Row, 1985.

Satinover, Jeffrey. *Homosexuality and the Politics of Truth*. Grand Rapids: Baker, 1996.

Schaeffer, Francis A. *The God Who Is There* (1968) *Complete Works*, vol. 1. Wheaton, IL: Crossway, 1982.

Schaff, Philip. *America: A Sketch of its Political, Social and Religious Character*, ed. Perry Miller. Cambridge, MA: Belknap Press, 1961.

Schmidt, T. E. *Straight and Narrow? Compassion and Clarity in the Homosexual Debate*. Downers Grove, IL: InterVarsity Press, 1995.

Schucman, Helen. *A Course in Miracles*. New York: Foundation for Inner Peace, 1975.

Sears, Alan and Craig Osten, *The Homosexual Agenda: Exposing the Principal Threat to Religious Freedom Today*. Nashville: Broadman and Holman, 2003.

Shapiro, Ben. *Porn Generation: How Social Liberalism Is Corrupting our Future*. Washington, DC: Regnery Publishing, 2005.

Singer, June. *Androgyny: Towards a New Theory of Sexuality*. London: Routledge and Kegan, 1977.

Sjoo, Monica and Barbara Mor. *The Great Cosmic Mother: Rediscovering the Religion of the Earth*. San Francisco: HarperSanFrancisco, 1987.

Spitzer, Robert L. *Archives of Sexual Behavior* 32 (Oct 2003).

Spong, John Shelby. *Why Christianity Must Change or Die: A Bishop Speaks to Believers in Exile*. San Francisco: Harper, 1999.

Stanton, Glenn T. *Why Marriage Matters: Reasons to Believe in Marriage in a Postmodern Society*. Colorado Springs: Piñon Press, 1997.

Steiner, Andy. "Out Early." *Utne Reader* (Jan/Feb 2001).

Steve Bruce, *God Is Dead: Secularization in the West*. Oxford: Blackwell, 2002.

Stoller, Richard J. *Presentations of Gender*. New Haven: Yale University Press, 1985.

Webb, William. "A Redemptive-Movement Hermeneutic: Encouraging Dialogue among Four Evangelical Views." *Journal of the Evangelical Theological Society* 48 (June 2005).

———. "Balancing Paul's Original-Creation and Pro-Creation Arguments: 1 Corinthians 11:11–12 in the Light of Modern Embryology." *Westminster Theological Journal* 66 (2004).

Westermann, Klaus. *Genesis 1–11: A Commentary*, trans. by J. J. Scullion. Minneapolis: Augsburg Press, 1984.

Whitchurch, Dale W. *Waking from Earth: Seeking Heaven, the Heart's True Home.* Kearny, NE: Morris, 1999.

Whitehead, Barbara Dafoe. *The Divorce Culture.* New York: Alfred A. Knopf, 1997.

Wilson, R. S. *Marcion: A Study of a Second-Century Heretic.* London: 1933.

Winner, Lauren F. *Real Sex: The Naked Truth about Chastity.* Grand Rapids: Brazos Press, 2005.

Wisdom, Alan F. H. "Let Marriage Be Held in Honor." *Theology Matters* 8/2 (March/April 2002).

Wolfe, Alan. *One Nation, After All: How the Middle Class Really Think about God, Country, and Family.* New York: Viking Press, 1998.

Wood, Glenn and John Dietrich. *The AIDS Epidemic.* Portland, OR: Multnomah, 1990.

Wyatt, "Nicholas. The Anat Stela from Ugarit and its Ramifications." *Ugarit Forschungen* 16 (1984).

Yancey, Philip. *Rumors of Another World: What on Earth Are We Missing?* Grand Rapids: Zondervan, 2003.

York, Michael. *Pagan Theology: Paganism as a World Religion.* New York: New York University Press, 2003.

NOTES

₪

INTRODUCTION
GOD AND SEX: AN ODD COUPLE

1. Justin Taylor, "Introduction," *Sex and the Supremacy of Christ*, eds. John Piper and Justin Taylor (Wheaton, IL: Crossway, 2005), 15, represents a welcome, healthy approach.
2. Christian de la Huerta, *Coming Out Spiritually: The Next Step* (New York: Tarcher/Putnam, 1999).
3. Craig Dunham, "A Church That's Too Embarrassed to Talk about Sex and Chastity," *By Faith* (July/August 2005), 21.
4. Ibid, 20.
5. Ed Thomas, "Pro-Homosexual UCC Leaders Are Pushing 'Counterfeit' Christianity," *Agape Press* (14 July 2005).
6. Jill Carattini, "Consuming Christianity," slice@sliceofinfinity.org (26 Aug 2005).
7. Lauren F. Winner, *Real Sex: The Naked Truth about Chastity* (Grand Rapids: Brazos Press, 2005), 30.
8. Jeffrey Satinover, *Homosexuality and the Politics of Truth* (Grand Rapids: Baker, 1996), 17.

PROLOGUE
THE BEGINNING OF THE STORY

1. Ernest Sanders, *Times Advocate* (16 July 1995).
2. Rom. 3:23.
3. Satinover, *Homosexuality*, 227.

CHAPTER 1
OUT WITH THE OLD: MAKE LOVE, NOT WAR

1. P. F. Sloan, "Eve of Destruction," recorded by Barry McGuire on *Eve of Destruction*, MCA, 1965.
2. For two excellent studies of this subject by E. Michael Jones, see

Degenerate Moderns: Modernity as Rationalized Sexual Misbehavior (San Francisco: Ignatius, 1993), and *Libido Dominandi: Sexual Liberation and Political Control* (South Bend, IN: St. Augustine Press, 2000).

3. Caleb Crain, "Alfred Kinsey: Liberator or Pervert?" *American Family Online* (3 Oct 2004).

4. See James H. Jones, *Alfred C. Kinsey: A Public/Private Life* (New York: W. W. Norton, 1997), and Jonathan Gathorne-Hardy, *Sex, the Measure of All Things: A Life of Alfred C. Kinsey* (Bloomington, IN: Indiana University Press, 2000). See also E. Michael Jones's review of James H. Jones, *Alfred C. Kinsey*, in *Culture War* 17/2 (1998) for an understanding of the importance of sexuality and the importance of Kinsey for the 1960s.

5. Crain, art. cit.

6. Cited in Crain, art. cit.

7. Jones, *Degenerate Moderns*, 104.

8. Ibid., 105.

9. He certainly saw no problem in pedophilia and bestiality—see Judith A. Reisman, *Kinsey: Crimes and Consequences: The Red Queen and the Grand Scheme* (Crestwood, KY: The Institute for Media Education, 1998), 226, 245–46.

10. Robert Peters, *Christian Wire Service* (8 Nov 2004), see mim@morality-inmedia.org.

11. Kinsey, cited by Cornelia Christenson in *Kinsey: A Biography* (Bloomington, IN: Indiana University Press, 1971), 9. See also Jones, *Degenerate Moderns*, 99.

12. See the remarkable research by Judith A. Reisman, *Kinsey: Crimes and Consequences*.

13. James E. Jones, "Annals of Sexology: Dr. Yes," *New Yorker* (1 Sept 1997), 113.

14. See the previously mentioned books by E. Michael Jones. See also Marjorie Coppock, *Wrestling with Angels: The Sexual Revolution Confronts the Church* (Eugene, OR: ACW Press, 2003); TFP Committee on American Issues, *Defending a Higher Law: Why We Must Resist Same-Sex Marriage and the Homosexual Movement* (Spring Grove, PA: TFP, 2004); Alan Sears and Craig Osten, *The Homosexual Agenda: Exposing the Principal Threat to Religious Freedom Today* (Nashville: Broadman and Holman, 2003); Patrick J. Buchanan, *The Death of the West: How Dying Populations and Immigrant Invasions Imperil Country and Civilization* (New York: Thomas Dunne Books/St. Martin's Press, 2002); Linda Grant, *Sexing the Millennium: Women and the Sexual Revolution* (London: HarperCollins, 1993); David Allyn, *Make Love, Not War: The Sexual Revolution: An*

Unfettered History (New York: Little, Brown and Co., 2000).

15. *60 Minutes*, "Porn in the USA," CBS (5 Sept 2004).

16. Peter Cheney, "Net Nightmare," *Australian Presbyterian* (March 2001): 6.

17. See the Web site, books.nap.edu.

18. Greg Taylor, "XXXMinistry," ChristianityToday.com (16 Aug 2005).

19. Ibid., 7.

20. NYTimes.com (11 Sept 2001).

21. *U.S. News & World Report* (27 May 2002).

22. USAToday.com (10 July 2001).

23. I take the term from Vigen Guroian, "Dorm Brothel: The New Debauchery, and The Colleges that Let it Happen," *Christianity Today* (Feb 2005), 46.

24. See Guroian, "Dorm Brothel."

25. Jamie Gadette, "Porn and Prejudice," *Salt Lake City Weekly* (17 March 2005).

26. Eric Rich, *Courant* (8 May 1999).

27. Ibid.

28. Ibid.

29. "Prostitutes Mean Business," *Netscape Highlights/Reuters* (6 Aug 2001).

30. "Femininity Betrayed: A Global Attack," *Life Issues* (13 Sept 2003).

31. Ben Shapiro, *Porn Generation: How Social Liberalism Is Corrupting our Future* (Washington, DC: Regnery Publishing, 2005).

32. "Abortion rate rises, leading to new calls for better sex education," Scotsman.com (25 May 2005).

33. "News and Issues," About.com.

34. Julia Duin, "Former Abortion Providers Provide Peace, Solace in Therapy," *Washington Times Weekly Edition* (26 Feb 2001).

35. J. Budziszewski, "Human Life, Natural Law, and Pastoral Care," *Theology Matters*, 7/1 (Jan/Feb 2001): 3–4.

36. *World* (5 May 2001), 12.

37. Cited in Joyce Milton, *The First Partner: Hillary Rodham Clinton* (New York: William Morrow, 1999), 59.

38. Professor Popenoe, professor of sociology at Rutgers University in *Life Without Father* (New York: The Free Press, 1996), 135.

39. Ibid.

40. Gerard Reed, *Reedings* 97 (Jan 2000), 3.

41. John Haskins, "Joining the Gay Movement Provides Fisting..." www.mass-news.com (27 March 2001). I am indebted to this article for the details that follow.

42. Warren Throckmorton, "GLSEN Distributes Gay Pornography to Youth at Massachusetts High School," *Education Reporter* (30 April 2005).

43. Ibid.
44. http://womensstudies.berkeley.edu/.
45. http://www.trincoll.edu/pub/academics/departments/gay_les_studies. html.
46. Philip Johnston, Home Affairs Editor, *Electronic Telegraph* (11 Feb 2000).
47. The Alliance for Marriage is seeking a constitutional amendment that defines marriage as between one man and one woman.
48. Chris Nutter, "How Gay Men Are Remodeling Regular Guys Post-Straight," *Village Voice* (8 Aug 2001). See also *Will and Grace*, NBC.
49. See the well-documented book by Sears and Osten, *The Homosexual Agenda*.
50. Ibid., 157–158.
51. See Joseph Cardinal Ratzinger, *The Ratzinger Report* (San Francisco: Ignatius Press, 1985), which is dated but amazingly prophetic.
52. Charles Colson, "Prom King Thinks She's a He," *Breakpoint* (17 May 2001).
53. Andy Steiner, "Out Early," *Utne Reader* (Jan/Feb 2001):17.
54. Deirdre N. McCloskey, "From Donald to Deirdre: How a Man Became a Woman—And What it Says about Identity," *Reason* (Dec 1999): 45.
55. "Schoolboy wins right to dress in drag," BBCWorldNews.com (16 Oct 2000).
56. BBCWorldNews.com (12 April 2000).
57. June Singer, *Androgyny: Towards a New Theory of Sexuality* (London: Routledge and Kegan, 1977), 267.
58. *The Humanist* (1983), the journal of the American Humanist Association.
59. Mikhail Gorbachev, *The Search for a New Beginning: Developing a New Civilization* (San Francisco: HarperSanFranciso, 1995), cited on the *State of the World Forum* Web page, www.worldforum.org.

CHAPTER 2
OUT WITH THE OLD: THE DEATH OF GOD

1. Steve Bruce, *God Is Dead: Secularization in the West* (Oxford: Blackwell, 2002).
2. Naomi Goldenberg, *Changing of the Gods: Feminism and the End of Traditional Religions* (Boston: Beacon Press, 1979), 41.
3. bell hooks, *Teaching to Transgress: Education as the Practice of Freedom* (New York: Routledge, 1994). The author spells her name without capitals in order to transgress the rules of grammar.
4. See Deena Metzger, "Revamping the World: On the Return of the Holy

244

Prostitute," *Anima* 12/2 (1986), cited in George Otis Jr., *The Twilight of the Labyrinth: Why Does Spiritual Darkness Linger Where it Does?* (Grand Rapids: Chosen Books/Baker, 1997), 107.

5.   James R. Edwards, "Earthquake in the Mainline," *Christianity Today* (14 Nov 1994), 39.

6.   Held at San Francisco's Episcopalian Grace Cathedral. Berit Kjos, "An Unholy Renaissance of Sacred Sexuality," *Southern California Christian Times* (July 1994), 9.

7.   Geraldine Coughlan, "Dutch Launch Sex Workers' First Union," *BBC World News* (2 Oct 2001).

8.   Julia Duin, "Morality matters to middle class; tolerance more so; Few use the language of absolutes," *Washington Times* (10 March 1998).

9.   Alan Wolfe, *One Nation, After All: How the Middle Class Really Think About God, Country, and Family* (New York: Viking Press, 1998), 27.

10. Tammy Bruce, *The Death of Right and Wrong: Exposing the Left's Assault on Our Culture and Values* (Roseville, CA: Forum/Prima Publishing, 2003), 162.

11. Ibid., 46.

12. Ibid., 57.

13. Ibid., 73.

14. Anne D. Neal, Jerry Martin, and Mashad Moses, *Losing America's Memory: Historical Illiteracy in the 21st Century* (Washington, DC: American Council of Trustees and Alumni, 2000), 2, cited in Bruce, *Death*, 176.

15. Ellen Sorokin, "University to Replace Western Civilization Classes," *Washington Times* (19 April 2002).

16. David Miller, *The New Polytheism: Rebirth of the Gods and Goddesses* (New York: Harper & Row, 1974), vii-x.

17. Ibid., vii. Such a declaration of independence brought us to the Clinton impeachment trial where the clash of worldviews was verbalized by commentator Margot Adler of National Public Radio. Guests on her program noted Congressman Henry Hyde's appeal to "the universal standard of truth," whereas the President's counsel, Sherry Mills, spoke of about ten versions of the truth.

18. *Ankh* means "life" in ancient Egyptian.

19. Jean Houston, *The Passion of Isis and Osiris: A Gateway to Transcendent Love* (New York: Ballantine/Wellspring, 1995), 7.

20. Ibid,, 28.

21. Jean Houston, "An Open Letter to President Bill Clinton," *Tikkun: The Journal of Noetic Sciences* (1997).

22. See also, "First Lady's 'Adviser' Says She's Not a Psychic," *Providence*

Journal Bulletin (25 June 1996), A3.

23. See David H. Lane, *The Phenomenon of Teilhard: Prophet for a New Age* (Macon, GA: Mercer University Press, 1996), 136–137.

24. Emily Culpepper, "The Spiritual, Political Journey of a Feminist Freethinker," *After Patriarchy: Feminist Transformations of the World Religions*, ed. P. Cooey (Maryknoll: Orbis Books, 1991), 164, citing Judy Grahn.

25. Internet Movie Database, "Memorable Quotes from Star Wars (1977)," http://www.imdb.com/title/tt0076759/quotes.

26. Surya Das, *Awakening the Buddha Within: Tibetan Wisdom for the Western World* (New York: Broadway Books, 1997), 16.

27. Ibid., 370.

28. Ibid.

29. The famous Buddhist phrase *Om Mani Padme Hung* expresses the essence of Mayana Buddhism.

30. Das, *Awakening the Buddha Within*, 377.

31. George Barna, *The Index of Leading Spiritual Indicators* (Word, 1996), cited in Jeremiah Greedon, "God With a Million Faces," *Utne Reader* (July/Aug 1998), 42–49.

32. Philip Schaff, *America: A Sketch of its Political, Social and Religious Character*, ed. Perry Miller (Cambridge, MA: Belknap Press, 1961), cited in Catherine L. Albanese, "Religion and the American Experience a Century After," *Church History* 57 (Sept 1988), 337.

33. See Donna Steichen, *Ungodly Rage: The Hidden Face of Catholic Feminism* (San Francisco: Ignatius Press, 1991), 32.

34. See Rosemary Radford Ruether, *Women-Church: Theology and Practice* (San Francisco: Harper & Row, 1985), 104.

35. Sister Dorothy Ollinger, S.S.N.D., quoted in Steichen, *Ungodly Rage*, 60.

36. Matt. 6:7, 24 (*mammon* here means "earthly things"). See also Rom. 1:25. See Michael P. Levine, *Pantheism: A Non-theistic Concept of Deity* (New York: Routledge, 1994).

37. See Peter Jones, *Spirit Wars: Pagan Revival in Christian America* (Mukilteo, WA: Winepress, 1997), 252–253.

38. See Jean Houston's Web site, www.jeanhouston.org. See also Steichen's *Ungodly Rage*, 251: "At Our Lady of the Angels Convent in Wheaton, Sister Gabriele has presented 'enlightenment' classes to 'explore' Jewish, Buddhist, Islamic, Indian, and Wiccan 'traditions' and rituals and to introduce the I Ching, a Chinese fortune-telling system. Sister Gabriele explained her quintessentially New Age motives: 'We no longer have the luxury of a leisurely religious search. We are in the process of unfolding a

new human identity, and in the balance hangs our ability to successfully navigate our initiation as planetary people. The convergence is upon us as surely as the evolution of the species.'"

39. For a brilliant analysis and critique of utopian thinking, see Thomas Molnar, *Utopia: The Perennial Heresy* (New York: University Press of America, 1990).

40. See G. McLeod Bryan, *Voices in the Wilderness: Twentieth-Century Prophets Speak to the New Millennium* (Macon, GA: Mercer University Press, 1999), 42. Smith commanded one of the largest and most enthusiastic audiences of the teachers of religion at the American Academy of Religion held in Nashville, November 2000.

41. The Sophia Summer Institute at Holy Names College, Oakland, California, in 2001 discussed the theme, "Birth of the Planetary Human," tracing the "outlines of a worldwide transformation of the human spirit." Speakers included Sally McFague, professor at Vanderbilt Divinity School, and Brian Swimme, a scientist and deep ecologist, author of *The Universe Is a Green Dragon*. Information taken from the program brochure.

42. Alvin and Heidi Toffler, *War and Anti-war: Survival at the Dawn of the 21ˢᵗ Century* (New York: Little, Brown and Co., 1993), 242.

43. William Greider, *One World Ready or Not* (New York: Simon and Schuster, 1997), 468. See also Scott Gillette, "A Glorious New Century? The Coming Age of Prosperity," *Ether Zone* (14 Aug 2001).

44. John Shelby Spong, *Why Christianity Must Change or Die: A Bishop Speaks to Believers in Exile* (San Francisco: Harper, 1999), xviii.

45. Lloyd Geering, *The World to Come: From Christian Past to Global Future* (Santa Rosa, CA: Polebridge Press, 1999), and *Tomorrow's God: How We Create Our Worlds* (Santa Rosa, CA: Polebridge, 2000).

46. Geering, *Tomorrow's God*, 130.

47. Geering, *The World to Come*, 107.

48. Geering, *Tomorrow's God*, 159.

49. C. S. Lewis, *Miracles* (New York: Macmillan, 1947), 82–83.

50. Geering, *The World to Come*, 157.

51. Ibid., 158.

52. Ibid., 157.

53. Rom. 1:25.

54. Geering, *The World to Come*, 161.

55. Ibid., 154: "All religious traditions will contribute...and those that can respond most flexibly...to the current challenges are likely to offer the most."

56. Ibid., 160.

57. Shulamith Firestone, *The Dialectic of Sex* (New York: Bantam Books,

1972), 12.

58. Joseph Nicolosi and Linda Ames Nicolosi, *A Parent's Guide to Preventing Homosexuality* (Downers Grove, IL: InterVarsity Press, 2002), 22.

CHAPTER 3
IN WITH THE NEW: THE COMING SEXUAL UTOPIA

1. Juggie Naran, "More Younger Children Are Having Sex," www.IOL.co.za (10 July 2005).
2. "Lust declared virtue, not vice," BBC (1 Jan 2004). Lust has been wrongly branded a vice and should be "reclaimed for humanity" as a life-affirming virtue, according to a top philosopher, Professor Simon Blackburn of Cambridge University. His campaign is part of an Oxford University Press project on the modern relevance of the seven deadly sins.
3. Spong, *Why Christianity Must Change*, 159.
4. Charles Pickstone, *The Divinity of Sex: The Search for Ecstasy in a Secular Age* (New York: St. Martin's Press, 1997), reviewed by John Attarian in *Culture Wars* (March 1998), 46ff. Pickstone is retracing the steps of Ezra Pound, who left the theism of Presbyterianism to seek spiritual freedom in Paris in the 1920s. He believed that sex, creativity, and mysticism were part of the spiritual quest, that "one comes to the divine through the senses," and so engaged in a life of debauchery in order to test his theory, but his "quest" ended in failure. See E. Fuller Torrey, *The Roots of Treason: Ezra Pound, and the Secret of St. Elizabeth's* (New York: McGraw Hill, 1984), 115, cited in Peter C. Moore, *Disarming the Secular Gods: How to Talk So Skeptics Will Listen* (Downers Grove, IL: InterVarsity Press, 1989), 45.
5. Neale Donald Walsch, *Conversations with God: An Uncommon Dialog,* Book 3 (Charlottesville, VA: Hampton Roads Publishing, 1998), 56. I am indebted to Lee Penn (see reference below) for introducing me to the writings of Walsch and Barbara Marx Hubbard.
6. Singer, *Androgyny*.
7. Ibid., 18.
8. Ibid., vii.
9. Ibid., 20, 22.
10. Ibid., 275.
11. This is exactly the point made by Fr. John C. Murray, *We Hold these Truths* (New York: Sheed and Ward, 1960), 208, who notes how utopians will use the democratic process for their own ends in a way not intended by the Founders: "All issues of human life—intellectual, religious, moral—are...

to be settled by the single omni-competent political technique of majority vote." If things are to be moved along this way, the pagan agenda must get hold of the organs of mass communication so as to determine the way people vote. This has happened.

12. Singer, *Androgyny*, 254.

13. See Daniel R. Heimbach, *True Sexual Morality: Recovering Biblical Standards for a Culture in Crisis* (Wheaton, IL: Crossway, 2004).

14. Ralph Waldo Emerson, *Self-Reliance* (1847), cited in Eugene Narrett, "Proud Ephemerals: Signs of Self Made Men," *Culture Wars* (Dec 1999), 4.

15. The quotations are from Saraha's *Treasury of Songs* in Edward Conze et al., eds., *Buddhist Texts through the Ages* (San Francisco: Harper Torchbooks, 1964), 24, 48, 64, 74.

16. Walsch, *Conversations with God*, Book 2, 167.

17. Ibid., Book 3, 146.

18. Ibid., Book 2, 79.

19. Helen Schucman, *A Course in Miracles* (New York: Foundation for Inner Peace, 1975), 47, 262.

20. Lee Penn, "United Religions: Globalists and New Age Plans," *SCP Journal* (Nov 1999): 45.

21. Metzger, "Revamping the World."

22. Terry Collins, "Boys face felony charges in videotaped sex case," *Minneapolis Star Tribune* (3 April 2001). The lecture was titled, "Defending Pornography: Free Speech, Sex, and the Fight for Women's Rights" and took place in Minneapolis on 3 April 2001.

23. Kevin Peraino, "Playboy Goes XXX," *Newsweek* (16 July 2001), 36.

24. Jon Ward, "Gay bishop backs Planned Parenthood," *Washington Times* (16 April 2005).

25. Ibid.

26. Ibid.

27. Ibid.

28. 1 Cor. 6:9. There are many who believe like Robinson. Planned Parenthood's clergy network currently has 1,400 pastors and clergy.

29. Bruce, *Death*, 7, 11.

30. Ibid., 27.

31. Cited in Shapiro, *Porn Generation*, 50.

32. Wolfe, *One Nation*, produces a stunning analysis of the death of moral relativism in America.

33. Ellen Goodman, *North County Times* (26 Jan 1999). This is moral limbo, but there is implicit disapproval—of those who dare to disapprove. There is only disapproval of disapproval and intolerance for those who

Reference List

Swidler, Arlene. ed., *Homosexuality and World Religions*. Valley Forge, PA: Trinity Press International, 1993.

Taylor, Justin. "Introduction." *Sex and the Supremacy of Christ*, eds. John Piper and Justin Taylor. Wheaton, IL: Crossway, 2005.

Taylor, Mark C. *Erring: A Postmodern A/Theology*. Chicago: University of Chicago Press, 1984.

TFP Committee on American Issues, *Defending a Higher Law: Why We Must Resist Same-Sex Marriage and the Homosexual Movement*. Spring Grove, PA: TFP, 2004.

Thomm, Nick. "Multi-Gendered Restrooms at UM." *CREDO: News for Catholic and Other Christians* (11 Feb 2002).

Thornton, Bruce S. *Eros: The Myth of Ancient Greek Sexuality*. Boulder, CO: Westview Press, 1997.

Throckmorton, Warren. "GLSEN Distributes Gay Pornography to Youth at Massachusetts High School." *Education Reporter* (30 April 2005).

Toffler, Alvin and Heidi. *War and Anti-war: Survival at the Dawn of the 21st Century*. New York: Little, Brown and Co., 1993.

Tooley, Mark. "Some Gays Say Multiple Partners Can Be Holy." *The Layman* (September 2003).

Turcan, Robert. *The Cults of The Roman Empire*, trans. by Antonia Neville. Oxford: Blackwell, 1996.

Van Til, Cornelius. *Christian Apologetics*, ed. William Edgar. Phillipsburg, NJ: 1976, 2003.

Vitagliano, Ed. "New Video Introduces Kids to Same-Sex Couples." *Theology Matters* 8/2 (March/April 2002).

von Hildebrand, Alice. *The Soul of a Lion: Dietrich von Hildebrand*. San Francisco: Ignatius Press, 2000.

Waller, Roy and Linda A. Nicolosi. "Homosexuality a Choice: Evidence Found for Effectiveness of Reorientation Therapy." *Narth* (Oct 2003).

Walls, Neal H. *The Goddess Anat in Ugaritic Myth*: SBL Dissertation Series 135. Atlanta: Scholars Press, 1992.

Walsch, Neale Donald. *Conversations with God: An Uncommon Dialog*, Book 3. Charlottesville, VA: Hampton Roads Publishing, 1998.

are intolerant.

34. Another example comes from CyberNOT, a censuring device that screens out offensive material on the Internet. Before 1995, censorship extended to sites run by gay activists. After the gays protested, the blocking of gay sites was lifted, and a member of GLAAD (Gays and Lesbian Alliance Against Defamation) was added to CyberNOT's board. Soon after, Don Wildmon's American Family Association, a Christian organization opposed to the homosexual agenda, was added to CyberNOT's list of censured sites. Again the disapprovers are formally disapproved. On this, see John Leo, "See No Evil, Surf No Evil," *US News & World Report* (1 Feb 1999), 18.

35. "Ethics, Enron and American Higher Education: A NAS/Zogby Poll of College Seniors," *National Association of Scholars* (July 2002).

36. Bruce, *Death*, 170.

37. Edith H. Jones, "American Legal System is Corrupt Beyond Recognition," MassNews.com (28 Feb 2004).

38. An interview with Walsch, cited in Lee Penn, "Dark Apocalypse, Blood Lust of the Compassionate," *SCP Journal* 24:2–24:3 (2000): 29.

39. Ibid.

40. Walsch, *Conversations with God*, Book 2, 105.

41. Ibid., 127.

42. Barbara Marx Hubbard, *The Revelation: A Message of Hope for the New Millennium* (Novato, CA: Natara Publishing, 1995), 166.

43. Jessie Bernard, *The Future of Marriage* (New York: World Publishing, 1972), 51.

44. Geering, *The World to Come*, 86.

45. Walsch, *Conversations with God*, Book 2, 97; and Book 3, 210.

46. Barbara Marx Hubbard, *Conscious Evolution: Awakening the Power of Our Social Potential* (Novato, CA: New World Library, 1998), 208.

47. Cited in Arthur W. Hunt, *The Vanishing Word: The Veneration of Visual Imagery in the Postmodern World* (Wheaton, IL: Crossway, 2003), 236.

48. Cited by Ed Vitagliano, "New Video Introduces Kids to Same-Sex Couples," *Theology Matters* 8/2 (March/April 2002): 6.

49. Alan F. H. Wisdom, "Let Marriage Be Held in Honor," *Theology Matters* 8/2 (March/April 2002). A wedding ceremony proposed by the gay Rev. Juan Oliver, canon missioner of the Episcopal Diocese of New Jersey (where John Spong was the presiding bishop), avoids traditional notions of commitment. It omits "until death do us part" and "forsaking all others." There is no mention of children or the role of parents.

50. Ibid., 4. See the statements of Rev. Marilyn McCord of Yale Divinity

School, defining the Trinity as "the Gay Men's Chorus" and suggesting it as an example the church should follow in "blessing" three or more persons engaged in a committed relationship.

51. Walsch, *Conversations with God*, Book 3, 35–36.
52. Lee Penn, "Dark Apocalypse," 12.
53. Barbara Marx Hubbard, *The Book of Co-Creation Part II* (privately published, 1993), 60, cited in Lee Penn, "Dark Apocalypse," 12.
54. "Androgyny," single from album "beautifulgarbage" (2 Oct 2001).
55. Cited in Satinover, *Homosexuality*, 121.
56. Satinover, ibid., 61. He cites as an example the San Francisco magazine *Anything that Moves*.
57. Virginia Ramey Mollenkott, *Omnigender: A Trans-Religious Approach* (Cleveland, OH: The Pilgrim Press, 2001), 41, 74.
58. One set is always defective, which means one is not truly both a male and a female, but this condition is a very rare, biological abnormality.
59. Mollenkott, ibid., 69, proposes this as a useful temporary strategy for young people unsure of their sexuality.
60. Ibid., 70.
61. Absent from this list is "polyamory," the love of more than one person at a time, which challenges the normative notion of monagomy.
62. Rev. Louis P. Sheldon, "Senate Panel Debates Need to Protect Traditional Marriage," TraditionalValues.org (9 Sept 2003). Sheldon gives a number of examples: "Mitchel Raphael, the editor of a Canadian homosexual magazine called *Fab*...noted: 'I'd be for marriage if I thought gay people would challenge and change the institution and not buy into the traditional meaning of "till death do us part" and monogamy forever'...Paula Ettelbrick says: 'Being queer means pushing the parameters of sex and family, and in the process transforming the very fabric of society.' Homosexual activist Michelangelo Signorile, writing in *Out!* magazine (Dec/Feb 1994) said that homosexuals should work for gay marriage as a way of subverting the entire institution of marriage. He says the most 'subversive action lesbian and gay men can undertake—and one that would perhaps benefit all of society—is to transform the notion of family entirely.'"
63. Ibid., 61.
64. Ibid., 79.
65. Ibid., 167.
66. Ibid.
67. The Student Union of the University of Michigan offers the choice of "multi-gendered restrooms" with numerous stalls and sinks for those with kinky lifestyles. See Nick Thomm, "Multi-Gendered Restrooms at

UM," *CREDO: News for Catholic and Other Christians* (11 Feb 2002). Kelly Garrett, coordinator of programs and student development in the Lesbian, Gay, Bisexual, and Transgendered Affairs Office, says, "People who don't fit into gender norms come to the Union specifically to use this bathroom. Our goal is to have a safe bathroom in every building on campus."

68. Mollenkott cites the bathrooms on the marine troop ship, USS *San Antonio*, which already has no urinals.

69. Mark Bergin, "Gender Blender," *World* (18 June 2005), 37.

70. Cited in Shapiro, *Porn Generation*, 38.

71. Ibid., 38. There is proof that Mollenkott is not a lone voice. In 2003 students at Smith College, an all-female school in Massachusetts, voted to remove all feminine pronouns from the school constitution and replace them with gender-neutral ones. The editing of the constitution is part of an effort to make transgender students feel more welcome on the campus. In the same year, Wesleyan University in Connecticut offered a "Gender Blind" dormitory floor for incoming students who aren't sure what sex they are. Students who ask for the floor will have roommates appointed without regard to their sex, perceived or otherwise. The rooms are set aside for transgender students, described as those students born with ambiguous genitalia or who don't identify with their physical sex.

72. Ibid., 169.

73. Ibid., 61.

74. Ibid., 80. Nicolosi and Nicolosi, *A Parent's Guide*, 16–17, on the contrary, argue that "normal" is "that which functions according to its design... [and] we are all designed to be heterosexual." Nicolosi (ibid., 99), a clinical psychiatrist, identifies what lies behind this call for omnigender and the end of normality. "Because gender is remembered as a source of pain in childhood, the annihilation of gender differences is, not surprisingly, a central demand of the gay culture."

75. Ibid., 81.

76. See the Web site *Article 8 Alliance*.

77. Kristin Rowe-Finkbeiner, *The F-Word: Feminism in Jeopardy: Women, Politics and the Future* (Emeryville, CA: Seal Press, 2004), 102.

78. Ibid., 82.

79. Ibid., 185. See also her *Sensuous Spirituality: Out from Fundamentalism* (New York: Crossroad, 1992).

80. In note 85, the deep cause is human pain, but I take the deepest level to be the religious and the theological.

81. This restriction is hardly an immense obstacle. Some time ago the British Parliament lowered the age of consent for homosexual sex in England

to sixteen.

82. Mollenkott, *Omnigender*, 70–71, fn. 66.
83. Judith Levine, *Harmful to Minors: The Perils of Protecting Minors from Sex* (Minneapolis: University of Minnesota Press, 2002).
84. "Familiar" is the technical term used to describe a "spirit-possessed" animal.
85. Fiona Horne, *Witch: A Magickal Journey: A Guide to Modern Witchcraft* (London: Thorstons, 2000), 77.
86. Ibid., 84.
87. Terence McKenna, *Food for the Gods: The Search for the Original Tree of Knowledge* (New York: Bantam, 1992), 40–41.
88. Otis, *The Twilight Labyrinth*, 175, citing a Paviotso shaman.
89. Mircea Eliade, *Shamanism: Archaic Techniques of Ecstasy* (Princeton, NJ: Princeton University Press, 1972), 328–29.
90. Stanley Kurtz, "Beyond Gay Marriage," *Weekly Standard* (8 April 2003), Web site version.
91. Ibid.
92. Ibid.
93. Ibid. Geri D. Weitzman, "What Psychological Professionals Should Know about Polyamory," www.Polyamory.org. Based on a paper presented at the 8th Annual Diversity Conference (12 March 1999), Albany, NY.
94. Mark Tooley, "Some Gays Say Multiple Partners Can Be Holy," *The Layman* (Sept 2003), 20.
95. Ibid.
96. Ibid.
97. The connection is not limited to this expression of pagan religion. In the Old Testament the worship of Baal was associated with sexual excess—see Num. 23, 25, 31; Deut. 4:3; Josh. 22:17; Ps. 106:28; 1 Cor. 10:7–8.
98. This was true for Tatian and Clement. See Kathy L. Gaca, *The Making of Fornication: Eros, Ethics and Political Reform in Greek Philosophy and Early Christianity* (Berkeley, CA: University of California Press, 2003), 223ff.
99. See Peter Jones, *Capturing the Pagan Mind* (Nashville: Broadman and Holman, 2003).
100. Nancy Sorkin Rabinowitz, "The Male Actor of Greek Tragedy: Evidence of Misogyny or Gender-Bending?" Hamilton College, Clinton, New York, E-mail: nrabinow@itsmail.hamilton.edu.
101. Gaca, *The Making of Fornication*, 77.
102. Ibid., 80.
103. Ibid., 81.

104. Ibid., 80.
105. See his treatise *Symposium*, where he finds lesbianism, homosexuality, and heterosexuality normal. He believes the myth that there were originally three kinds of people, a man, a woman, and an androgynous being. Zeus divided all three in half so that the two parts of the man looked for each other (explaining homosexuality) just as did the two parts of the woman (explaining lesbianism). The androgynous being explains for him the origin of heterosexuality. On Plato's views of sexuality, see David M. Halperin, "Plato and Erotic Reciprocity," *Classical Antiquity* 5 (1985): 60–80; also Halperin, "Platonic Eros and What Men Call Love," *Ancient Philosophy* 5 (1985): 161–204.
106. Horne, *Witch*, 332–34, reveals how witchcraft and lesbianism can be closely identified. She describes the celebration of the Goddess where forty skyclad (naked) women "weave in and out of each others' arms, kissing one another," chanting, "Virgin, needing no other! Virgin complete in herself...virgin but not celibate."

CHAPTER 4
HOMOSEXUALITY: THE SEXUAL SACRAMENT
OF RELIGIOUS PAGANISM

1. John Leo, "Media Groupthink: How Gay 'Household' Numbers Are Distorted," *U.S. News & World Report* (23 July 2001).
2. See Nicolosi, *A Parent's Guide*.
3. Marvin Olasky, "From Mental Disorder to Civil-Rights Cause," *World* (19 Feb 2005). In Plato's *Laws* 636c male-to-male sex is described as *para phusin*, the same term Paul uses. See Simon Goldhill, *Foucault's Virginity*, 51, 53. It seems that while Plato found homosexuality "unnatural," he promoted it.
4. A. Dean Byrd, PhD, Shirley E. Cox, PhD, and Jeffrey W. Robinson, PhD, "The Innate-Immutable Argument Finds No Basis in Science: In Their Own Words: Gay Activists Speak about Science, Morality, Philosophy," *Salt Lake City Tribune* (27 May 2001).
5. Art. cit.
6. See Satinover, *Homosexuality*, 31–37. Two years later the American Psychological Association followed suit.
7. Nicolosi, *A Parent's Guide*, 14. "A furious egalitarianism...compelled psychiatric experts to negotiate the pathological status of homosexuality with homosexuals themselves." See also *Psychology Today* (Jan./Feb.

2003), ed. Robert Epstein, PhD; Christopher Rosik, PhD, "Conversion Therapy Revisited: Parameters and Rationale for Ethical Care," *Journal for Pastoral Care*, 55 (Spring 2001): 47–67; Roy Waller and Linda A. Nicolosi, "Homosexuality a Choice: Evidence Found for Effectiveness of Reorientation Therapy," *Narth* (Oct 2003); and Dr. Robert L. Spitzer, *Archives of Sexual Behavior*, 32 (Oct 2003): 403–17. Spitzer challenges the assumption that homosexual orientation is an "intrinsic part of a person's identity that can never be changed."

8. In August 2003 Lawrence v. Texas was struck down. See also the decision in favor of Romer v. Evans in 1996.

9. Linda Harvey, "What Homosexual 'Marriage' Will Mean to America's Children," *Choice for Truth* (Sept 2003): 1–2.

10. Note the popularity of such shows as *Queer Eye for the Straight Guy*.

11. Hugh Hewitt, "Exiled Voices," *World* (June 2005), 9.

12. Nicholas A. Jackson, "The Ex-Gay Gene?" *Mission America* (5 July 2005).

13. Robert Spencer, "Cartoon Rage vs. Freedom of Speech," FrontPageMagazine.com, 2 February 2006.

14. "Canadians Legalize Same-Sex Marriage," *Los Angeles Times* (21 July 2005), A8.

15. Karl Giberson, "The Real Assault on Marriage," *Science and Theology News* (July/Aug 2005): 6.

16. De la Huerta, *Coming Out Spiritually*, 7.

17. After legalization of gay marriage in Massachusetts, a large billboard ad for a gay Web site featured two naked men wrapped in an American flag.

18. De la Huerta, *Coming Out Spiritually*, 11.

19. Even ancient Greece did not legalize gay marriage. Marriage was for procreation and the maintenance of the city state.

20. Paula Ettelbrick, quoted in William B. Rubenstein, "Since When Is Marriage a Path to Liberation?" *Lesbians, Gay Men, and the Law* (New York: The New Press, 1993), 398, 400.

21. T. E. Schmidt, *Straight and Narrow? Compassion and Clarity in the Homosexual Debate* (Downers Grove, IL: InterVarsity Press, 1995), 1.

22. Chris Hinkle, "More Than a Matter of Conscience: Homosexuality and Religious Freedom," *AAR* (2000): 112.

23. Some conservatives within the mainline churches oppose the general trend. See Dr. Robert Sanders, *Virtueonline: The Voice for Global Orthodox Anglicanism*, for a reasoned, theological opposition.

24. "Homosexuality is Divinely Ordered, says Anglican Catechism," *Religion Today* (14 June 2001).

25. Edward Walsh, "Presbyterian Board Alters Gay Policy," *Washington Post*

(16 June 2001), A01.

26. Minutes of the 199th General Assembly (1987), United Presbyterian USA, 776, cited in David W. Jones, "Egalitarianism and Homosexuality: Connected or Autonomous Ideologies?" *Journal for Biblical Manhood and Womanhood* VII (Fall 2003): 7.

27. See Alan Charles Raul, "How Legalizing Gay Marriage Undermines Society's Morals," *The Christian Science Monitor* (9 Dec 2003).

28. See the *Religion Today* article, "Homosexuality is Divinely Ordered...": "Homosexual Christian believers should be encouraged to find in their sexual preferences such elements of moral beauty as may enhance their general understanding of Christ's calling." See also Walsh, art. cit.: "Removing the ban" against homosexuals in the ordained ministry, says the liberal John Buchanan, a former General Assembly moderator of the Presbyterian, "creates space to live and work together."

29. Peter J. Gomes, *The Good Life: Truth that Lasts in Times of Need* (San Francisco: HarperSanFrancisco, 2002), 308. Gomes cites the witness of Richard Halloway, bishop of Edinburgh, who seeing other Anglican Christians opposing homosexuality before a group of university students by citing Bible verses, made the previous judgment and added, "I am fairly certain that [these students'] encounter with Christianity that day scandalized them."

30. Ibid., 310–11.

31. Swiss voters approved the same inheritance and tax rights for homosexual couples as for married heterosexual couples. See "Swiss vote to ease border control," BBC (5 June 2005). Great Britain followed, though the head of state is also defender of the (Christian) faith, and Christian bishops sit in the House of Lords.

32. See Satinover, *Homosexuality*; Nicolosi and Nicolosi, *A Parent's Guide*; Sears and Osten, *The Homosexual Agenda*. Satinover, *Homosexuality*, 103, argues that if homosexuality were genetically determined, its presence in the population would tend to diminish. See also 109–17.

33. Cited in Otis, *The Twilight Labyrinth*, 180.

34. Ibid.

35. Nicolosi, *A Parent's Guide*, 100.

36. Christian de la Huerta, "Articles of Faith: In the Spirit of Pride," www.thetaskforce.org (16 June 2005).

37. Ibid.

38. Ibid.

39. Ibid.

40. Cited in Robert Turcan, *The Cults of The Roman Empire*, trans. by Antonia

Neville (Oxford: Blackwell, 1996), 58.

41. De la Huerta, *Coming Out Spiritually*, 34.
42. Frederic Baue, *The Spiritual Society: What Lurks beyond the Postmodern* (Wheaton, IL: Crossway, 2001), 16.
43. Shirley MacLaine, *Going Within: A Guide for Inner Transformation* (New York: Bantam Books, 1989), 197.
44. Monica Sjoo and Barbara Mor, *The Great Cosmic Mother: Rediscovering the Religion of the Earth* (San Francisco: HarperSanFrancisco, 1987), 67–68.
45. Culpepper, "Feminist Freethinker," 164.
46. Mollenkott, *Sensuous Spirituality*, 42, 166.
47. Ibid., 19, 24.
48. A form of Chinese divination—see ibid., 16.
49. *The (London) Daily Record*, 11 December 1999.
50. Cited in Steichen, *Ungodly Rage*, 302.
51. Henry Makow, "The Vagina Monologues and the Clash of Civilizations," *Toogood Reports* (24 Oct 2001).
52. "A Report," *Good News* (Jan 1994), 2. Judy Westerdorf, a United Methodist clergywoman, made this statement to the two thousand mainline Christian women at the pagan-"Christian" feminist RE-Imagining Conference in Minneapolis in 1993. For a scholarly and sympathetic evaluation of modern witchcraft, see Helen A. Berger, *A Community of Witches: Contemporary New-Paganism and Witchcraft in the United States* (Columbia, SC: University of South Carolina Press, 1999).
53. Much of this information is also to be found in Peter Jones, "Androgyny: The Pagan Sexual Ideal," *Journal of the Evangelical Theological Society* 43 (September 2000): 443–69.
54. Michael York, *Pagan Theology: Paganism as a World Religion* (New York: New York University Press, 2003), 42. York refers to the work of Eliade, *Shamanism*.
55. See *passim*, Eliade, *Shamanism*. This evaluation is echoed by De la Huerta, *Coming Out Spiritually*, 31, states, "Throughout many epochs and widespread across different cultures, homoerotically inclined and gender-variant individuals have directly fulfilled spiritual functions, assuming the role of shamans, healers, seers, diviners, spiritual teachers, priests, priestesses, and sacred prostitutes." For additional examples, see 31–43.
56. York, *Pagan Theology*, 42.
57. Besides the seminal work of Eliade, see the more recent work of Arlene Swidler, ed., *Homosexuality and World Religions* (Valley Forge, PA: Trinity Press International, 1993).
58. I am indebted to Martti Nissinen, *Homoeroticism in the Biblical World:*

A Historical Perspective (Minneapolis: Fortress Press, 1998), 28. See also Helmer Ringgren, *Religions of the Ancient Near East*, trans. by John Sturdy (Philadelphia: Westminster Press, 1973), 25, who speaks of naked "eunuchs" associated with the cult to the Sumerian goddess Inanna (Istar).

59. Nissinen, *Homoeroticism*, 30.

60. Ibid., 32.

61. Neal H. Walls, *The Goddess Anat in Ugaritic Myth*: SBL Dissertation Series 135 (Atlanta: Scholars Press, 1992), 83.

62. Ibid., 107. On Cybele, see below.

63. Ibid., 86.

64. See Nicholas Wyatt, "The Anat Stela from Ugarit and its Ramifications," *Ugarit Forschungen* 16 (1984): 331.

65. Augustine, *City of God*, vii: 26.

66. Eliade, *Shamanism*, 125. See also Nissinen, *Homoeroticism*, 34.

67. Ibid., 352.

68. See Serena Nanda, *Neither Man nor Woman: The Hijras of India* (Belmont, CA: 1990), xv. Cited in Nissinen, ibid. According to Tal Brooke, *Avatar of Night* (Berkeley, CA: End Run Publishing, 1999), 331, Sai Baba, a leading Hindu guru and Goddess-worshipper (see 193, 200), with whom he was closely associated before his Christian conversion, was androgynous and practiced homosexuality with a number of his disciples.

69. Mircea Eliade, *The Two and the One* (New York: Harper, 1969), 118.

70. Ibid.

71. Das, *Awakening the Buddha Within*, 140; cf. 384. Das notes that in the past, Buddhism "looked askance at...homosexual sex. Yet most contemporary dharma teachers feel [such] behavior...within bounds and karmically workable" (209).

72. Mollenkott, *Omnigender*, 155.

73. Web site, Southeast Alaska Gay and Lesbian Alliance, http://www.ptialaska.net/~seagla/perspective/Testimonies.htm. See Walter Williams, *The Spirit and the Flesh: Sexual Diversity in American Indian Culture* (Boston: Beacon Press, 1986).

74. In 1576 the European explorer Pedro de Magalhaes de Gandavo noted the presence of transgendered warriors among the Tupinamba Indians; Roman Catholic missionary Father Marquette described the Illinois *berdache* in 1673. See Robert M. Baum, "The Traditional Religions of the Americas and Africa," in Swidler, *Homosexuality and World Religions*, 14–15.

75. Baum, art. cit., provides a systematic discussion and a useful specialized bibliography.

76. Mircea Eliade, "Androgynes," *The Encyclopedia of Religion*, vol. 1, ed. Mircea Eliade (New York: Macmillan, 1987), 277.

77. Ibid.

78. See Wendy Doniger O'Flaherty, *Women, Androgynes and Other Mythical Beasts* (Chicago: University of Chicago Press, 1980), 285–89. See also Baum, "Traditional Religions," 19–32. Baum looked at fifty African societies.

79. Baum, art. cit., 21.

80. See Randy P. O'Connor, *Blossom of Bone: Reclaiming the Connections between Homoeroticism and the Sacred* (San Francisco: HarperSanFrancisco, 1994).

81. Baum, art. cit., 15. See also Edward Carpenter, "On the Connection between Homosexuality and Divination, and the Importance of the Intermediate Sexes Generally in Early Civilizations," *Revue d'ethnographie et de sociologie* 11 (1910): 310–16, and *Intermediate Types among Primitive Folk: A Study in Social Evolution (London, 1919)* (Manchester, New Hampshire: Ayer Co. Pub., 1975); Williams, *The Spirit and the Flesh*.

82. C. G. Jung, *Mysterium Coniunctionis: An Inquiry into the Separation and Synthesis of Psychic Opposites in Alchemy*: Bollingen Series XX: trans. by R. F. C. Hull (Princeton: Princeton University Press, 1970), 244–45, identifies this same phenomenon though not directly associated with sexuality.

83. Francis A. Schaeffer, *The God Who Is There* (1968) *Complete Works*, vol. 1 (Wheaton, IL: Crossway, 1982), 37.

84. Richard Noll, *The Jung Cult: Origins of a Charismatic Movement* (Princeton: Princeton University Press, 1994), 41–42, 269–73.

85. Satinover, *Homosexuality*, 46–47, notes how Jung saw the spiritual aspect of homosexuality.

86. O'Flaherty, *Women, Androgynes*, 294.

87. The Christian attempt to "love the sinner and hate the sin" (as Augustine put it) is often rebuffed. Pagan spirituality demands that one *love* one's sin and embrace one's antinomies in a mystical experience of oneness.

88. George Lucas recognized Campbell, a frequent guest at the Skywalker Ranch, as a spiritual mentor.

89. In a 1980s PBS series. Taxpayer money promoted a deeply religious, anti-Christian apology for pagan spirituality.

90. Joseph Campbell and Bill Moyers, *The Power of Myth* (New York: Doubleday, 1988), 57.

91. Ibid.

92. Eliade, *Shamanism*, 352. Baptist minister and presidential counselor the Rev. Tony Campolo makes a remarkable pronouncement: "Not only do I

love the feminine in Jesus, but the more I know Jesus, the more I realize that Jesus loves the feminine in me.... Society has brought me up to suppress the so-called feminine dimension of my humanness. But when Jesus makes me whole, both sides of who I am meant to be will be finally realized. Then and only then will I be fully able to love Jesus." Tony Campolo, *Carpe Diem: Seize the Day* (Dallas: Word, 1994), 87–88.

93.   Margo Anand, *The Path of Sacred Sexuality for Western Lovers* (New York: Tarcher/Putnam, 1989), 4.

94.   Nicolosi, *A Parent's Guide*, 99, cites a gay cross-dresser who says, "Being involved in cross-dressing is a way of laying claim to all the possible archetypes of the universe.... In the divide between men and women, I like being on the fence, able to sense and experience both sides and to implicitly point out that the divisions are artificial."

95.   The term *soft (malakoj)* is the Greek word used for "homosexual" in 1 Cor. 6:9—see Dale B. Martin, "Asenokoitês and Malakos: Meaning and Consequences," in *Biblical Ethics and Homosexuality: Listening to Scripture*, ed. Robert L. Brawley (Louisville, KY: Westminster/John Knox Press, 1996): 117–36.

96.   Eliade, *The Two and the One*, 112, mentions homosexual practice in ritual androgynous initiation.

97.   Plato in the *Symposium*, 192E, has one of his speech-makers, Aristophanes, say, "The desire for all is to be one, not two...not to be divided by night or by day...formerly...we were one; but now, for our sins, we are all dispersed."

98.   Ibid., 154.

99.   J. Michael Clark, "Gay Spirituality," *Spirituality and the Secular Quest*, ed. Peter H. Van Ness (New York: Crossroads/Herder, 1996), 337.

100.   Ibid., 338.

101.   A radical "Christian" feminist honestly stated, "No woman can serve two authorities, a master called Scripture and a mistress called feminism." Cited without reference in Mary Kassian, *The Feminist Mistake: The Radical Impact of Feminism on Church and Culture* (Wheaton, IL: Crossway, 2005, reprint of *The Feminine Gospel*), 278.

102.   Clark, "Gay Spirituality," 342.

103.   Ibid. This is similar to the Navajo *nadle*, known as the "reconciler."

104.   Islam disavows homosexuality, but its monist variant, Sufism, is growing in popularity in the West. A progay Muslim makes this interesting observation: "Religious gays in the realm of Islam...would have to take recourse in the antinomian Sufism [mysticism...in which] all that counts is union with the divine through mystic exaltation. On that level it becomes immaterial whether a believer is hetero- or homosexual"—see Khalid

Duran, "Homosexuality and Islam," in Swidler, *Homosexuality and World Religions*, 196.

105. De la Huerta, *Coming Out Spiritually*, 39.
106. Ibid.
107. Christians will protest: God is in control, and paganism cannot win. Every knee *will* bow to the name of Jesus Christ, but the Bible does not guarantee that any one country will remain faithful, nor does it promise that we will not undergo suffering and oppression at the hands of pagan powers.
108. See the report of Rosemary Radford Ruether's lecture "Globalization, Christian Ecofeminism and World Religions," in Charles A. Coulombe, "Truth is Divisive," *Mission* 12 (2003): 10.
109. This song was played at the ceremonies marking the new millennium, presided over by then President Clinton—no heaven, no hell, no religions, just oneness.
110. Eliade, "Androgynes," 279.
111. Jonathan Goldberg, *Reclaiming Sodom* (New York: Routledge, 1994). See also Stephen D. Moore, "Que(e)rying Paul: Preliminary Questions," *Auguries: The Jubilee Volume of the Sheffield Department of Biblical Studies*, eds. David J. A. Clines and Stephen D. Moore, in *JSOT*, Supplement Series 269 (Sheffield: Sheffield Academic Press, 1998): 253.
112. Geering, *The World to Come*, 105.
113. Allan Dobras, "Prescription for Tolerance: Is Moral Judgment a Mental Disorder?" See *MissionAmerica* (2 Feb 2006). See also "Psychiatry Ponders Whether Extreme Bias Can Be an Illness," *Washington Post* (10 December 2005).

CHAPTER 5
UNINTENDED DESTRUCTIVE CONSEQUENCE

1. The State of the World Forum, the brainchild of Mikhail Gorbachev, reflects a similar utopian thinking. In a panel on "Cosmology, Culture and Social Change," a new "integral culture" was proposed where "all roles and relationships will be redefined" along the paradigm of the "integration of masculine and feminine archetypes"—see "1997 State of the World Forum: Cosmology, Culture and Change—Final Report," Internet document, www.worldforum.org/1997/forum/Cosmologyandculture.html., 2.
2. Mollenkott, *Omnigender*, 174.
3. Ibid., 162.
4. See Anne Hendershott, professor of sociology at the University of San

261

Diego, *The Politics of Deviance* (San Francisco: Encounter Books, 2004).

5. Mollenkott, *Omnigender*, 80.

6. Ibid., 185, citing Proverbs 29:18 KJV.

7. Mark C. Taylor, *Erring: A Postmodern A/Theology* (Chicago: University of Chicago Press, 1984), 158–59.

8. Ibid., 157–58.

9. See David Cave, *Mircea Eliade's Vision for a New Humanism* (New York: Oxford, 1993), 3.

10. Eliade, *The Two and the One*, 123, n. 1.

11. Taylor, *Erring*, 158–59.

12. Philip Yancey, *Rumors of Another World: What on Earth Are We Missing?* (Grand Rapids: Zondervan, 2003), 77.

13. Cited by John R. Diggs, Jr., MD, in "The Health Risks of Gay Sex," for the Corporate Resource Council, dfacr.org.

14. Shapiro, *Porn Generation*.

15. Ibid., 7, 45.

16. Rick Fitzgibbons, "Medical Downside of Homosexual Behavior: A Political Agenda is Trumping Science." Zenith.org, (18 Sept 2003).

17. Diggs, art.cit.

18. See the Web site http://www.virtualcity.com/youthsuicide/, whose goal is to show the homophobic cause of gay suicide.

19. J. Michael Bailey, "Homosexuality and Mental Illness," *Archives of General Psychiatry*, 56 (1999): 883–84.

20. D. Island and P. Letellier, *Men Who Beat the Men Who Love Them: Battered Gay Men and Domestic Violence* (New York: Haworth Press, 1991), 14.

21. In a survey of 1,099 lesbians, the *Journal of Social Service Research* found that slightly more than half of the lesbians reported that they had been abused by a female lover-partner. Gwat Yong Lie and Sabrina Gentlewarrier, "Intimate Violence in Lesbian Relationships: Discussion of Survey Findings and Practice Implications," *Journal of Social Service Research* 15 (1991): 46.

22. Bailey, art. cit., 884.

23. See the well-documented article by Dr. Timothy J. Dailey, Senior Research Fellow at the Center for Marriage and Family Studies of Family Research Council, "Comparing the Lifestyles of Homosexual Couples to Married Couples," *Family Research Council* (1 June 2005).

24. Cited in Diggs, art. cit.

25. An interview with Walsch, cited in Lee Penn, "Dark Apocalypse, Blood Lust of the Compassionate," *SCP Journal* 24:2–24:3 (2000): 29.

26. Diggs, art. cit.

27. Ibid.
28. "Survey Finds 40 Percent of Gay Men Have Had More Than 40 Sex Partners," *Lambda Report*, January 1998, 20. See also Roger Magnuson, *Are Gay Rights Right?* (Portland, OR: Multnomah, 1990), 43, citing "The AIDS Epidemic," *Newsweek* (18 April 1983), 74–79 and Glenn Wood and John Dietrich, *The AIDS Epidemic* (Portland, OR: Multnomah, 1990), cited in Ron Gleason, *What Homosexuals Do*, an unpublished manuscript kindly shared by the author.
29. Diggs, art. cit.
30. Ibid.
31. Ibid.
32. Bruce, *Death*, 97.
33. Diggs, art. cit.
34. *Journal of the American Public Health Association*, 93 (June 2003).
35. See the article by A. Dean Byrd, president of NARTH (National Association of Research and Therapy of Homosexuals), "Journal of the American Public Health Highlights Risks of Homosexual Practices," www.narth.com.
36. Mary E. Northbridge, "HIV Returns," Editor's Choice section, *Journal of the American Public Health Association*, 93 (June 2003): 860.
37. Michael Gross, "When Plagues Don't End," *Journal of the American Public Health Association*, 93 (June 2003): 861–62.
38. Ibid., 872–81.
39. Fitzgibbons, "Medical Downside."
40. Charles Colson, *Breakpoint* (7 June 2005).
41. Barbara Dafoe Whitehead, *The Divorce Culture* (New York: Alfred A. Knopf, 1997).
42. Cited in Glenn T. Stanton, *Why Marriage Matters: Reasons to Believe in Marriage in a Postmodern Society* (Colorado Springs: Piñon Press, 1997), 20.
43. Ibid., 24.
44. Sarah Lyall, "Europeans Opting Not to Marry," *New York Times* (24 March 2002).
45. Matt Magio, "Jesse Jackson Endorses Illegitimacy!" *Almanac Independent*, January 2001.
46. *Good News, Etc.* (July 2001), 8.
47. Bruce, *Death*, 204, citing a professor at the University of Missouri-Kansas City.
48. See "Casual Attitude Towards Adult-Teen Sex by GLSEN," www.agape-press.org (May 2005).

49. Bruce, *Death*, 195.
50. Janet Shamlian, "Parents alarmed that books are more 'Sex in the City' than 'Nancy Drew,'" *NBC News* (15 Aug 2005).
51. Alan and Osten, *The Homosexual Agenda*, 67.
52. Cited in Beverly Eakman, "Telling Kids They Might Be Gay," NewsWithViews.com (29 July 2004).
53. Ibid.
54. John Leo, "Stealth Language at the U.N. is Dangerously Undemocratic," *Jewish World Review* (11 Sept 2001).
55. Eakman, art. cit.
56. Hendershott, *The Politics of Deviance*. This comment is from an interview with Hendershott in "Standard deviance—redefinition of bad behavior as 'normal' (thanks to 'progressive' liberals)," *World Magazine* (6 June 2005).
57. Donna Rice Hughes, *Kids Online: Protecting Your Children in Cyberspace* (New York: Revell, 1998), cited on Protectkids.com.
58. This title is no longer in print, but the original material is available in the title *Spirit Wars: Pagan Revival in Christian America* (reprint Escondido, CA: Main Entry Editions, 2014).
59. Jane Lampman, "Churches confront an 'elephant in the pews,'" *Christian Science Monitor* (25 Aug 2005).
60. From a mailing from Traditional Values Coalition, P.O. Box 97088, Washington, DC 20090-7088.
61. See Kevin McCullough, "The secret lives of Christian school boys," WorldNetDaily.com (May 2005).
62. Psychologist David de Vaus of Melbourne's La Trobe University, "Study Finds Married Men Live Longer," www.health.discovery.com/news/afp/20020930/feminists.html. See also well-respected psychologist Winifred B. Cutler, PhD, *Love Cycles: The Science of Intimacy* (New York: Villard Books, 1991), and George Gilder, "In Defense of Monogamy," *Commentary*, 58 (Nov 1974): 22–39.
63. See E. Michael Jones, *Dionysos Rising: The Birth of Cultural Revolution out of the Spirit of Music* (San Francisco: Ignatius Press, 1994).
64. Apparently 46 million unborn babies are aborted worldwide every year.
65. Peter G. Peterson, *The Gray Dawn: How the Coming Age Wave Will Transform America—and the World* (New York: Random House, 1999).
66. Michelle Roberts, "Infertility Time Bomb Warning," *BBC News* (22 June 2005).
67. Peterson, *Gray Dawn*, 28.
68. Ibid., 42.
69. Ibid., 47.

70. Ibid., 12–14.
71. Ibid., 77.
72. Ibid., 111.
73. Ibid., 202.
74. Ibid., 207, 217–20.
75. Ibid., 187.
76. Rom. 1:25.
77. It is true that not all pagan societies have shown an automatic tendency to embrace sexual liberation. Things are doubtless more complicated. The creational "image of God" restrains cultures from going all the way. Societies are inconsistent. Rosemary Radford Ruether is shocked at the "poignant contradictions" she finds in the Hindu culture where images of the goddess are more prevalent than in any other culture, and yet she finds also a strict subordination of women—see Rosemary Radford Ruether, *Integrating Ecofeminism, Globalization and World Religions* (New York: Rowman and Littlefield, 2005), 49. There is, however, a ruthless consistency in certain forms of ancient paganism—see the ancient mystery religions or many forms of tribal animism (see the previous chapter)—that now reappears in the programmatic agenda of neopaganism.
78. Rom. 1:25.
79. Yancey, *Rumors of Another World*, 88.
80. 2 Cor. 5:20; 1 Tim. 4:4. See Jones, *Capturing the Pagan Mind*.
81. Rom. 1:25.
82. See Peter Jones, *Stolen Identity* (Colorado Springs: Victor, Cook Communications, 2006).

CHAPTER 6
GOD AND SEX

1. "Church doesn't think like Jesus: Survey shows only 9 percent of Christians have biblical worldview," WorldNetDaily.com (3 Dec 2003).
2. Schaeffer, *The God Who Is There.*
3. Campbell and Moyers, *The Power of Myth*, 58.
4. Lewis, *Miracles*, 85, says, "The pantheist is led to state that either everything is God or that nothing is God, but in neither case is he unable to give any precise meaning to his concept."
5. Roshi Joan Halifax, "Excerpts from Buddhist Peacework: Creating Cultures of Peace," Boston Research Center for the Twenty-First Century: Newsletter 14 (Winter 2000): 10–11.

6. Apparently a snake sheds its skin once every two or three months.
7. Campbell and Moyers, *The Power of Myth*, 55.
8. Ibid., 53. See Jones, *Spirit Wars*, 126–30, on the various pagan uses of the serpent symbol.
9. Gen. 3:1–5.
10. Lewis, *Miracles*, 90–91.
11. Isa. 29:16; cf. Rom. 9:20–21.
12. Ibid., 87.
13. 2 Chron. 23:6.
14. Ex. 28:4: "They are to make these sacred garments for your brother Aaron and his sons, so they may serve me as priests."
15. Isa. 66:1; cf. Matt. 5:35; Acts 7:49.
16. Isa. 57:15 ESV.
17. Matt. 6:9.
18. Ex. 20:7.
19. Ps. 89:7.
20. Isa. 6:1–3.
21. Isa. 6:5.
22. Isa. 33:14.
23. Ex. 20:3–5 NKJV.
24. Rom. 1:25.
25. Prov. 9:10.
26. 1 Kings 18:39.
27. Isa. 46:5; cf. 40:18.
28. Ps. 86:8.
29. Ps. 89:6.
30. Ex. 20:4–5.
31. Deut. 6:4. Many Jewish homes still say this in Hebrew: Sh'ma Yis-ra-eil, A-do-nai E-lo-hei-nu, A-do-nai E-chad.
32. Deut. 5:2; Josh. 3:10; 2 Kings 19:4, 16; Ps. 42:2; 84:2. See also in Jewish literature, Philo, *Decalogue* 67; 2 Maccabees 15:4; Sybilline Oracles 3:763. In the New Testament, the phrase occurs in Acts 14:15; 2 Cor. 3:3; 6:16; and 1 Thess. 1:9–10.
33. For a fascinating study of the previous texts, see Mark J. Goodwin, *Paul: Apostle of the Living God* (Harrisburg, PA: Trinity Press International, 2001).
34. 1 Thess. 1:9–10.
35. Geering, *Tomorrow's God*, 189.
36. He used the synonym "naturalism."
37. J. Gresham Machen, *Christianity and Liberalism* (Grand Rapids:

Eerdmans, 1923), 62–63.

38. Even New Age, occultic astral travel does not come close to divine omnipresence.

39. Ps. 50:21.

40. Isa. 55:8.

41. Ps. 96:9.

42. 1 Cor. 8:6; cf. Eph. 4:6: "One God and Father of all, who is over all and through all and in all."

43. Deut. 32:6.

44. Mal. 2:10. According to Rudolf Bultmann, *Theology of the New Testament* (New York: Charles Scribner's Sons, 1955), 69, God is described as essentially the Creator, often in expressions of the Old Testament or Judaism. See extensive references to what Bultmann calls "the Hellenistic church aside from Paul," 69–70, but which include many references to Paul and to the early church fathers.

45. Cited in Uwe Siemon-Netto, "Poll Shows Protestant Collapse," *UPI* (28 June 2001).

46. Singer, *Androgyny*, 61.

47. See Jean Naudou, "Sexualité et Ascèse," *Sexualité et Religions*, ed. Marcel Berrnos (Paris: *Editions du Cerf,* 1988), 32.

48. John 1:1–3.

49. Colin E. Gunton, *The Triune Creator: A Historical and Systematic Study* (Grand Rapids: Eerdmans, 1998), 9.

50. Ibid., 10.

51. J. Gresham Machen, *The New Testament: An Introduction to Its Literature and History* (Edinburgh: Banner of Truth, reprint 1992), 319.

52. Rev. 3:20; cf. Matt. 7:7.

53. Isa. 40:25–26.

54. Geering, *Tomorrow's God*, 50.

55. Gen. 1:1.

56. Rom. 1:19–20.

57. Gunton, *Triune Creator,* 3.

58. Ibid., 7.

59. Klaus Westermann, *Genesis 1–11: A Commentary*, trans. by J. J. Scullion (Minneapolis: Augsburg Press, 1984), 127.

60. Geering, *Tomorrow's God*, 62.

61. Dan Cohn-Sherbok, *The Jewish Messiah: The Future of a Delusion* (London: Dr. Williams' Trust, 1999), 16, citing Mordecai Kaplan, the founder of Reconstructionist Judaism.

62. Ibid., 15.

63. Gunton, *Triune Creator*, 9.

64. Ibid., Paul in Rom. 4:17.

65. Spong, *Why Christianity Must Change*, 21—see Larry Witham, "What Path for Christianity? Three Theologians, Three Views," *Washington Times* (29 Feb 2000).

66. On Gnosticism, see Hans Jonas, *The Gnostic Religion* (Boston: Beacon, 1963); Kurt Rudolph, *Gnosis: The Nature and History of an Ancient Religion* (Edinburgh: T&T Clark, 1983); Jones, *Spirit Wars*, chapters 5, 7, 9, 11, 13, and 15.

67. On Marcion, see R. S. Wilson, *Marcion: A Study of a Second-Century Heretic* (London: 1933).

CHAPTER 7
THE BIRTH OF SEX

1. Gen. 2:20.

2. Spong, *Why Christianity Must Change*, 90.

3. Song 4:3–4.

4. Prov. 5:18–20.

5. Song 5:1 CEV.

6. Eph. 5:22–33.

7. 1 Cor. 7:1–5.

8. See Rebecca Jones, *Does Christianity Squash Women? A Christian Looks at Womanhood* (Nashville: Broadman and Holman, 2005). See also Piper and Taylor, *Sex and Supremacy* (see chap. 1, n. 1).

9. Bruce S. Thornton, *Eros: The Myth of Ancient Greek Sexuality* (Boulder, CO: Westview Press, 1997), 69.

10. Gen. 3:20.

11. See Prov. 31.

12. For the various references to the Greek writers and their comments, see Thornton, *Eros*, 69–73.

13. Prov. 31:25–26.

14. Prov. 31:10 NJB.

15. Rom. 1:20.

16. Isa. 6:3

17. Lev. 11:45; cf. 1 Pet. 1:16.

18. Gen. 1:2: "The earth was formless and empty."

19. Gen. 1:4 ESV.

20. Gen. 1:6, 14.

21. Gen. 1:21. See also Prov. 8:27 which describes creation, and in the Greek text uses the verb *separate*.

22. Gen. 1:24.
23. Gen. 1:25. The term is used many times later on to distinguish between "clean" and "unclean," see Lev. 11:22 and 29.
24. Gen. 1:5, 8, 10; Isa. 40:26.
25. Gen. 2:19, with the same verb.
26. Gen. 1:26.
27. Ps. 8:1, 5–6.
28. Num. 8:14.
29. 2 Chron. 23:6.
30. See Jacob Milgrom, *Leviticus 1–16: The Anchor Bible* (New York: Doubleday, 1991), 689: "Creation...was the product of God making distinctions (Gen. 1:4, 6, 7, 14, 18). This divine function is to be continued by Israel: the priests to teach it (Lev. 10:10–11) and the people to practice it (Ezek. 22:26)."
31. Lev. 23:2, 21.
32. Gen. 17:1–2.
33. Gen. 2:15–17.
34. Gen. 2:18 ESV.
35. Ex. 19:6.
36. Isa. 66:19: "They will proclaim my glory among the nations." See also Gen. 12:3; 18:18; Deut. 2:25; Ps. 98:2; Lev. 26:45; cf. Isa. 52:10.
37. Lev. 20:26; cf. 20:24.
38. Lev. 10:10. See also Isa. 35:8.
39. *Kosher*, now often applied to particular Jewish food preparation, means "that which is fitting or proper," or "something properly done"—see Kasher, *Encyclopedia Judaica*, vol. 10 (Jerusalem: Keter Publishing House, 1972), 806.
40. Lev. 11:47; Deut. 14:21.
41. Lev. 19:19.
42. Ibid.
43. Ibid.
44. Ezek. 48:9. See also Ex. 29:24, 27; 36:37; Lev. 10:15; 14:12; Num. 15:19; Ezek. 44:29.
45. Ex. 20:8–11.
46. Lev. 20:7–8, 23–25.
47. John 1:1–3 ESV; cf. Rev. 22:13.
48. Heb. 1:3.
49. 1 Cor. 8:5–6 ESV.
50. Col. 1:17 ESV.
51. See the treatment of the effects of modern feminism on the culture by

Kassian, *The Feminist Mistake*, 51–59.

52. 1 Cor. 15:38.

53. Lev. 15:2.

54. 1 Thess. 4:7.

55. 1 Cor. 6:13. On the importance of the body, see Lauren Winner, *Real Sex*, 32–34 (see chap. 1, n. 7).

56. Rom. 6:19.

57. 1 Thess. 4:4.

58. 2 Tim. 2:21.

59. Mark 7:6; John 5:23.

60. 1 Tim. 1:17; 6:16; Rev. 5:13.

61. 1 Cor. 6:20.

62. 2 Cor. 4:10.

63. Phil. 1:20.

64. 1 Cor. 6:19.

65. Gen. 1:27.

66. Molnar, *Utopia*, 63. See also 123: In the pagan utopia, according to Molnar, "everything is equal with everything else." He cites G. K. Chesterton's description of the views of theosophist Annie Besant: "According to Mrs. Besant the universal church is simply the universal church itself. It is the doctrine that we are really all one person; that there are no real walls of individuality between man and man. If I may put it so, she does not tell us to love our neighbor; she tells us to be our neighbors.... The intellectual abyss between Buddhism and Christianity is that, for the Buddhist or theosophist, personality is the fall of man, for the Christian it is the purpose of God, the whole point of his cosmic idea"—from G. K. Chesterton, *Orthodoxy* (New York: Mead and Company, 1927), 244–45.

67. Eph. 4:15.

68. Rom. 12:1.

69. 1 Thess. 5:23.

70. Gen. 1:27.

71. Gen. 2:23.

72. Gen. 2:23.

73. Gen. 2:20 NJB.

74. Marianne Szededy-Maszak, "A Distinct Science," *Los Angeles Times* (9 May 2005), special women's health section.

75. Gen. 3:20.

76. 1 Tim. 2:15.

77. See for example, *Dialogue of the Savior* 144:15–21, in Robinison, *Nag Hammadi Library*, 237.

78. See on this general subject Peter Jones, *The Gnostic Empire Strikes Back: An Old Heresy for the New Age* (Phillipsburg, NJ: P&R, 1992), and Jones, *Spirit Wars*.
79. Firestone, *Dialectic of Sex*, 81.
80. Gen. 1:27.
81. Gen. 5:2.
82. Gen. 6:19.
83. Lev. 27:5.
84. Matt. 19:4.
85. Richard Hove, *Equality in Christ: Galatians 3:28 and the Gender Dispute* (Wheaton, IL: Crossway, 1999), 83.
86. Ibid.
87. 1 Cor. 15:38–39.
88. Molnar, *Utopia*, 63.
89. Acts 17:24–27.
90. Spong, *Why Christianity Must Change*, 140, 147.
91. Tillich, when asked shortly before he died, whether he prayed, replied, "No, but I meditate." See Schaeffer, *The God Who Is There*, 79. Spong identifies Tillich as his spiritual father—see *Why Christianity Must Change*, 174.
92. Isa. 54:5.
93. Hos. 2:16. See also Jer. 3:14; 3:20; 31:32; Ezek. 16:32; Hos. 2:2.
94. 2 Cor. 11:2.
95. Rev. 21:2.
96. Jer. 3:20.
97. Jer. 3:1. See also Isa. 57:3; Deut. 20:18; 23:18; 32:16; 2 Kings 9:22; Isa. 1:21; Jer. 2:20; 3:9; 13:27; 19:13; Ezek. 6:9; 16:25; 16:36–37.
98. Gen. 2:24.
99. Matt. 19:5–6 ESV; cf. Mark 10:8 ESV, a parallel passage.
100. 1 Cor. 6:16; Eph. 5:31 ESV.
101. Ex. 24:3.
102. 2 Chron. 30:12 ESV.
103. Ezek. 37:22.
104. Gal. 3:28.
105. Eph. 2:14, 15, 16 and 18, using either "two" or "both."
106. Gen. 1:28.
107. Eph. 2:15.
108. Eph. 3:10.
109. 1 Cor. 3:8.
110. Gen. 2:23–24 ESV.
111. Eph. 5:30.

112. Eph. 2:15.
113. Eph. 5:31.
114. While the marital union is the biblical norm, other relationships, such as singleness, can derive principles from marriage to establish relationships of genuine union.
115. Richard J. Stoller, *Presentations of Gender* (New Haven: Yale University Press, 1985), 183, cited in Nicolosi, ibid., 24.
116. Nicolosi and Nicolosi, *A Parent's Guide*, 22. See also his *Reparative Therapy of Male Homosexuality* (Northvale, NJ: Jason Aronson, Inc., 1991).
117. Nicolosi, *A Parent's Guide*, 23. These are simple things, but they are also profound as Mollenkott's attempt to deliver us from such pronouns indicates. See also my article about the importance of gender-distinct language in biblical translation: Peter Jones, "The TNIV: Gender Accurate or Ideologically Egalitarian," *Journal for Biblical Manhood and Womanhood*, ed. Bruce A. Ware (May 2003) TNIV Special Edition (Louisville, KY: Council on Biblical Manhood and Womanhood). Though published by InterVarsity Press, which has made a significant commitment to the egalitarian view of gender and ministry, Nicolosi nevertheless makes a statement about the importance of gender distinction in language: "We see this gender confusion...in the drive to purge all language of gender-specific terminology...[and the rejection of] the possibility of a benevolent male acting as head of a family" (Ibid., 68–69).
118. Ibid., 29.
119. In the light of these statements by clinical psychiatrists, one wonders what to make of Tony Campolo's word to young Christians: "Not only do I love the feminine in Jesus, but the more I know Jesus, the more I realize that Jesus loves the feminine in me.... Society has brought me up to suppress the so-called feminine dimension of my humanness. But when Jesus makes me whole, both sides of who I am meant to be will be finally realized. Then and only then will I be fully able to love Jesus." See Campolo, *Carpe Diem*, 87–88. Nicolosi, ibid., 40, without reference to Campolo, gives a damning judgment of such counsel: "With today's confused approach to gender issues...teachers may tell [boys] to embrace their 'feminine side' or 'androgynous nature,' or, worse...identify themselves as gay."
120. Nicolosi, ibid., 30, speaks of the need for boys to grow up with the model of a "salient" male figure. He defines "salient" as joining two things: strength and benevolence. This, of course, is the perfect description of the male elder-pastor and husband in Scripture—Eph. 5:22–23 and 1 Tim. 3:1–7.
121. Prov. 31:28 ESV.

122.   Isa. 54:5.
123.   Eph. 5:22–23.
124.   Gen. 1:31; cf. Gen. 1:4 NKJV, 10, 12, 18, 21, 25.
125.   Ps. 19:1; 8:1.
126.   1 Tim. 4:4.
127.   Rom. 1:25.
128.   "Praise God, from Whom All Blessings Flow" ("Doxology"), Bishop Thomas Ken (1709).

CHAPTER 8
THE DEATH OF SEX

1.   Rom. 8:22.
2.   Rom. 8:23.
3.   John 11:33; 38–39.
4.   Matt. 27:51.
5.   Text of presiding Bishop Griswold's Friday Sermon at the 74th General Convention, Episcopal News Service (8 Aug 2003).
6.   "Jesus would Vote with Me in Favour of Gay 'Marriage' Says Canadian Senator," LifeSiteNews.com (8 July 2005).
7.   Ibid.
8.   Andrew Wang, "Making the Case for Full Inclusion of Homosexuals," *Los Angeles Times* (9 July 2005), B2.
9.   Matt. 4:1–11.
10.   1 Thess. 4:5.
11.   Larry B. Stammer, "Gay Bishop, Rabbi Discuss Religion, Sex," *Los Angeles Times* (5 Nov 2003), B5.
12.   Eph. 4:17–19.
13.   Rom. 1:18–21.
14.   Rom. 1:18.
15.   Rom. 5:19.
16.   Gen. 2:15–17; 3:1–7.
17.   Rom. 1:22–23 ESV.
18.   Rom. 1:25.
19.   Acts 19:27.
20.   Josh. 4:24; Jonah 1:9 ESV.
21.   Num. 16:9 NKJV.
22.   See also Matt. 4:10; cf. Deut. 6:13.
23.   The exact Greek terms are not always identical but certainly synonymous.

24. See Deut. 11:16 ESV. I take issue here with the NIV translation of Rom. 1:25, which reads, "They exchanged the truth of God for a lie," because the Greek has the definite article before truth and lie, and thus, the text should read, "They exchanged the truth of God for the lie." At this most basic level there is only one truth and there is but one lie.

25. Caìtlin Matthews, *Sophia, Goddess of Wisdom: The Definite Feminine from Black Goddess to World-Soul* (London: The Aquarian Press/Harper Collins, 1992), 332, 327.

26. Josh. 24:14. See also 1 Kings 3:9.

27. Dan. 3:28 ESV.

28. Matt. 6:24.

29. Matt. 12:26.

30. Matt. 7:13–14.

31. Rom. 1:25.

32. 2 Cor. 6:14.

33. Rom. 1:22–23.

34. Ex. 20:4 ESV.

35. 2 Kings 11:18.

36. Ezek. 7:20 ESV; see Deut. 4:16.

37. Thomas Berry, *The Great Work: Our Way into the Future* (New York: Bell Tower, 1999), 73.

38. Ibid., 88, 22.

39. Stanislav Grof, *Future of Psychology: Lessons from Modern Consciousness Research* (New York: State University of New York Press, 2000), 149.

40. See Cornelius Van Til, *Christian Apologetics*, ed. William Edgar (Phillipsburg, NJ: 1976, 2003), 62, who notes, "There are two and only two classes of men. There are those who worship and serve the creature, and there are those who worship and serve the Creator."

41. Rom. 1:26–27.

42. Richard B. Hayes is George Washington Ivey Professor of New Testament at Duke Divinity School. See his article, "Relations Natural and Unnatural: A Response to John Boswell's Exegesis of Rom. 1," *Journal of Religious Ethics* 14 (Spring 1986): 186.

43. Art.cit., 191.

44. From *The Testament of the Twelve Patriarchs*. The prophet Hosea, 4:7ff., speaks about exchanging glory resulting in pagan idolatry and sexual perversions.

45. Rom. 1:26–27. See previously, chapter 5. See also the article by Richard B. Hayes mentioned previously.

46. Jude v. 7.

47. Jude v. 8 states, "They serve as an example of those who suffer the punishment of eternal fire."
48. Rom. 1:26–27 ESV.
49. Satinover, *Homosexuality*, 173, calls homosexuality "a spiritual state," which, as rebellion against God constitutes a "sin." Satinover, ibid, 184, quotes his colleague, Joseph Nicolosi, who describes homosexuality as "a disordered way of being-in-the-world." If these opinions are true, the massive attempt in our day to normalize and legalize homosexuality is a notable example of "the lie," to quote Paul.
50. This is argued by a number of well-known Bible scholars.
51. This term is used especially of creation and the "re-creation" after the flood—see Gen. 5:2; 6:19–20; 7:2–3, 9, 16.
52. Lev. 18:22; 20:13.
53. Matt. 19:4; Mark 10:6 ESV.
54. Gal. 3:28.
55. The further mention of birds, animals, and reptiles is also an obvious recalling of Genesis 1:26, where these very terms occur (minus "fish") in the same order.
56. The verb is *metalassw*. It is used only here in Romans 1:25–26 and twice in Esther 2:7, 20.
57. Rom. 3:23.
58. Rom. 2:1.
59. Rom. 2:17–26.
60. Rom. 5:12.
61. Matt. 19:4–6. Here Jesus quotes Genesis 2:24 in the defense of heterosexual marriage as the work of God.
62. Eph. 5:31, where Paul cites Genesis 2:24 to illustrate Christ's work of redemption.
63. Berry, *The Great Work*, 159.
64. Singer, *Androgyny*, 18.
65. This, of course, does not mean that all homosexuals are practicing pagans or that all monogamous heterosexuals are Christian believers. Paul is dealing with worldview, especially the order of creation that should bring us to God the Creator.
66. Gen. 2:25 ESV.
67. Gen. 3:20; 1 Tim. 2:15.
68. In a very persuasive article, David W. Jones, "Egalitarianism and Homosexuality," 5–19, shows how biblical egalitarians are exposed to homosexual arguments by denying the relationship between gender identity and gender roles. They agree that God created gender identity distinctions,

but refuse to see the biblical evidence that identity assumes role. One could argue that gender identity is granted real significance in Scripture by the assigning of gender-specific roles. Otherwise, gender identity is rendered virtually meaningless in the realizing of God's purposes for the universe.

69. 1 Cor. 11:3; Eph. 5:23. See also Rom. 5:12–19, which describes Adam's "federal" headship.
70. 1 Tim. 2:14.
71. Gen. 2:24.
72. Gen. 3:6.
73. Gen. 3:12.
74. Gen. 3:13.
75. Eph. 4:19.
76. 1 Thess. 4:7.
77. 1 Cor. 5:1–5.
78. 1 Cor. 6:12–20.
79. 1 Cor. 6:16.
80. The quotations are from Saraha's *Treasury of Songs* in Conze, et al, *Buddhist Texts*, 48, 24, 64, 74.
81. 1 Cor. 6:18.
82. 1 Thess. 5:23.
83. 1 Cor. 6:17. See also Phil. 2:2.
84. 1 Cor. 6:18.
85. 1 Cor. 5:5; 2 Cor. 4:11; 1 Tim. 1:20; 2 Peter 2:4.
86. Ezek. 18:15 ESV speaks also of the true believer who "does not eat upon the mountains or lift up his eyes to the idols of the house of Israel, does not defile his neighbor's wife."
87. Gen. 3:14–19.
88. Gen. 3:15.
89. Gen. 3:20.

CHAPTER 9
BORN-AGAIN SEX AND THE FUTURE

1. See Peter Jones, *Capturing the Pagan Mind: Paul's Blueprint for Thinking and Living in the New Global Culture* (Nashville: Broadman and Holman, 2003), 192–93.
2. Ibid., 181–207.
3. C. S. Lewis, "Learning in War-Time," cited by Tim Keller on his church Web site, Redeemer.com.
4. Molnar, *Utopia*, 237.

5. Ps. 8:6.
6. Cited in Geering, *Tomorrow's God*, 189.
7. 1 Cor. 15:19.
8. Col. 1:16.
9. Eph. 3:9; cf. Col. 3:10.
10. Col. 1:20.
11. See 1 Cor. 15:45–46 for an explicit scriptural statement.
12. 1 Cor. 15:3.
13. 1 Cor. 6:11.
14. Oliver O'Donovan, *Resurrection and the Moral Order: An Outline for Evangelical Ethics* (Grand Rapids: Eerdmans, 1994), 14.
15. Heb. 10:5.
16. Luke 22:19. See also Eph. 2:16: "And in this one body to reconcile both of them to God through the cross, by which he put to death their hostility." See also Col. 1:22: "But now he has reconciled you by Christ's physical body through death to present you holy in his sight, without blemish and free from accusation"; Heb. 10:10; 1 Peter 2:24.
17. Mark 9:2–8. The transfiguration, as 9:1 indicates, is a prophetic anticipation of Jesus' resurrection.
18. 2 Cor. 5:10.
19. Rom. 8:21–23.
20. 1 Cor. 14:33, 40.
21. Fritjof Capra, *The Turning Point: Science, Society and the Rising Culture* (New York: Simon and Schuster, 1982; reprint New York: Bantam, 1983), 371.
22. Rev. 4:11.
23. 1 Cor. 15:38–39.
24. 1 Cor. 15:40.
25. Jer. 5:22. The Greek text uses the verb *tassw*, "to set in place."
26. Job 38:12. Here the text has the noun *taxis*, "place," which is derived from the verb *tassw*.
27. The same term, *taxis*, "place," is used here behind the English translation "turn."
28. 1 Cor. 15:22–23.
29. The verb in Greek is *hupotassw*, "to set under," and is a compound of *tassw*, "to set or place."
30. Rom. 8:20.
31. Gal. 3:13.
32. Gal. 4:4 ESV.
33. Ps. 8:6; cf. Ps. 18:38–39.

34. Ps. 18:9.
35. Ps. 110:1. See also Dan. 7:27.
36. 1 Cor. 15:27–28; Eph. 1:20–22; Heb. 2:8; cf. 1 Peter 3:22 where the same verb (place under, or submit) of the psalm is used, so this could be counted as a fourth reprise of Ps. 8.
37. Ps. 22:16, alluded to in Matt. 26:24; cf. Phil. 3:2.
38. 1 Cor. 15:27. Paul uses a number of times the same verb, "submit," *hupotassw* that occurs in Psalm 8.
39. Eph. 1:20–22.
40. 1 Peter 3:22.
41. Gen. 1:26; cf. 1:28.
42. O'Donovan, *Resurrection*, 14.
43. Heb. 2:5.
44. Heb. 2:6.
45. Heb. 2:7–8.
46. O'Donovan, *Resurrection*, 15.
47. Col. 1:20.
48. Eph. 3:9.
49. Gen. 1:1.
50. Eph. 1:10.
51. O'Donovan, *Resurrection*, 32–33.
52. Dan. 7:27. Again the verb is *hupotassw*.
53. O'Donovan, *Resurrection*, 32–33.
54. 1 Cor. 15:28.
55. The verb, in transliterated Greek, is *hupotassw*, to set under. *Tassw* means "to set in place."
56. Rom. 1:4.
57. Mark 1:24; Luke 4:34; Acts 3:14.
58. Rom. 6:10.
59. Richard Gaffin, *Redemption and Resurrection: A Study in Pauline Soteriology* (Phillipsburg, NJ: P&R, 1987), 124–25.
60. 2 Cor. 5:21.
61. Rom. 6:10.
62. John 14:1–4.
63. 1 Cor. 1:30.
64. Eph. 4:24.
65. 1 Peter 1:16.
66. 1 Thess. 3:13.
67. Rom. 6:22.
68. Col. 1:12.

69. Heb. 12:10.
70. Heb. 12:14.
71. Rev. 21:8; cf. the Old Testament perspective of the future in Isa. 52:1. See also Eph. 5:5; 1 Cor. 6:9; Rev. 22:15.
72. Jer. 31:23 ESV.
73. Rev. 21:2–5.
74. Molnar, *Utopia*, 241.
75. 1 Cor. 2:6.
76. 1 Cor. 2:9.
77. Luke 20:33.
78. Gen. 1:28.
79. Matt. 19:8.
80. Matt. 24:38.
81. Luke 20:34–35.
82. New Age physicist Capra, *The Turning Point*, 371, describes the goal of pagan spirituality as the state of consciousness "in which all boundaries and dualisms have been transcended and all individuality dissolves into universal undifferentiated oneness."
83. Rev. 19:7; 21:2.
84. Randy Alcorn, *Heaven* (Wheaton, IL: Tyndale House, 2004), 339.
85. Dale W. Whitchurch, *Waking from Earth: Seeking Heaven, the Heart's True Home* (Kearny, NE: Morris, 1999), 95, cited in Alcorn, *Heaven*, 336.
86. Matt. 22:30.
87. See the *Gnostic Gospel of Thomas: The Nag Hammadi Library in English*, ed. James Robinson (San Francisco: Harper & Row, 1977), 114.
88. Matt. 22:30.
89. Of course, even if this is the intended parallel, such a statement does not declare resurrected human beings to be "sexless." It only describes them as no longer needing marriage.
90. Luke 20:36.
91. Gal. 3:28.
92. See Hove, *Equality in Christ*, for a very timely discussion of the issues.
93. Eph. 5:22–33.
94. 1 Tim. 2–3.
95. John Frame, "Men and Women in the Image of God," *Recovering Biblical Manhood and Womanhood: A Response to Evangelical Feminism* (Wheaton, IL: Crossway, 1991), 232, gives "a weak vote" in favor of what I am affirming, and says, "I rather suspect that we will still be male and female in the resurrection."
96. Luke 24:31, 36–43; John 21:1–14.

97.   1 Cor. 15:53.
98.   1 John 3:2.
99.   Phil. 3:21.
100. Ezek. 42:20.
101. The same Hebrew verb, *badal,* "to separate," used in Genesis about the original creation, is used here of the new creation.
102. Rev. 4:8.
103. Alcorn, *Heaven,* 235.
104. 1 Cor. 13:12.
105. Ibid.
106. See John Piper, *What's the Difference?: Manhood and Womanhood Defined According to the Bible* (Wheaton, IL: Crossway, 2001), 17–21, who cites strong statements by Emil Brunner and Paul Jewett. See also Alcorn, *Heaven,* 338: "We'll be male and female," and Lewis, *Miracles,* 159–60, who is of the same opinion.
107. Eph. 5:26; 2 Cor. 11:2.

CHAPTER 10
BORN-AGAIN SEX AND THE PRESENT

1.   Matt. 15:19; Acts 15:29; 1 Cor. 5:9; 6:9; 6:13, 15–16, 18; 7:2; 10:8; 2 Cor. 12:21; Gal. 5:19; Eph. 4:19; 5:3; 5:5; Col. 3:5; 1 Thess. 4:3; 7:7; 1 Tim. 1:9–10; Heb. 12:16; 13:4; Rev. 2:20; 21:8.
2.   1 Cor. 15:38.
3.   Lev. 15:2.
4.   1 Thess. 4:7.
5.   1 Cor. 6:13.
6.   Rom. 6:13.
7.   2 Tim. 2:21.
8.   Mark 7:6; John 5:23.
9.   1 Tim. 1:17;6:16; Rev. 5:13.
10.   1 Cor. 6:20.
11.   2 Cor. 4:10.
12.   Phil. 1:20.
13.   1 Cor. 6:19 ESV.
14.   Gen. 12:3 has not been repealed, as Isa. 42:6; 49:6; 51:4 show.
15.   Aristophanes (ca. 450–385 BC) coined this verb to indicate to what extent Corinth was known for sexual immorality. See Gordon Fee, *The First Epistle to the Corinthians* (Grand Rapids: Eerdmans, 1987), 2. C. K.

Barrett, *The First Epistle to the Corinthians* (New York: Harper & Row, 1968), 2, observes that "words derived from the name Corinth seem to have been used in the Old Comedy with the meaning *to practice fornication, whoremonger*, and the like."

16. 1 Cor. 6:9–11.
17. 1 Cor. 1:2. See also Acts 20:32; 26:18; Heb. 10:10. In all these texts, notice the past tense.
18. See 1 Cor. 5–6.
19. See also 1 Peter 1:2.
20. Rom. 11:16; Eph. 2:19.
21. 2 Cor. 6:17–18, a citation from Isa. 52:11; Ezek. 20:34, 41; 2 Sam. 7:14, 8.
22. 2 Cor. 6:14–16.
23. Deut. 18:9.
24. 1 Cor. 5:9–10.
25. Gen. 19.
26. 2 Cor. 7:1.
27. 1 Thess. 4:3 ESV.
28. 1 Cor. 10:26, citing Ps. 24:1; cf. 50:12; 89:11.
29. 1 Peter 1:15. See also 2 Tim. 1:9; 1 Thess. 4:7.
30. Matt. 6:9.
31. Matt. 23:9. Names make us special. Speaking God's name as Father recognizes him as holy or special, set apart.
32. 1 Cor. 6:20.
33. Eph. 5:23.
34. 1 Cor. 7:14.
35. 1 Tim. 2:15.
36. 1 Tim. 4:10 ESV.
37. Isabel Lyman, "Oklahoma City Doctor Finds Her Way Home (To Homeschooling/Stay-at-home!)," *Oklahoma Council on Public Affairs*, 2 August 2005.
38. Isa. 7:15 ESV.
39. 1 Cor. 7:14.
40. Ps. 127:3.
41. Arthur W. Hunt, *The Vanishing Word*, 230.
42. Eph. 5:32.
43. Luke 14:34.
44. 1 Tim. 5:25; 6:18.
45. Phil. 3:21.
46. Luke 10:17.
47. Rom. 16:20; Deut. 15:6; Isa. 14:2.

48. Elizabeth Johnson, "Apocalyptic Family Values," *Interpretation* 56 (2002): 34ff., argues that Gal. 3:28 is a baptismal formula and that "baptism represents the very end of the created order." Such an interpretation does no justice to the organic character of biblical theology as developed by Paul and comes very close to the gnostic denial of the goodness of creation.

49. Heb. 2:8.

50. Heb. 2:5: "It is not to angels that he has subjected the world to come, about which we are speaking."

51. Matt. 5:13–16.

52. 1 Tim. 4:3–4.

53. See the very helpful study by Timothy G. Gombis, "A Radically New Humanity: The Function of the *Haustafel* in Ephesians," *Journal of the Evangelical Theological Society*, 48 (June 2005): 317–50, who rightly affirms that Paul does not throw out the creational structures, like patriarchy and submission, but fills them with "new creation dynamics" (324). In the same journal, William Webb, "A Redemptive-Movement Hermeneutic: Encouraging Dialogue among Four Evangelical Views," *Journal of the Evangelical Theological Society*, 48 (June 2005): 351–64, makes the fatal mistake of both failing to see the social context in Ephesians of pagan deconstruction and the importance of the maintenance of the creational structures. Using his "redemptive-movement hermeneutic," which allows him to imagine where Paul's argument would have ended up had he followed it to its logical conclusion, he argues that Paul would have rejected both submission and hierarchy as imperfect forms. Alas, this is where you can arrive when Paul's doctrine of God the Creator is downplayed—which is also the case of his article, "Balancing Paul's Original-Creation and Pro-Creation Arguments: 1 Corinthians 11:11–12 in the Light of Modern Embryology," *Westminster Theological Journal* 66 (2004): 275–89.

54. Gen. 4:7; cf. Rom. 6:12.

55. Berry, *The Great Work*, 159.

56. Ibid, 181.

57. 1 Cor. 14:33.

58. Paul exhorts Christians to "submit *yourselves*."

59. This is the force of Eph. 5:21: "Submit to one another out of reverence for Christ." See below.

60. Luke 2:51.

61. 1 Cor. 15:28.

62. In the Old Testament the term is used twenty-seven times.

63. See Marilyn Gottschall, "The Ethical Implications of the Deconstruction of Gender," *Journal of the American Academy of Religion* 70 (2002): 279–99.
64. See for example, Gordon D. Fee, "The Cultural Context of Ephesians 5:18–6:9," *Priscilla Papers* 16 (2002): 3–8. See the helpful critique of this position by Timothy Gombis, "A Radically New Humanity," 317–19, where he argues that Paul is not seeking common ground with the pagan culture but rather shows its "absolute incompatibility."
65. See also Gombis, art. cit.
66. "An Interview with Margaret Miles," *GTU Currents*, Summer 2001, 2.
67. Rom. 6:15–19.
68. Elaine Woo, "Catalyst of Feminist Revolution," *Los Angeles Times* (5 Feb 2006), 1, 26–27. Friedan's daughter, Dr. Emily Friedan, called her mother "a mass of contradictions." Karen Matthews, "Friends, Family Eulogize Feminist Friedan," *ABC News* (6 Feb 2006), http://abcnews.go.com/US/wireStory?id=1586990.
69. Margalit Fox, "Betty Friedan, Who Ignited Cause in 'Feminine Mystique,' Dies at 85," *New York Times* (6 Feb 2006).
70. Woo, art. cit., 27.
71. See Moore, "Que(e)rying Paul," 253.
72. See the Web site Christianlesbians.com, which seeks to maintain this position. The author, an ex-fundamentalist, is now enrolled in a liberal theological school and has already found liberal exegetical methods essential and liberating for her new-look Bible study method.
73. Henry Makow, "Confessions of a Survivor of the (Homo)sexual Revolution," *Toogood Reports* (16–18 Nov 2001).
74. For extensive bibliography, see The Council on Biblical Manhood and Womanhood and its Web site www.cbmw.org.
75. Ps. 8:6.
76. 1 Chron. 29:24; Ps. 36:7 ("be still" actually translates "submit yourself to"); 47:3.
77. Rom. 13:1; Titus 3:1; and 1 Peter 2:13; cf. 1 Tim. 2:3. Note that every one of the following references includes the Greek verb *hupotassw*, "to submit," or its cognates.
78. 1 Cor. 16:15–16; 1 Peter 5:5.
79. 1 Cor. 14:34; Eph. 5:23; Col. 3:18; 1 Tim. 2:11; Titus 2:5; 1 Peter 3:1, 5.
80. 1 Tim. 3:4; Luke 2:51; cf. Eph. 6:1–3.
81. Titus 2:9; 1 Peter 2:18; cf. Eph. 6:5–8; 1 Tim. 3:4–7.
82. Rom. 8:7; cf. 1 Tim. 1:8.
83. Eph. 5:24.
84. Heb. 12:9; James 4:7.

85. Rom. 13:2.
86. Ps. 62:5; cf. 61:2.
87. 2 Cor. 9:13 ESV.
88. Alice von Hildebrand, *The Soul of a Lion: Dietrich von Hildebrand* (San Francisco: Ignatius Press, 2000), 137.
89. 1 Cor. 14:33, 40.
90. 1 Cor. 14:33, 40—"according to its structure or place—*taxin*," a derivative of *tassw*, "to set in place," from which we get *hupotassw*, literally "to set in place under."
91. Col. 2:5 ESV—"your order—*taxin*," also a derivative of *tassw*.
92. Rom. 13:5 ESV.
93. Rom. 8:7.
94. Rom. 13:2. These terms—*oppose* and *ordain*—also are cognates of the verb *hupotassw*, "to submit."
95. 1 Thess. 5:14—without structure.
96. 1 Tim. 1:9; Titus 1:6, 10: the adjective, based on the root *tassw* literally means "without submission."
97. 1 Tim. 4:3–4 ESV.
98. Heb. 13:4.
99. Usually, when Paul uses the term *Father* it contains the notion of God as Creator or source—see Eph. 3:14.
100. Eph. 5:20.
101. Eph. 5:21–22.
102. Rom. 1:21.
103. Ernest Sanders, *Times Advocate*.
104. The Eucharist means "thanksgiving." See 1 Cor. 11:24.
105. Col. 3:17.
106. 1 Tim. 4:4.
107. Ibid. See also 1 Cor. 8:1–13; 10:14–22, 25–32; 11:2–16; 15:45.
108. 1 Tim. 4:9–10. See Steven M. Baugh, "Savior of All People—1 Timothy 4:10 in Context," *WTJ* 54 (1992): 331–40. Baugh shows that this is not a "universalistic" statement about final salvation, but a declaration of God's "common grace"—see Matt. 5:45; Acts 14:16–17; Ps. 145:9; cf. Rom. 9:22. "Savior" in the Greco-Roman world has "as its primary meaning 'a generous benefactor.'"

CHAPTER 11
AWESOME SEX: FEAR NOT

Chapter 11: Awesome Sex: Fear Not

1. Ex. 20:20 ESV.
2. Ex. 15:11; cf. Deut. 10:17; Job 37:22.
3. Gen. 31:42, 53.
4. Deut. 10:17 ESV.
5. Jer. 10:5 ESV. See also Isa. 41:23.
6. 2 Cor. 5:11 ESV.
7. Prov. 1:7.
8. Deut. 10:12–13 ESV.
9. Phil. 2:12 ESV; cf. Rom. 11:20; 2 Cor. 5:11.
10. Ps. 22:23; 40:3; 66:3; 96:4; Rev. 19:5.
11. Ps. 85:9; 145:19.
12. Ps. 25:14.
13. Ps. 99:3; cf. Rev. 15:4.
14. Ps. 103:11, 13, 17; 118:4; 147:11.
15. Ps. 115:11.
16. Ps. 130:4.
17. Jer. 44:10.
18. Ex. 20:20; Prov. 3:7.
19. Deut. 6:24; Ps. 111:5; 128:4; Eccl. 8:12–13.
20. Ps. 33:8; cf. Ex. 14:31.
21. Jer. 5:22.
22. Gen. 9:2.
23. Micah 7:17; Ex. 23:27; Deut. 2:25.
24. Prov. 24:21. See also Rom. 13:3; 1 Peter 2:17.
25. Eph. 5:33 ESV: "Let the wife see that she respects (fears) her husband," cf. 1 Peter 3:1–2.
26. Eph. 6:5; Col. 3:22; 1 Peter 2:18.
27. Rom. 13:7 ESV.
28. 1 Peter 2:17.
29. Rom. 13:1–3; Eph. 5:22, 33; 1 Peter 2:13, 18.
30. Ps. 86:1.
31. Ps. 102:1, 11–12.
32. 2 Sam. 22:28; Ps. 18:27; 76:9; 149:4.
33. Ps. 25:18.
34. Ps. 119:153; Isa. 66:2.
35. Ps. 31:7 ESV.
36. Ps. 69:1–2; alluded to in John 19:29–30; cf. Mark 15:36.
37. Isa. 49:6, 13.
38. Matt. 5:3.
39. Num. 12:3 ESV.

40. Matt. 21:5; citing Zech. 9:9.
41. Matt. 11:29.
42. Matt. 5:5; cf. Ps. 37:11.
43. 1 Peter 3:1–4.
44. 1 Peter 3:4.
45. 1 Peter 3:1–2.
46. Ps. 24:1.
47. Isa. 6:1–3.
48. Rev. 4:8–11.
49. Ibid.
50. See Jack Rogers' statement, as he was elected moderator of the PCUSA, summer, 2001. See Deb Price, "Editorial," *The Detroit News* (22 June 2001): "I believe if we read the Bible in the same way we learned to read it in order to accept the equality of...women, we will be forced to the conclusion that gay and lesbian people are also to be accepted as our equal."
51. Richard N. Ostling, "The Evangelical Lutheran Church in America orders its first major study on whether to endorse homosexual relationships," *Associated Press* (13 August 2001).
52. Clark, "Gay Spirituality," 342.
53. De la Huerta, *Coming Out Spiritually*.
54. Ibid., 39.
55. Titus 1:6–9 ESV.
56. 1 Peter 3:1–7 ESV.
57. Ps. 127:3.

EPILOGUE
THE REST OF THE STORY

58. Gen. 1:27–28, 31 ESV.
59. Ps. 8:4–6 ESV.
60. Rev. 4:11; 15:3 ESV.

₪

If you have enjoyed this book,
or if it has had an impact on your life,
we would like to hear from you.

Please contact us at:

TRUTHXCHANGE
PO Box 416
Escondido, CA 92133-0416

Or visit our Web site:
www.truthXchange.com